Traditional
THEISM
and its Modern Alternatives

Edited by Svend Andersen
with an introduction by D.Z. Phillips

ACTA JUTLANDICA LXX:1
THEOLOGY SERIES 18

AARHUS UNIVERSITY PRESS

Copyright: Aarhus University Press, 1994
Printed on permanent paper conforming to ANSI
standard Z39.48-1984 by the Alden Press, Oxford
ISBN 87 7288 482 7
ISSN 0065 1354 (Acta Jutlandica)
ISSN 0106 0945 (Theology series)

ACTA JUTLANDICA is published by Aarhus University Press
on behalf of the Learned Society of Aarhus (founded 1945).

Editorial address:
Aarhus University Press
Building 170
University of Aarhus
DK-8000 Aarhus C, Denmark

Fax + 45 86 19 84 33

Preface

The contributions to this volume are the papers from the Ninth European Conference on Philosophy of Religion, held in August, 1992. As the title indicates, the conference was one of a series, but it was also one of the arrangements by which the 50th anniversary of the Faculty of Theology in the University of Aarhus was celebrated.

The sequence of the papers follow the order of the conference programme. According to the established way of procedure at the conferences, a first paper is commented on in the second paper. Normally, the organisers accept great liberty as to the definition of 'comments'.

A remark is necessary on the contribution by professor Keith Ward, 'A Defence of Metaphysical Theism'. It is not the paper he actually read at the conference. This paper, with the title 'A Defence of Traditional Theism', has been published elsewhere. In consequence of this fact — for which no one but the editor can be blamed — the comments of professor Kodalle relate to the original paper. This might puzzle the reader somewhat. I think, however, that Kodalle catches the spirit of Ward's new paper. If the reader wants to check the tenability of Kodalle's criticism precisely, he or she must consult Keith Ward's original paper, published as 'God as a Principle of Cosmological Explanation' in Robert John Russell et al. (ed.), *Quantum Cosmology and the Laws of Nature* (University of Notre Dame Press, 1993).

I am very pleased to be able to publish the papers as a volume of *Acta Jutlandica*. I want to thank first of all the authors for their work and for their permission to publish the papers. Also, I want to express my gratitude to the Faculty of Theology and to the Danish State Research Council for the Humanities for contributing to the funding of the conference. The council also provided support for the production of this volume, for which I am particularly thankful.

I hope that when this volume appears in the year of the tenth conference, a European association for philosophy of religion will exist. For fruitful cooperation also in this respect I want to thank my colleagues Vincent Brümmer, Utrecht; Ingolf Dalferth, Frankfurt; and Michael Durrant, Cardiff.

Aarhus, May 1994   *Svend Andersen*

Contents

Introduction:
Piety, theism and philosophy

D.Z. Phillips

The papers in this collection come from the Ninth European Conference on the Philosophy of Religion held at the University of Aarhus, Denmark in August, 1992.

The theme of the conference was Theism and its Modern Alternatives. Why alternatives? There is no agreement on the answer to that question. Before outlining the nature of the disagreements, we need to distinguish between theism, where it means some belief in God, and theism as a certain kind of philosophical response to that belief. If 'theism' is to be spoken of in both contexts, the following question arises: Is philosophical theism an adequate response to religious theism? It is to *that* question that four answers emerged in the papers and in discussions of them.

According to the *first* answer, philosophical theism should be one, single, coherent response to religious belief. The fact that there is disagreement about its formulation is understandable, but intellectually regrettable. If we were all capable of unblemished rational reflection, this disagreement would not exist. How could it, since philosophical theism's task is to provide *the* foundation religious belief needs if it is to be rational. There can, therefore, be no more than one adequate philosophical response to religious belief.

According to the *second* answer, philosophical theism is indeed an appropriate philosophical response to religious belief, but the lesson of cultural change over the centuries is that we must be flexible about its content. This answer differs from the first in the suggestion that philosophical theism is a far more general and flexible mode of intellectual argumentation than the first answer would suggest. For example, it may constitute, not simply the foundation of religious belief, but also a conceptual elucidation of its content. Philosophical theism is not a static, ahistorical mode of argument. Its place in contemporary, pluralistic culture, may be as one option among others. Further, its role may be a deconstructed one, involving decontextualisation and recontextualisation. The decontextualisation comes from recognising that much of the legacy of philosophical theism is a legacy of magnificent errors, which is no longer at the centre of our culture. This situation can be a blessing if we are prepared to learn from it. We can be brought to see that religion has still something distinctive to say about values which neither politics nor economics alone can provide. This new emphasis is the recontextualisation of philosophical theism, but one which, it is said, does not abandon the notion of a religious ontology.

According to the *third* answer, those who offer the second answer have failed to appreciate how problematic philosophical theism is. When they see what is wrong with it, and suggest that it should be more flexible, they are like doctors who recommend cosmetic surgery for a patient who is terminally ill. We cannot patch up philosophical theism. It simply will not do. It was *never* philosophically adequate, even at the time it dominated the intellectual scene. So it must be replaced. But by what? Some want to replace philosophical theism with pantheism, but this is found to be inadequate. What we need is to take advantage of the resources available in Process Thought. Perhaps the new option should be called Panentheism, but whatever the name, what is vital is to go beyond the bankrupt categories of philosophical theism, since they can still cause real harm. There is no contradiction in saying that confused philosophical beliefs can have harmful historical and spiritual results. As Peter Berger says, '...non-existent sticks can draw real blood'.[1]

According to the *fourth* answer, all three answers considered so far must be rejected. It agrees with the third answer in thinking that no form of philosophical theism will do either as a foundation or elucidation of religious belief. Where it differs from it is in rejecting the need to replace one 'ism' with another. Philosophy has a far more modest task, namely, the task of grappling with scepticism which denies *the possibility* of religious meanings, and grappling with other forms of philosophical confusion which obscure those meanings from us.[2] Religion is a mixed bag, not only as between religions, but within religions. Conceptual clarification may well reveal confusions. It will certainly reveal differences. Philosophy, as such, can go

---

1. Peter Berger, *Invitation to Sociology*, Harmondsworth 1975, p. 185.
2. A word of explanation is necessary. This view emerged in discussions of papers, rather than in the papers themselves, although some approximate to such a view. Further, it is a view which I hold. For the final session of the conference, I had been asked to give a general perspective on it, both expository and critical. Later, I was asked whether the remarks I made then could be used as an introduction to this collection. This explains why the introduction takes this form.

no further, but theology must. A theologian speaks from within some religious community or other. Philosophy grapples with the grammar of religious belief, while theology is the guardian of some set of religious beliefs.

Given these four answers, there will be correspondingly different accounts of the relations which exist between religious belief (or religious piety, as many speakers called it), and philosophical responses to that belief. Let me illustrate this by reference to what I shall call *the story of piety*. My four illustrations feature philosophical theism, flexible philosophical theism and panentheism. All three share a common assumption, namely, that the story of piety needs philosophical endorsement in some way. For obvious reasons, the conception of philosophy as conceptual clarification cannot feature in the four illustrations in the same way. It is present *in* the way the other suggestions are discussed.

The first response says that the story of piety is not enough, since we have to ask whether the story corresponds to 'what is the case'.

Saying this is unobjectionable as long as 'what is the case' is not placed beyond all epistemic contexts. A story may fall in face of what is the case, but the content of the story will have been shown to be open to that kind of criticism. The story said such-and-such was the case when it was not. But if you forget the qualifying such-and-such, and simply speak of 'what is the case', as though its meaning is context-free, you are chasing a metaphysical chimera. It is a logical howler of the first order to think that if we say, 'Pain is something', 'Physical objects are something', 'Love is something', 'Banking is something', we are thereby predicating pain, physical objects, love, banking, to some one subject called Something. This fascination with the general subject is one of the sins of philosophical realism. Some have suggested that when we give it up we lose our ontological innocence. What we actually do is to repent of one sin of philosophical mystification. We may say, 'This is what we mean by ...', but neither 'This' nor 'Something' is the name of anything. We cannot say '"Something" is something' or 'This is "this"'.

When Socrates speaks in terms of myth when speaking of divine judgement, he has no option in the type of discourse he employs. It is not a second best. He says that he believes his story is true, but adds, I believe ironically, that he won't insist on all the details. This reminds us of Wittgenstein's philosophical joke concerning Michelangelo's Creation of Adam. Taking it as a picture (i.e. as a portrait), he said that Michelangelo, being very good, could be relied on to have done his best in getting the details right. But to say God is in the picture, is not to say that it is a picture of God. It is to say that the picture shows you, for example, in the near-naked figure of the Creator, a spiritual truth. But Wittgenstein was too optimistic in saying that *obviously* no one would take this to be a portrait or diagram. That is precisely how J.L. Mackie did take such paintings. He said that in order for there to be an event called the Last Judgement, the details, as depicted by Michelangelo, would at least have to approximate to what will be the case. Here is an empirical use of 'what is the case' being applied to what is the case spiritually.

At this point, I am fairly confident that someone will say that spirituality, as used in this context, is no more than 'advocacy of a way of life'. That remark rolls off the tongue, but what does it mean? My death and my state after death are different if I am judged in the way Socrates or Michelangelo depict. If we are not careful, 'what is the case' may not even be allowed for ordinary matters of fact. What is the case when I sit on a chair will be settleable only at a sub-atomic level, while sitting on a chair will be a feature of a way of life. Think of Socrates asking whether a physiological account would explain what he was doing in sitting in his cell awaiting his execution. Think of Wittgenstein reminding us that part of the grammar of 'chair' is that we call this 'sitting on a chair'. Is a person's bleeding a perception of 'what is the case', while seeing a person in such distress is advocacy of a way of life? Behind realism there often lurks a crude positivism. We need to be reminded of how the spiritual can change 'what is the case'. When critics accused the American poet Wallace Stevens of not portraying what is the case in his art, which he called 'the blue guitar', he responded thus:

> They said, 'You have a blue guitar,
> You do not play things as they are.'
>
> The man replied, 'Things as they are
> Are changed upon the blue guitar.'

The second response says that the story of piety is not enough because, as yet, it is a story without an ending.

Piety is an inadequate response to suffering. Theism promises an explanation. We haven't got it; we'll never get it on earth; but we believe there is one, and that is what keeps us going. But if God has an explanation of why children have died, an explanation which will bring new understanding to Rachel weeping for her children in Ramah, refusing to be comforted, it seems monstrous that he does not make it known. That hidden explanation is not religious mystery. That is the picture of a God who invites us to a game at which we lose a lot, while he keeps the decisive card up his sleeve. Suffering seems to be *for* something. To many, such an instrumental view of suffering is immoral. We need to explore non-explanatory and non-compensatory responses to suffering. This is not the place to do that. For me, by comparison with them, the theodicies of theism seem morally and spiritually bankrupt.

No doubt it was difficulties of this kind which led some in the conference to speak of religious belief as the conviction that the universe is moving in the direction of the harmonisation of values. I confess that as a philosophical thesis, I do not know what this means. Some things improve, others decline, from time to time. The general claim is problematic. The view may be an expression of optimism. In that case, I do not share it. Someone explained the difference between an optimist and a pessimist thus: The optimist says, 'After all, this is the best of all possible worlds', and the pessimist replies, 'Yes, that's right'.

The third response says that the story of piety is not enough because it tries to tell an impossible story.

How can imperfect beings tell a story of perfection? How can we speak of the Absolute in a fragmented world? Does not this difficulty confuse a metaphysical absolute, unthinkable because it is a chimera, with a religious absolute? When the Psalmist says of God's ways, 'Such knowledge is too wonderful for me; it is high, I cannot attain unto it' (Psalm 139), no statement is being made *about* human language. It is an expression of praise *in* religious language. The Psalmist is not saying that because of the imperfection and fragmentariness of our language, God cannot be praised. Praising God is precisely what the Psalmist is doing.

The fourth response says that the story of piety is a risky story, because it can only be told in a pragmatic manner.

It would indeed be foolish to think that the needs of all people, no matter what their circumstances, can be met by some general philosophical theory. Whether piety can tell a story often depends on the imaginative use of a situation. It *is* risky, nothing can be guaranteed. Of course, we have the language of scripture, but it has to speak in *this* situation. The possibilities of the incarnate logos cannot be planned in advance. I sympathise with many of these sentiments. But there is a danger of importing pragmatism into the content of the story. Whether a story *can* be told at a certain time may be a pragmatic matter, but it does not follow that the truth in the story is a pragmatic matter. Christianity tells a hard story which offers salvation. It is a complicated story. Of it, Kierkegaard reminds us, Jesus said on the Cross, 'It is finished'. He did not say it is probably finished, that it was becoming accumulatively obvious that it was finished, that it was emerging towards a finish. No, he said, 'It is finished'.

In this introduction, I have not named any participants. This leaves it open for anyone to say, 'That wasn't me he was talking about'. But the final references in the introduction must surely be to the great nineteenth century thinker, native of the country where we held the conference, Søren Kierkegaard. According to Kierkegaard, on the one hand we have a pious story, which says it has a message which every person stands in need of. On the other hand, we have philosophical cathedrals in which, it is said, the pious story must be read if it is to be a proper lesson. Kierkegaard argued that such cathedrals are marked for demolition. Wittgenstein called them houses of cards.

To illustrate their status, another story concerning Kierkegaard which I have told too often: Wanting to get his suit pressed, Kierkegaard took it to a shop which had a sign in the window, 'Suits pressed here'. He came out disappointed. Only the sign was for sale. At the end, we are brought back to our beginning. 'Philosophical theism' is a philosophical sign. A sign does not give life to practice. It is practice which gives life to a sign. So do religious practices give a point to the philosophical signs, or do such signs obscure these practices from us?

That is the issue about which, in the papers in this collection, participants have disagreed and about which philosophers and theologians will continue to disagree in the future.

The Historical Roots of Theism

Ingolf U. Dalferth

1. Theism defined

1. Theism, i.e. the belief in the existence of a supreme and beneficient being who is the creator and sustainer of the universe, is not a practical religious faith but a philosophical theory of relatively recent origin. As far as I know the term first occurred in the preface of Cudworth's *The True Intellectual System of the Universe, ... wherein all the Reason and the Philosophy of Atheism is confuted* (London 1678). It was coined in reply to the rise of atheism in the Renaissance and early Enlightenment that had occupied thinkers since the middle of the 16th century.[1] 'The realm', Carlton wrote in his *Discourse on the Present State of England* in 1572, 'is divided into three parties, the Papists, the Atheists, and the Protestants. All three are alike favoured: the first and the second because, being many, we dare not displease them; the third, because having religion, we fear to displease God in them.'[2] Atheism is contrasted here not with theism but with the opposing parties of Western Christianity. It denies what they affirm, and it depends on them for what it rejects. It has its own patron saints, in particular Epicurus and Lucretius. But just as these had questioned particular forms of religious belief and philosophical theology, so particular views, e.g., the intervention of providence in the world and not (at least not at the beginning) the existence

---

1. Cf. Th. Campanella, *Atheismus Triumphatus, seu Reductio ad Religinem per Scientiarum Veritates*, Rome 1631; *Dissertatio de Fulcris Atheismi sub praeside Chr. Colbio*, Königsberg 1655; Th. Spitzel, *Scrutinium Atheismi Historico-Aetiologicum*, Augsburg 1663. The term seems first to have been introduced into English by Sir John Cheke in 1540 in his translation into Latin of Plutarch's *On Superstition*. Cf. G.T. Buckley, *Atheism in the English Renaissance*, New York 1965, p. 64. For the theological reactions see H.-M. Barth, *Atheismus und Orthodoxie. Analysen und Modelle christlicher Apologetic im 17. Jahrhundert*, Göttingen 1971, for the philosophical debate M.J. Buckley, *At the Origins of Modern Atheism*, Yale 1987.
2. Quoted in Buckley, *Origins*, p. 10.

of god as such were at issue in the debates between Renaissance atheism and Christian theology. Atheism, in short, is the rejection of a particular religion, or religious view, and derives its meaning entirely from the affirmation(s) which it negates.

What is true of atheism is also true of theism: it does not stand alone. Just as atheism is essentially parasitic upon some religious or theological understanding of God or some particular religious doctrine or set of doctrines, so theism as a philosophical position is parasitic upon the atheist denial of the God worshiped by Jews, Christians, Moslems, or by any other particular religion. Before philosophical theism there was atheism, both as a term and as a fact, and just as atheists denied the existence of a benevolent governing principle or mind in the universe, so theists affirmed it. In Shaftesbury's words: 'To believe that every thing is govern'd order'd, or regulated *according to the best*, by a designing Principle or Mind, such as is good and eternal, is to be a perfect *Theist*'.[3] The meaning and content of theism is thus defined by what is denied by atheism, and as atheists can and do reject various tenets of religious belief, the content of theism varies accordingly.

Of course, in a vague and imprecise sense everything that can and did become the object of the denial, scepticism, or uncommitted opinion of atheists can be called 'theism'. But then theisms multiply beyond recognition and the term becomes hopelessly vacuous. As a philosophical term 'theism' is a name, not of a religious faith, but of a philosophical position reacting to the atheist denial of a given religious faith, and it is in this sense that I propose to use the term. In this philosophical sense theism began its post–Renaissance career in Europe as a negation of atheism, not vice versa. Hobbes and Spinoza — however unjustified their popular denunciation as atheists may have been — preceded Newton, Locke, Bentley,[4] and Clarke.[5] Their theism was a philosophical response to the atheist denial of basic religious convictions such as the existence of God, or the denial of the personal God proclaimed by the monotheistic religions, the dependence and divine order of the world as creation, and the wisdom and benevolence of God's rule of the world. However, theism was never the only answer but

---

3. Shaftesbury, *An Inquiry Concerning Virtue*, London 1699, p. 7.
4. R. Bentley, *Confutation of Atheism*, London 1692.
5. S. Clarke, *A Demonstration of the Being and Attributes of God, More Particularly in Answer to Mr. Hobbs, Spinoza and their Followers*, London 1705.

stood alongside religious and theological reactions to atheism worked out and presented in the doctrinal systems of the time.[6]

2. The semantic opposition between theism and *atheism* remained a fundamental trait of the term, but not the exclusive one. When atheism became more clearly distinguished from scepticism, theism was also differentiated from *agnosticism*, the refusal to answer any questions about the ultimate ground of the universe. None of these contrasts distinguished theism from *deism*, which Voltaire and others used interchangeably with theism throughout the 18th century.[7] Diderot sought to distinguish deism, which denied revelation, from theism, which allowed it.[8] But it was Kant who systematically distinguished the two terms. A deist, according to him, only knows a transcendental theology, i.e., believes in an ultimate ground of everything. A theist, on the other hand, also holds a natural theology, i. e., conceives God in analogy to human intelligence as the supreme intelligence that actively participates in the course of the world. He briefly summarised the difference in the formula: 'the *deist* believes in *God*, the *theist* believes in a *living God'*.[9] Kant implied the singularity of the living God, so theism in his sense is incompatible with *polytheism* and *dualism* of any sort, including henotheism which holds that there are many gods but restricts allegiance to only one of them. Theism is closer to *monotheism*, which is often used as a synonym for theism but only justly so if it is taken to mean belief not only in a singular deity but in singular living or personal deity. As a personal deity the theistic God stands over against the world as its creator, and this transcendence of God's personal agency marks theism off from *pantheism* as well as those kinds of monistic absolutism that equate the Absolute with all that exists. Whether theism is also incompatible with *panentheism* is a matter of debate and definition. On the one hand theism stresses not only God's transcendence over against the world but also God's immanence and activity in the world. On the other hand it is by no means clear that panentheism has to conceive God in impersonal rather than personal terms or is unable to safeguard the distinction between God and world, divine creativity and

---

6. Cf. e.g. J.F. Buddeus, *Theses Theologicae de Atheismo et Superstitione*, 2nd ed., Jena 1722.
7. First used by P. Viret, *Instruction Chrestienne*, Geneva 1564.
8. D. Diderot, *Oeuvres*, ed. J. Assézat, Paris 1875-77, vol. I:13, p. 479.
9. I. Kant, *Critique of Pure Reason*. Trans. N. Kemp Smith, London 1933, B 659.

worldly creation. So there are good reasons for Hartshorne to oscillate between 'New Pantheism' and 'Neoclassical Theism' in characterising his own pantheistic position.

3. Even more complicated than the relationship between theism and the philosophical conceptions mentioned is the relationship between theism and Christian trinitarian thought. While nobody seriously denies that they are different, opinions diverge as to whether they are compatible or incompatible. Those who believe in their compatibility argue that, unlike pantheism, both views hold that God is personal and different from the world; that, unlike deism, God is personally active in the world; and that their positions differ only in that Christian trinitarianism comprises further beliefs about God than those held by the theist.[10] By reference to the dogmatic tradition of separating discussion of 'the one God' from the discussion of 'the triune God', begun by Aquinas, theism is thus presented as an independent elaboration of the tract *De deo uno*, a philosophical exposition of the basic beliefs about God which are a necessary, though not sufficient, part of trinitarian belief. This reading is rejected by others as a profound misunderstanding of the actual role and function of the tract *De deo uno* in Christian dogmatics. It cannot be separated, they argue, from its trinitarian context without being distorted because it is not an independent theistic *praeambula* to trinitarian (or some other richer) belief in God but an integral part of it. When taken in isolation, therefore, the treatise presents a unitarian view of God based not on the Christian experience of God's salvific activity in history but on the new science of the 17th century, i.e., its universal mathematics (Descartes), experimental methodology (Bacon) and universal mechanics (Newton). But a unitarian theism of this sort is not a necessary ingredient of trinitarian theology but strictly incompatible with it. For this reason theism and trinitarianism are said to be the incompatible, at least if by compatibility one means to imply that Christian trinitarianism comprehends theism as a proper subclass. Orthodox Christianity does not differ from philosophical theism in that it holds some additional beliefs about God but shares its theistic convictions. The meaning and truth of a belief like 'God is a person', for example, does not remain unaffected by its transposition from a theistic into a trinitarian context. In trinitarian theology God is not a person but three persons in one substance; God is not externally related to

---

10. Cf. R. Swinburne, *The Coherence of Theism*, Oxford 1977, p. 1.

us but closer to each of us than any person can ever be; and while God may possess personal properties, he is as the creator of everything other than himself 'as far beyond being a person as the infinite is beyond the finite', as Keith Ward has rightly pointed out.[11] Moreover, it is a mistake to assume that we can abstract a central core of self-contained theistic beliefs from trinitarian accounts of God, and thereby isolate what is accessible to reason from the trinitarian mystery which is beyond reason or understanding. This does not only leave us with an abstract theistic account of God, devoid of religious significance and increasingly superfluous as an explanatory hypothesis (as the well known exchange between Napoleon and Laplace popularly epitomizes). It also reduces the doctrine of the trinity to practical insignificance, as Barth and Rahner have argued in their respective ways, and it accounts for the doctrine's isolation and widespread sterility in the Western tradition.

The roots of this development extend, of course, much further back than Enlightenment theism. Since Augustine and scholastic Augustinianism, trinitarian thought has taken on an abstract air, and since the separation of the discussion of 'the one God' from the discussion of 'the triune God' the doctrine of the trinity has been increasingly in danger of becoming a doctrine alongside others rather than the frame of reference or the grammar of all the others. The Reformation did not achieve a restoration of trinitarian thought, and at the beginning of the 19th century Schleiermacher rightly observed that it was still one of the unfulfilled tasks of Protestant theology to do so. In the meantime the Western inclination towards a unitarian formulation of the doctrine of God had been greatly increased by the Enlightenment, which subordinated discussions of the trinity to preoccupation with the unitary being of God. Where the doctrine of the trinity was not held on merely traditionalist grounds, it was discarded altogether, or it assumed a speculative life of its own. Thus 19th century attempts to defend trinitarian thought against the natural theology of a philosophical theism, which was widely taken over by Christian theologians, led to the absorption of trinitarian thought into the speculative discussion of the being of God as Absolute, i.e., the absolute unity of transcendence and immanence, unity and difference, singularity and diversity. But this speculative trinitarianism estranged it even further from

---

11. K. Ward, Is God a Person?, in: G. van den Brink et. al. (eds.), *Christian Faith and Philosophical Theology. Essays in Honour of Vincent Brümmer*, Kampen 1992, pp. 258-66, p. 265.

the life of the church, and it left the figurative language of faith without adequate conceptual form. What it failed to perceive is that the difference between theism and trinitarianism is not merely (or primarily) a theoretical matter of different sets of belief about God, but fundamentally a practical problem and a difference of practical function: Whereas theism is a philosophical theory as distinct from a practical religious faith, trinitarianism is a theological doctrine and as such an expression and manifestation of religious faith. Whereas theism is based on common features of our everyday life and shared experience (the structure of experience as such, the reliable order of the world), and on fundamental (transcendental) explanatory requirements of our scientific accounts of the world (the existence of the world, the regularity and/or teleological structure of the processes in the world), trinitarianism is anchored in the life of the Christian community and the specific experience of Christian faith. In other words, whereas theism can be held without participating in a religious cult or the life of a religious community, trinitarianism is intrinsically dependent on the worship, doxology, and practice of the Christian faith. Whereas theism attempts to explain or to ground the scientific accounts of the world since the Renaissance in terms of a secular theology, trinitarianism explicates the meaning of Christian experience and seeks to guide Christian life by specifying the fundamental grammar of religious practices such as prayer, worship, faith in God, trust in love, and hope for the ultimate overcoming of evil.

Theism, in short, is a philosophical theory that seeks to explain the world better than atheistic attempts to do so without reference to god or God. The unfortunate effect of this is that in theism god/God is reduced to an explanatory hypothesis, conjecture, presupposition, or interpretation of our world; and insofar as theories must be assessed by their explanatory power, the theistic account of god/God is always in danger of being discarded if the problems sought to be solved, the questions sought to be answered, and the phenomena sought to be explained, can be solved, answered or explained more adequately otherwise. Trinitarian theology, on the other hand, is the doctrinal summary of the Christian experience and practice of faith. It seeks to elucidate the meaning of our experience, to guide our lives, and to help us orient ourselves reliably in a world understood to be God's creation and realm of salvific activity. It is to be assessed not by its explanatory power but by its capacity to disclose sufficiently and adequately the way reality is conceived in faith, to interpret our experience of the world meaningfully in the light of this experience, and to orient our lives in this world adequately and coherently. It stands or falls not with a theistic account of god/God but with christology and pneumatology, i.e. with both the communal and personal experience of God's salvific activity in Jesus Christ. As Blaise Pascal has put it: 'All of those who seek God apart from Christ, and who go no further than nature, either find no light to satisfy them or come to devise a means of knowing and serving God without a mediator, thus falling into either atheism or deism, two things almost equally abhorrent to Christianity.'[12] In a Christian context, what God is, and even that God is, cannot be answered apart from Christ and the Christian community's experience of the Spirit. Hence the God confessed and addressed in Christianity cannot be affirmed, criticized or supported adequately without taking into account the reality of Christian life and practice, the reality of living faith.

2. Historical Roots and Development

Theism, I have argued, arose in reaction to the atheist rejections of the views of God in the religious and philosophical traditions and debates of the 16th and 17th century, and it based its anti-atheist arguments for its versions both of natural and rational theology on the same mechanistic and mathematical premises of modern science and methodology whence modern atheism had begun. So just as there are many forms of atheism, so too there are many forms of theism. Whereas practical atheists denied the trinitarian God of orthodox Christianity by questioning the authority of scripture (*liber scripturae*), theoretical atheists went even further and denied any theological reading of the book of nature (*liber naturae*) as well. They took the new science to be capable of explaining the mysteries of nature and of grounding the legal, political and social orders of society without recourse to the hypothesis of God. Thus Renaissance Epicureanism was convinced that if there is a God, God is not interested and involved in what happens in the world and in human society, so that the understanding of nature and the foundation of the political and social order must be based on non-theological principles as Machiavelli and Hobbes had argued in their respective ways. Moreover, the reemergence of the Aristotelian doctrine of the eternity of the world together with the mystical-theosophical speculations of philosophers of nature such as Paracelsus and Giordano Bruno dissolved the idea of divine

12. Blaise Pascal, *Pensées*, trans. with an introduction by A.J. Krailsheimer, London 1977, no. 449, pp. 169—70.

transcendence and paved the way towards a pantheistic identification of God and world which was merely an intermediate step to the secular replacement of God by the world. While religious indifferentism was greatly advanced by the confessional differences and religious wars of the period, the question of truth in religion became increasingly pressing in light of the growing awareness of other religions and faiths in other parts of the world stimulated through commerce and trade. Finally, the anti-Aristotelian epistemology and methodology epitomized in Descartes' philosophy, Galileo's scientific endeavour, and Bacon's *Novum Organum* opened the way to a new view of reality. The mechanization and mathematization of the universe replaced the Aristotelian understanding of the universe as a hierarchy of forms, dominant in the Scholastic period, by means of a combination of such multifarious scientific ideals as the Pythagorean-Platonic tradition of arithmetizing the structure of the universe; the Stoic view of the universe as a quasi-animated, organic, purposeful whole whose parts are held together by forces of universal sympathy; the Atomist reduction of all causes to atoms-in-motion and the elimination of all final causality;[13] and the mechanistic materialism and sensational psychology of the French *philosophes*, as epitomized in Holbach's *Système de la Nature*, which brought all this to its secular conclusion.

Philosophical theism reacted to this twofold atheism, its foundations and consequences, in both its natural and rational theology versions by concentrating exclusively on the *liber naturae* and the *lumen naturale*, the book of nature and the requirements of human reason to interpret nature properly. This reversed the traditional order between the two books. The book of scripture was no longer taken to provide the key to the book of nature but the other way round. And this for three major reasons.

1. The wars of religion had proved the book of scripture to be fundamentally contested and contestable. Far from providing a common and unambiguous ground for theological consensus among the conflicting religious parties, its status, authority and proper understanding had themselves become a major object of conflict and controversy. Protestants who insisted on the clarity, inerrancy and sufficiency of scripture held it to be the ultimate judge in all matters of faith. Roman Catholics assigned this role to the teaching office of

---

13. Cf. A. Funkenstein, *Theology and the Scientific Imagination from the Middle Ages to the Seventeenth Century*, Princeton 1986.

the church which they claimed to be indispensable for a coherent and authoritative interpretation of scripture. And enthusiasts of various sorts rejected both the authority of the church and of scripture in terms of the inner light and personal illumination by the spirit But if the book of scripture was thus unable to serve as a common authority even among those who called themselves Christians, how could it provide a unifying basis for the social cohesion of people of different confessional and religious orientation in a state or an authoritative key to the understanding of the world at large?

2. With the displacement of the book of scripture from the centre of agreement and religious unity concensus in religion and society had to be sought along different lines. The most influential attempt was to specify the common ground in terms of fundamental beliefs held by all parties concerned. Within the Christian system of beliefs this resulted in a radical distinction, variously drawn, between fundamental and non-fundamental articles of faith, i.e. those which demand agreement by all Christians and those in which they may differ without loss of salvation or fear of condemnation or exclusion. However, since fundamental beliefs were also taken to be more universal, the search for fundamentals inevitably led beyond the confines of the Christian traditions. The consensus of society had to be based not on particular religious convictions, even fundamental ones, but on beliefs common to all people, i.e. beliefs based on publicly accessible evidence (*experience*) and universally valid criteria of reasonableness (*reason*). The contrast between fundamental and non-fundamental articles of faith was thus deepened into the more radical contrast between faith and reason, private (religious) convictions and rational (theistic) belief, with reason as the ultimate arbiter and guide in everything. All beliefs, including religious beliefs, had to be vindicated by experience and reason, i.e. by public standards of reasonableness established independently of Christian commitments.

This explains the remarkable interest in pre-Christian and extra-Christian religions and religious thought in the 17th century. Cicero's *De natura deorum* became one of the most popular philosophical books of the time, and the natural religion of the Indians[14] as well as the rational wisdom and morality

---

14. Cf. La Hontan, *Gespräche mit einem Wilden*, Frankfurt 1981; A. Pagden, *The Fall of Natural Man. The American Indian and the Origins of Comparative Ethnology*, Cambridge 1982.

of Confucius[15] were hotly debated topics in academic circles and public coffee-houses alike. For many the natural religion and morality of ancient and contemporary people outside Judaism, Christianity and Islam vindicated the claims of human reason, proved the sufficiency of moral principle and suggested a universal human consensus on such questions as the existence and attributes of God, the immortality of the soul and human freedom and morality.

None of this had to be known through the book of scripture, all of it was or could be held on the basis of the book of nature alone.

3. Finally, just as the book of scripture was displaced by natural religion so supernatural revelation was superseded by natural theology. When human reason gained independent access to the book of nature it had no longer need for the book of scripture as its key. The Augustinian tradition had argued that the *liber mundi*, originally a fully sufficient source of knowledge, became unintelligible to us because of our sin and fall; but God in his mercy has given us the *liber scripturae* which shows us the meaning of everything written in the book of nature and thus allows us to regain the knowledge which we have lost.

This implied that the world in all its natural, historical, and cultural dimensions, with their infinite details and inexhaustible perspectives, can be conceived as a meaningful whole and ordered cosmos which can, in principle at least, be understood. If we fail to understand all its infinite detail to belong to one coherent and intelligible pattern, it is our fault, not nature's. But to conceive and interpret the world in this way requires us to see nature as God's creation that points to the true nature of its maker, and this we cannot do clearly and unambiguously unless we know its creator in the first place. Without that knowledge we can have no clear knowledge of the world as creation, and hence no knowledge of its unity and intelligibility. For the singularity of God is what guarantees the world's unity, and his revealed will its intelligibility; and revelation is what guarantees a single author of the book of revelation and the book of nature, by revealing the God who saves to be the God who creates.

---

15. Cf. N. Malebranche, Entretien d'un philosophe chrétien et d'un philosophe chinois sur l'existence et la nature de Dieu, *Oeuvres complètes de Malebranche*, Paris 1962ff, 15:39; G.W. Leibniz, *Discours sur la theologie naturelle des Chinoises*, trans. with introduction and notes by D.J. Cook and H. Rosemont, Honolulu 1977.

The Augustinian argument for the epistemic necessity of the book of scripture and its priority over the book of nature sought to show God to be the common author of nature and revelation. It broke down when the focus of interest changed from their common author to their different languages. For the book of nature, as Galileo pointed out, is 'written in the language of mathematics' (*scritto in lingua matematica*)[16] and the book of scripture is obviously of little use in deciphering that language. It has to be studied on its own — independently of the book of scripture. Only so can we hope to arrive at a proper understanding of it. Hence Descartes' decision, according to his *Discours de la méthode*, to give up 'l'étude des lettres' (including theology) in order to devote himself totally to the study of himself (moi-même) and of the 'grand livre du monde'.[17] This independent study of the book of nature by calculation and experiment was the beginning of modern science; and the independent study of the self and its capacities by critical self-reflection the beginning of modern philosophy. Thus what began as an attempt to integrate nature, and the natural knowledge of the world, into the theological perspective, ended by freeing the study of the book of nature from domination by the book of scripture.

However, the scientific study of the book of nature continued to operate on the assumption that nature was a unity and the world an ordered and intelligible whole. But it had lost the traditional theological justification for these fundamental assumptions, i.e. the revelation of God the saviour as God the creator, and of the world as creation, thus establishing the unity and intelligibility of the world by contrasting it as creation with its creator. Parallel to the rise of modern science, therefore, philosophy sought to provide new justifications for its fundamental assumptions. This was first done in terms of a natural theology or theism independent of, and increasingly in contrast to, the revelational theology of the Christian tradition because it was based on ontological, cosmological and teleological analyses of the structure of the world and the self. And when these attempts broke down under the impact of Hume's and Kant's critical philosophies, it was

16. G. Galilei, Il Saggiatore, *Opere* VI. Rome, 1923, pp. 197-372, p. 232.
17. R. Descartes, Discours de la méthode. *Oeuvres des Descartes*, vol. VI, ed. C. Adam and P. Tannary, Paris 1897-1913, pp. 1-78, p. 9.

done by deriving constitutive and/or regulative principles of human mind and knowledge from a transcendental analysis of the capacities and presuppositions of human understanding and reason. In either case nature now illuminates revelation, and not vice versa; the book of nature is the key to the book of scriptures; and reason, not revelation, is the final arbiter.

For much of the formative period of modern Western culture, therefore, the idea of an independent study of the book of nature promoted the rise not only of science but also of philosophical theism, i.e. a philosophical *natural theology* and a scientific *theology of nature* independent of the theological doctrines of God and creation based on the book of scripture. This also accounts for their different reactions to atheism. While theology argued against (practical) atheism from the authority of scripture and revelation, philosophical theism started from non-theological premises such as the innate idea of God, the experience of the existence, regularity, and natural order of the world, or from what now would be called 'comparative religion'. Accordingly, to mention only some English writers, Lord Herbert of Cherbury was one of the first to describe religion and its basic knowledge of God as the one to be worshiped as a universal human phenomenon in his *De Veritate* (1624) and *De Religione Gentilium* (1645). At about the same time the Cambridge Platonists had recourse to a Platonist psychology and cosmology as *An Antidote against Atheism* (Henry More, 1656) and the key to *The True Intellectual System of the Universe* (Ralph Cudworth, 1678). In a different way John Locke showed *The Reasonableness of Christianity* (1695) on the empiricist basis established in his *Essay concerning Human Understanding* (1689) by arguing that we have intuitive knowledge of ourselves, demonstrative knowledge of God, and sensitive knowledge of the world of nature. Similarly Newton, like Descartes, More, or Spinoza, was convinced that he knew several things of God, the source of all power and ruler of the universe, clearly and distinctly. Unlike Descartes' his God was not merely a Deist originator of the world, but actually interfered in his creation to correct endangered planetary orbits. This again enraged Leibniz, who opposed the Newtonian image of God as an imperfect maker of a wordly mechanism in constant need of repair and replaced it with a view of God as the Monad-in-Chief, which, because of its maximal power, wisdom, and goodness, by necessity creates the best of all possible worlds. Thus while Locke's theism is based on *a posteriori* inferences (natural theology), Leibniz's is grounded on *a priori* arguments (rational theology). In short, theism, as even these few hints suffice to make clear, is by no means a homogeneous doctrine but takes different and sometimes opposing forms.[18] Yet they are all meant to solve specific problems, and hence comprise a number of typical components.

3. Basic Components

Theism arose as a philosophical reaction to modern atheism. In as much as atheism is not a positive doctrine in itself, it varies in scope and content with the religious beliefs that it rejects. Often it is nothing but a polemical characterisation of those who do not believe in the gods or God of a given religion, and in this sense most religions, including ancient China, India, the Greek and Roman world, Judaism, Christianity, and Islam have known the phenomenon of atheism or have described those who disagreed with their views as atheists. Since the times of the pre-Socratics there have been sceptics who doubted or denied the existence of the Greek or Roman gods. The Christians were called ἄθεοι because they refused to participate in the state cult of the Roman Empire. In the 14th century Nicolaus de Autricuria had to renounce his atheist materialism and Epicurean atomism because he held that 'in the processes of nature there is nothing to be found but the motion of the combination and separation of atoms'.[19] In the 17th century Mersenne declared that there were as many as 50,000 atheists in the Paris of his time but 'the majority of these were called atheists simply because they declined to accept any longer the authority of Aristotle'.[20] Similarly, Spinoza's philosophy was accused of being atheist, and this conviction continued well into the 19th century.[21] So atheism varied with the religious standard from which it departed, and not all philosophical reactions to these various sorts of practical and theoretical atheism can aptly be termed theism. Historically theism arose in reaction to modern atheism, which only slowly took shape since the Renaissance and its new scientific discoveries. Atheism's basic tenets were (1) the doubt or negation of the existence of God, (2) the denial of a universe ordered by a caring mind or intelligence and not merely by natural laws, (3) the affirmation of inexplicable evil and unjust suffering in the world as fundamental reasons against all belief in God, and (4) the

18. Cf. the exemplary controversy between Leibniz and Clarke: *The Leibniz-Clarke Correspondence*, ed. H.G. Alexander, 3rd ed., Manchester 1976.
19. Cf. F.A.Lang, *History of Materialism*, London 1877, vol. I, p. 225.
20. C.B. Upton, Atheism and Anti-Theistic Theories, *Encyclopedia of Religion and Ethics*, vol. II, 2nd ed., Edinburgh 1930, pp.173-83, p. 177.
21. Cf. Fr.H. Jacobi, *Werke* 1/4, Leipåzig 1812-25, repr. Darmstadt 1968, p. 216.

independence of morality from belief in God. Each of these became the major
concern and philosophical preoccupation of theism as well, which for this
reason can be summarized as comprising the following four components:

1. Theism elaborates and defends a *concept of God* succinctly summarized by
Swinburne: By 'God' a theist understands something like a 'person without
a body (i.e. a spirit) who is eternal, free, able to do anything, knows
everything, is perfectly good, is the proper object of human worship and
obedience, the creator and sustainer of the universe'.[22] This concept of God
results from three basic motifs of theism, two of which are directed against
the tenets of atheism, the third against the difference and particularity of
opposing religious traditions. First, there is the *cosmological motif*, which
makes God, not matter-in-motion as in Hobbes, the ultimate cause and
explanation of the world. Accordingly rational theology explains the intelligibility and unity of the world by appealing to a self-explanatory being
'whose sheer nature explains its existence, as well as the existence of
everything else'.[23] Similarly natural theology seeks to explain order and
harmony in the world by appealing to a purposive mind behind it. Second,
there is the *religious motif*, which takes God to be not coextensive with the
universe but transcendent, a personal being worthy of worship, able to act
not only in creating the world but in the created world, and hence free to
respond to prayers.[24] Finally, there is the *philosophical motif*, which seeks to
conceive God in terms not of any given historical religion and its appeals to
particular revelation but in more general terms as the common core of
different religions, at least as the central core of Jewish, Christian, and
Muslim beliefs in God. In concentrating on those aspects of belief in God on
which these historical religions cannot agree to differ without falling into self-
contradiction, philosophical theism was and is the attempt to offer a rational
principle to bridge the gap between opposing views and convictions of
different religious traditions, both beyond (Jews, Moslems) as well as within
Christianity (Roman Catholics, Protestants, Eastern Orthodox). All three
motifs conceptualize God and God's relationship to the world by using
certain models: the models of *Personal Explanation*, in terms of actions and

22. Swinburne, *Coherence*, Oxford 1977, p. 1.
23. Ward, *Rational Theology*, p. 8.
24. V. Brümmer, *What Are We Doing When We Pray? A Philosophical Inquiry*, London,
    1984.

intentions, and of *Mind and Body*; the models of *Mind, Subject* and the *Elusive Self or Soul*; the models of *Personal Agency* and *Personal Communicator*. The models used determine the divine properties attributed to God such as infinity, eternity, freedom, omniscience, omnipotence, benevolence, creative activitiy, incorporeality, etc. These motifs, and the models of God based on them, are usually combined because theism is thought to be defensible only insofar as it can meet the requirements of explaining the world as well as the religious and philosophical requirements. Consequently the analogy between human persons as finite, but free and creative moral agents, and God as the Supreme Creative and Beneficent Agent becomes the key element in theistic conceptions of God.

This can clearly be seen, to give but one example, in Samuel Clarke's classic theistic *Demonstration of the Being and Attributes of God*.[25] The argument, which takes its methodology and basic convictions from Newton, proceeds in two steps, the first establishing the being, the second the principal attributes of the divine nature. From the phenomena of experience Clarke argues by way of analysis to the underlying forces which establish the being of God; he subsequently argues by way of synthesis to the God of providence by conjoining the existence and the personal attributes of God. This movement of analysis and synthesis occurs again in each part of the concatenated argument, i.e., in establishing the being of God and its impersonal attributes, and in establishing the intelligent and free being of God and God's personal attributes of power, wisdom, and providence.

I. The Being of God
A. Analytic Movement:
    Prop. 1:   That Something has existed from Eternity.
    Prop. 2:   That there has existed from Eternity some one Immutable and Independent Being.
    Prop. 3:   That that Immutable and Independent Being, which has existed from Eternity, without any External Cause of its Existence, must be Self-Existent, that is, Necessarily-Existing.
B. Synthetic Movement:
    Prop. 4:   What the Substance or Essence of that Being, which is Self-Existent or Necessarily-Existent, is, we have no Idea, neither is it at all possible for us to comprehend it.

25. I follow the reconstruction and analysis of the argument given in Buckley, *At the Origins*, pp. 174-5.

Prop. 5:   That though the Substance or Essence of the Self-Existent Being is itself absolutely incomprehensible to us, yet many of the Essential Attributes of his Nature are strictly Demonstrable, as well as his Existence. As in the First Place, that He must of Necessity be Eternal.

Prop. 6:   That the Self-Existent Being, must of Necessity be Infinite and Omnipresent.

Prop. 7:   That the Self-Existent Being must of Necessity be but One.

II. The Principal Attributes of the Divine Nature:
A. Analytic Movement:

Prop. 8:   That the Self-Existent and Original Cause of all Things must be an Intelligent Being. This, the main Question between us and the Atheists.

Prop. 9:   That the Self-Existent and Original Cause of all Things, is not a Necessary Agent, but a Being imbued with Liberty and Choice.

B. Synthetic Movement:

Prop. 10:   That the Self-Existent Being, the Supreme Cause of all Things, must of Necessity have Infinite Power.

Prop. 11:   That the Supreme Cause and Author of all Things must of Necessity be Infinitely Wise.

Prop. 12:   That the Supreme Cause and Author of all Things must of Necessity be a Being of Infinite Goodness, Justice and Truth, and all other Moral Perfections; such as become the Supreme Governor and Judge of the World.

Clarke's argument starts from the fact that something now exists and explains it in terms of something that has existed from all eternity by using the principles (1) that all temporal being is the result of becoming or production (principle of causation), and (2) that to be produced without a producer is intrinsically contradictory (principle of noncontradiction). The explanatory model underlying his argument is that of personal explanation in terms of an agent producing something. Clarke does not say so explicitly. But it becomes clear from the two conclusions for which he argues. The first is that there is a being that is eternal, immutable and independent, and self-existent or necessary. However, to accept this is not sufficient for theism. We may agree that these predicates are coherent and that there is something to which they apply, and yet insist that the proper subject of these predicates is not God, but the world or nature or matter. This is precisely how the atheist argues. Hence Clarke rightly locates the major issue at stake in the debate between theism and atheism in his eighth proposition or, more generally, by means of his second major conclusion: That only an intelligent and free agent can be the proper subject of the impersonal theistic attributes established. For theism, it is not enough to show the necessity of an original cause of all things temporal and to avoid the fallacy of explaining contingent existence in terms of necessary existence. What it has to demonstrate is that the 'Supreme Cause' for which it argues is an '*Author* of all Things', i.e., a Supreme Creative and Beneficient *Agent*. For theism to be possible such a personal conception of God must be shown to be coherent, as Clarke has clearly seen. But he was also aware that its coherence is not adequate to rebut the atheist. This brings us to the second point.

2. The coherence of this concept of God is required for the second major component of theism: its *arguments for the existence of God*. To show a Supreme Creative and Beneficent Agent to be possible is not enough; there must be good reasons for asserting the existence of such a being. Thus arguments for and against the existence of God have become a major topic of philosophical argument since the Enlightenment. Without reasons for belief in the existence of God no further theistic beliefs can be reasonable. Of the numerous rational bases proposed for belief in the existence of God, the ontological and cosmological arguments, and the arguments from design, are especially important. They all argue as follows:

(a) that the concept of God is coherent and the existence of such a supreme being is possible (arguments for the possibility of God);

(b) that such a being actually exists either because it absolutely must (ontological arguments for the necessity of God) or has to, given the existence and character of the world (cosmological arguments and arguments from design for the actuality of God);

(c) that there can only be one such being, because the unity and singularity of the world allows for only one creator and providential lord of nature and history (arguments for the singularity of God).

The three sets of problems of the *possibility, necessity* and/or *actuality*, and *singularity* of God are central to theism and have remained at the focus of debates in Anglophone philosophy of religion since the days of Samuel Clarke. For the question of the possibility of God implies fundamental questions about meaning, the coherence of concepts, and the use of words; the question of the necessity and/or actuality of God fundamental questions about logic, ontology, cosmology and the character of the world; and the question of the singularity of God raises fundamental questions about the unity and plurality of worlds, the difference between actual and possible worlds, and the identity of individuals in different worlds. Thus theism is a philosophical construction which places the problem of God at the centre of philosophical debate with intimate links to virtually every philosophical topic. Consequently, it is particularly sensitive to changes in these areas.

Arguments for the existence of God are a central but not the only area of epistemic debate in theism. Insofar as they seek to demonstrate the fundamental explanatory principle of the existence, order or structure of the world, and/or our experience of the world, they imply a notion of the world, its unity, order and structure, and a conception of the relation between God and world spelled out in terms of, on the one hand, divine creation and government, intervention and revelation, inspiration and redemption, and, on the other, worldly dependence, corruption, sin, correction and perfection.[26] But how can we know about God and God's relation to the world? Neither God nor the world are phenomena or (actual or possible) data of experience. Only myths present gods as phenomena, but God is not one of the gods, and philosophy not mythology. Similarly, only a naïve realism understands the world as a thing, the most complex thing that there is, but the totality of things is not a thing, and, for the theist, as Swinburne points out, 'the world' can only mean 'all logically contingent things apart from God' or, in a narrower sense, 'all physical things which are spatially related to the earth'.[27] Whether we agree or not, what cannot be denied is that theism implies a notion of the world which is such that the relationship between God and the world is different in kind from any relationship between things in the world, so that perceiving and knowing things in the world must be different in kind from knowing God. Yet if God cannot be perceived in fact, God is no *datum* (actual existent), and if he cannot be perceived in principle, God is no *dabile* (possible existent). Consequently, knowledge about God cannot be inferred from what we know in experience because — as Hume and Kant have shown — we can argue from things experienced to things that might be experienced, but not to something that is beyond our experience

26. Cf. the illuminating discussion of these and related problems by Chr. Schwöbel, *God: Action and Revelation*, Kampen 1992.
27. Swinburne, *Coherence*, pp. 129f.

altogether. But then, if God is no *dabile*, can God only be a *cogitabile*,[28] i.e.,

— something that, although incapable of being phenomenally given, allows us to explain otherwise puzzling facts about phenomena or about those who experience phenomena (a *theoretical construct* like electrons or the Ego); or

— something that could not be otherwise,

  — given the structure of our actual world (something necessary in our actual world: a *contingent (structural) necessity* or ultimate brute fact like the nature of our spatio-temporal manifold);

  — given the structure of our actual experience of our world (something necessary in our experiencing our actual world: a *transcendental necessity* or ultimate reflective fact like the categorial schemes in terms of which we experience);

  — given the structure of our acting in our actual world (something necessary for us as agents: a *practical necessity* like freedom);

— something that could not fail to be as it is (something necessary in all possible worlds: an *absolute (structural, transcendental, or practical) necessity*)?

In either of these cases the character of our knowledge of God, and the epistemic questions that can meaningfully be asked depend on whether our conceptions of God are mere constructions of something possible (fiction), or theoretical constructs (useful fictions), or reconstructions of a contingent, transcendental, practical, or absolute necessity. But it seems obvious that God cannot be a theoretical construct because the term 'God' does not (any longer) function in scientific theories which aim at explaining facts about the world or ourselves. Electrons have a place in physical theory because they throw light on a particular area of reality, suggest new lines of enquiry, and allow for experimental testing; the *Ego* is used in (some) psychological theories because it helps to explain a number of puzzling facts about our acting, believing, and knowing. But this is not so in the case of God. 'God' functions in metaphysical theories which are not tied to particular areas but seek to provide an overall understanding of reality, and 'God' is used in order to throw a particular light on the whole of reality and to suggest a certain attitude toward all experience. But then the use of 'God' cannot be

---

28. F. Wagner, *Was ist Religion? Studien zu ihrem Begriff und Thema in Geschichte und Gegenwart*, Gütersloh 1986, pp. 575ff.

strictly parallel to that of theoretical or practical constructs but must be understood differently.

Some, like J. Hick or R. Swinburne, have taken God to be a contingent necessity or ultimate brute fact. Accordingly for Hick 'the existence of purposive intelligence' is 'an ultimate fact' which explains everything but is 'not a candidate for explanation' itself.[29] Similarly, Swinburne has argued that God is the ultimate brute fact that explains the universe better and with a higher probability than any rival hypothesis. Yet he does not hold that God is a logically necessary being, not only because he believes this to be an incoherent idea but because 'the non-existence of God is logically compatible with the existence of the universe'.[30]

Many theists have rejected this, albeit for different reasons. Some follow Kant in taking the idea of God to be a transcendental necessity demanded by the general conditions of the possibility of human knowledge. Understood in this way 'God' is not a concept applicable to reality but an indispensable regulative idea of our knowledge of reality: we require it in order to give completeness and unity to our theoretical knowledge of what is true about the world of our experience. 'God is not' as Kant put it, 'a Being outside of me, but merely a thought within me'.[31] Yet it is not an arbitrary thought because the tendency of our mind to see the world of experience as a unified and connected whole naturally leads us to explain it in terms of 'an all-sufficient necessary cause' or God. We only have to be careful not to reify this regulative principle and mistake it for an actual entity. For although the ideal of a unity in the explanation of the world is necessary, it 'is not an assertion of an existence necessary in itself'.[32]

More recently, Alvin Plantinga has offered a relativistic version of this type of argument by describing belief in God as a properly basic belief which may be part of the foundation of a person's noetic structure.[33] According to him, a belief is rational if it is evident with respect to the beliefs that form the basis of our noetic structure; this may be the case either by being supported by some foundational beliefs or by being itself part of the

---

29. J. Hick, *Arguments for the Existence of God*, London 1979, p. 50.
30. R. Swinburne, *The Existence of God*, Oxford 1979, p. 120.
31. I. Kant, *Opus Postumum, Kants handschriftlicher Nachlaß*, vol. 8, Berlin 1936, p. 145.
32. I. Kant, *Critique of Pure Reason*. Trans. N. Kemp Smith, London 1933, B 647.
33. A. Plantinga, Is Belief in God Rational? in C.F. Delany (ed.), *Rationality and Religious Belief*, Notre Dame 1979, pp. 12f; Is Belief in God Properly Basic? *Nous* 15, pp. 41-51.

foundational set of beliefs on which we rely as evidence for non-basic beliefs. Belief in God is rational in the latter sense. But, whereas for Kant, God is a regulative idea of human knowledge as such irrespective of the concrete form it takes in a given person, belief in God understood in Plantinga's sense may be basic to some persons but not to others, so that — as J. Kellenberger has pointed out — it will be rational for one to believe in God and for another not to believe in God.[34]

Similarly, some have followed Kant in taking God to be a practical necessity, i.e., a necessary postulate of practical reason. The highest good which is the object and final end of pure practical reason can be attained only if morality (the fulfillment of our moral obligations) and happiness coincide. But this is obviously not the case in this life; therefore, we have to postulate both our immortality and the existence of God or otherwise we 'would have to regard the moral laws as empty figments of the brain, since without this postulate the necessary consequence which is itself connected with these laws could not follow'.[35] God, then, is necessary not for morality as such but for the bringing about of the highest good. This, however, leaves us without any (theoretical) knowledge about God because we cannot make any truth claims about God.

This Kantian attempt to reconcile freedom and reason by distinguishing sharply between knowing and acting, theoretical and practical reason and, accordingly, the impossibility of theoretical knowledge of God and the necessity of postulating God as a regulative idea of morality and the unity of knowledge has met with little approval. Philosophers in the onto-theological tradition like Hegel, Hartshorne, or Ward have argued in different ways that God cannot be practically necessary but theoretically unintelligible. If God is possible at all, God is necessarily actual because God cannot fail to exist. The concept of God differs from all other concepts in that we cannot accept it as coherent and remain agnostic about whether it is actually instantiated or not: God is either impossible or a logically necessary being. Thus if there is to be any knowledge about God at all, it must be knowledge not about whether the concept of God is actually instantiated but rather whether this concept is meaningful and coherent, and being coherent is enough for it to be instantiated because it 'is a conceptual truth that any

34. J. Kellenberger, *The Cognitivity of Religion. Three Perspectives*, Berkeley 1985, pp. 102f.
35. Kant, *Critique*, B 839.

possibly necessary being is actual'.[36] However, the cogency of this argument depends on the interpretation of the notion of the possibility of God as meaning: 'Possibly it is necessary that there is a God', rather than 'Possibly it is not necessary that there is a God'. In the latter case the same type of ontological argument would establish not the necessary existence but the necessary non-existence of God. But there seem to be no theoretical or *a priori* reasons for choosing one of the two interpretations rather than the other.[37] So theists are forced to fall back on some version of the cosmological argument, or, if they agree with Swinburne that the non-existence of God is logically compatible with the existence of the universe, to have recourse to some version of the argument from design. Since this presupposes an argument to design in the light of the ambiguities of our actual experience of beauty and order as well as evil and suffering in the world it requires a closer consideration of the *problem of evil*.

3. The theoretical nature of theism and its dependence on particular views about the nature and character of the world are manifest in its preoccupation with the *problem of evil* in the specific form of *theodicy*. There has always been evil, pain, suffering, and injustice in the world. They have been a major driving force in the formation of religious convictions, but in religious rather than philosophical contexts they have usually inspired belief and trust in God, deepened our understanding of God, and generated hope for a better reality to come. For theism, however, they constitute a fundamental threat and insurmountable stumbling block because they lead us to question the nature and reality of God rather than the nature and reality of the world. In Epicurus' old questions rephrased by Hume: 'Is God willing to prevent evil, but not able? Then he is impotent. Is he able, but not willing? Then he is malevolent. Is he both able and willing? Whence then is evil?'[38] Posed in this way the problem of evil is transformed into a problem of the logical compatibility of certain beliefs about God and the world, i.e., the beliefs that:

36. K. Ward, *Rational Theology and the Creativity of God*, Oxford 1982, p. 26.
37. Cf. I.U. Dalferth, *Gott. Philosophisch-theologische Denkversuche*, Tübingen 1992, pp. 202-13, 219-24.
38. David Hume, *Dialogues Concerning Natural Religion* (1779). Ed. N.K. Smith .2nd ed., London 1947, p. 147, pt. X.

(a) God exists;
(b) God is omnipotent;
(c) God is omniscient;
(d) God is wholly good;
(e) There exists evil in the world.

This is a theoretical problem, and it has a number of theoretical solutions.[39] If we drop (a) or (e), the problem does not arise; if we give up the idea of infinity in (b) to (d), the problem disappears. Less radical solutions attempt to reject the alleged incompatibility in various ways. It may be argued, e.g., by Plantinga,[40] that beliefs (a) to (d) do not entail that God does not create, or has no reason to create, beings who perform evil deeds; that the existence of some evil is necessary for the existence of certain sorts of values and second-order goods; that the existence of morally free agents necessarily entails the possibility of moral evil ('Free Will Defence'); or that an infinite number of actions and interactions, both between agents in the world and between worldly agents and God, necessarily produces effects beyond the control of any individual agent, including God (Hartshorne).

None of these solutions is uncontested, but the theoretical way the problem is posed leaves all the suggested solutions with a ring of practical insignificance: even if belief in God in the face of evil and suffering could be made plausible, it would still not tell the believer how to cope with evil, or how to establish the truth of (a) through (d). The alleged incompatibility of (a) through (e) matters only if they are all true, which is not at all obvious in the case of (a) through (d). All theoretical reflection can hope to show is 'that no amount of evil will contradict the existence of a perfect God, as long as the requirement is met, that it is necessarily implied in the existence of a world which leads to overwhelming good'.[41] But how can this be supported by our actual experience of the world? The world gives little or no reason to suppose that it leads to overwhelming good. Moreover if we had reason to believe in the existence, power, wisdom and goodness of God, we could

39. Cf. I.U. Dalferth, *Religiöse Rede von Gott*, München 1981, pp. 538ff.
40. A. Plantinga, The Free Will Defence, in M. Black (ed.), *Philosophy in America*, London 1965, pp. 204-20; *God and Other Minds. A Study of the Rational Justification of Belief in God*, Ithaca 1967, chaps. 5 and 6; *The Nature of Necessity*, Oxford 1974, chap. 9; *God, Freedom and Evil*, London 1975.
41. K. Ward, *Rational Theology*, pp. 206f.

agree with Leibniz that this is compatible with the evil and suffering in the world. But Hume has shown that we have little or no reason to infer these beliefs from our ambiguous experiences of the world, and Kant has shown that (a) through (d) are not the sort of beliefs whose truth could even in principle be established by theoretical reason.

So theism indeed faces a dilemma. The compatibility of belief in God with our experience of the world is not enough to justify belief in God: we need independent arguments to sustain this belief. But the arguments of rational and natural theology for the existence of God do not stand up to examination. The *a posteriori* arguments of natural theology from the actual world to God cannot justify asserting the perfect existence, power, wisdom and goodness of God in the face of evil, pain, and suffering. Therefore the argument of design, based on our experience of order and disorder in our world, participates in the ambiguity of the world; and the cosmological argument cannot justify the assumed intelligibility of the world independently of its inference to a self-explanatory being who makes it intelligible. The *a priori* arguments of rational theology, which conceive God to be either impossible or necessary, either cannot justify the premise (1) 'It is possible that God exists' rather than the premise (2) 'It is possible that God does not exist' and thus can no more prove the necessary existence of God than they can prove his necessary non-existence, or they too must rely on *a posteriori* arguments for (1) rather than (2) which fact — because all the evidence available is as compatible with (2) as with (1) — only manifests a question-begging religious perspective on the world. In short, without convincing arguments for the existence of God the theoretical enterprise of theism fails. Natural theology breaks down because, given the facts of evil, it cannot prove that our world is intelligible in a way that unambiguously points to God, and rational theology breaks down because it cannot make plausible why God should necessarily exist rather than necessarily not exist.

Theism stands or falls with its arguments for the existence of God. It insists that it conceptualizes the very God addressed in faith and reflected upon in theology, and that this is borne out by both its concept of God as a perfect personal being and its arguments for the existence of this God so that, in Shaftesbury's words, nobody can be 'a settled Christian' who is not 'a good theist' in the first place.[42] Now it is true that both faith and theology talk to and about God in particular ways, and that both presuppose him to

42. *Op. cit.,*p. 7.

exist. But then the theistic reformulation of Christian faith cannot restrict its conceptualization to the semantic dimension of the understanding of 'God' which emerges from faith and theology. It must also take into account that faith and theology presuppose God to exist, and this is the function of its arguments for the existence of God. Thus just as the theistic understanding of God seeks to conceptualize (part of) the semantics of the religious use of 'God', so its arguments for the existence of God seek to conceptualize (part of) its pragmatics. But theism fails in both respects. 'God has now become 'a personal being" where before God was absolute Being (not *a* being) in three persons (not *a* person)'[43] and belief in his existence has now become a separate topic of discussion where previously it was the inseparable presupposition of the Christian doctrine of God and all other doctrines. No Christian doctrine is (or should be) without foundation in experience, although this is not to say that each doctrine by itself reflects a separate kind of experience. Only the whole system of doctrines together expresses the Christian experience of reality. The theistic concentration upon God and God's existence in isolation is bound to distort the integrating view of faith, and to conceptualize beliefs about God irrespective of their wider experiential and doctrinal contexts can only result in misconceptions. This is borne out by the theistic arguments for the existence of God, which represent, under misleading disguises, isolated aspects of the internal views of faith, but distort the overall picture. For instance, the ontological argument represents the Christian experience of the reality, singularity, and unsurpassable sovereignty of God in terms of ontological necessity, but it breaks down because (amongst other things) it fails to provide adequate means for determining God's identity in the sense of bringing us to know who God is.[44] The cosmological argument represents the Christian experience of total dependence on the sovereign will of God as the metaphysical dependence of the contingent on the necessary, but it breaks down because it confuses different understandings of contingency.[45] Finally, the argument from design represents the Christian experience of the caring guidance of God as

43. T.W. Jennings, *Beyond Theism. A Grammar of God-Language*, New York 1985, p. 19.
44. Cf. J. Hintikka, Kant on Existence, Predication, and the Ontological Argument, in S. Knuutila and J. Hintikka (eds.), *The Logic of Being. Historical Studies*, Dordrecht 1986, pp. 249-67.
45. J. L. Mackie, *The Miracle of Theism. Arguments for and against the Existence of God*, Oxford 1982, p. 84.

an underlying purposive order of nature and history, but it breaks down because all this can be explained without reference to God.[46] In short, theism fails because it begins with abstractions and ends by committing what Whitehead has called the 'fallacy of misplaced concretness'.

4. Finally, theism could not prevent or correct but even furthered the view that morality is independent of religion and belief in God. While Samuel Clarke held that morality is not arbitrary but belongs to the objective order of the universe, Shaftesbury inisted that there is a sense of right and wrong in every person, 'the moral sense' which is not derived from religion but belongs to human nature as such. The doctrine of the moral sense as an auto-nomous human faculty was developed and defended against criticism by Francis Hutcheson in his *Essay on the Nature and Conduct of the Passions and Affections, with Illustrations on the Moral Sense* (1728). Whereas Joseph Butler tried to re-interpret it theistically by equating the moral sense with the voice of God in human conscience, the whole approach was decisively criticized by David Hume who insisted on a radical disjunction between is and ought and on the impossibility of deriving principles of morals from statements about human nature and conscience. Hume's criticism of moral naturalism was in no way meant as a return to a theist grounding of morality. On the contrary, he insisted even more radically on the autonomy of morality as the moral sense tradition and thus paved the way to Kant's ethics of human autonomy, free will and self-determination. Traditional Christian theology had grounded its moral reflections in its understanding of the goodness of God within the framework of God's creative and salvific activity. Theism, on the other hand, derived its account of the goodness of God from its under-standing of human goodness by way of analogy. But the more the philo-sophical understanding of the natural world and human morality drifted apart, the less theism was able to bridge the gap in its account of God. It utterly failed in its attempt 'to find a 'natural' and 'neutral' universal foundation for morality and then add the specifically Christian emphasis as an optional extra'[47] because its unitarian conception of God was unable to overcome the antinomy between divine heteronomy and the autonomy of human morality. On the contrary, by creating an alternative between auto-

46. Dalferth, *Religiöse Rede*, pp. 532ff.
47. Chr. Schwöbel, God's Goodness and Human Morality, *Nederlands Theologisch Tijdschrift* 43, 1990, pp. 122-38, p. 137.

nomous morality and heteronomous theism it contributed heavily to the process of secularization and the increasing loss of interest in a theistic framework for human life. Not only was theism not needed for morality, it even proved to be incompatible with morality. Hence it had to be discarded in the name of human autonomy.

4. A Future for Theism?

In discussing theism in the sense proposed it is useful to distinguish between the prehistory, history and posthistory of philosophical theism. Its prehistory includes such diverse factors as Platonist dualism, the Aristotelian pattern of causality, Stoic immanentism, Philonean personalism, Neoplatonist negative theology and Sozinian antitrinitarianism. Its history begins with Bacon's scientific methodology, Galileo's scientific discoveries, and Descartes' search for epistemic certainty. They all argue that complex problems must be broken down into basic units which are certain beyond doubt because they are known *clare et distincte*; and they conceive God either to be one of these fundamentally clear ideas (Descartes) or to be inferable from them. Theism blossoms with Newton's scientific achievements and their theistic interpretations in the 18th century: God is seen as the most simple principle of explanation, self-evident in itself, and necessarily required by our (complex) experiences of ourselves and of the world and in this sense the common core of civil religion in a multi-religious and multi-confessional society. Theism begins to decline with the philosophical critiques of Hume and Kant, the growing awareness of its incompatibility with moral autonomy and the onto-theological alternatives of Hegel and Schelling. It forfeits its basis by the overcoming of Newtonian science in our own century, its point through the dissolution of Cartesianism in contemporary philosophy, its persuasiveness as a philosophical undertaking by the insight and discovery that if religion has no intrinsic justification it cannot be justified externally, its attraction owing to atheism's becoming a tradition alongside a diversity of religious traditions rather than a revolution of all religion, and its public function by undermining the autonomy of morality and being stripped of its apologetic claim to be an anavoidable truth for all reasonable persons.

Are we to conclude, therefore, that philosophical theism is of interest only as a piece of history, that 'The Rise and Fall of Theism'[48] is a topic for the

48. Jennings, chap. 2.

historian of ideas but not for the philosopher? Not necessarily, as history
teaches us. In the 17th and 18th centuries theism served as the point of
contact between (Christian) theology and Enlightenment philosophy and
science. Now Jennings is surely right in saying 'it is necessary to recognize
that theism can no longer serve as the middle term in building an apologetic
bridge between Christian faith and contemporary culture'[49] because, as John
Clayton has argued convincingly,[50] theism is unable to provide a common
foundation on which to build belief in God in an age of religious and cultural
pluralism. But just as mission is not the only way for a religion or theology
to relate to other religions, so apologetics is not the only way to relate to
religion's cultural matrix. Rational or argumentative relations are rarely
central, and never basic to religion, but always presuppose more fundamental practical interactions and involvements of a religion with its cultural
contexts. On the other hand religious and theological arguments themselves
can serve more than solely justificatory ends: 'they may be used polemically
within a tradition to correct heresy or, more positively, to edify members of
the community; they may also be used to assist with the interpretation of
texts or to express awe and wonder'.[51] The same is true of theistic arguments of philosophy: they may serve apologetical, polemical, and explanatory
purposes, but also pursue critical, hermeneutical, or grammatical ends.
Accordingly, of all the factors that led to the development of theism, one of
the weightiest was the need to formulate a concept of God which was
beyond the idiosyncracies of the opposing versions of Roman Catholic and
Protestant Christianity.[52] Such a generic concept of God was more than just
a piece of apologetics as in those versions of theism which, like Samuel
Clarke's, were primarily designed to combat atheism. It was an attempt to
establish a public domain of reasonable discourse which allowed one to
clarify, contest, and evaluate religious and other claims, and this without
having to claim to be or to expound the only true religion.

   This, I think, remains an important task for philosophy of religion after
the decline of philosophical theism in the sense described, much more so in
any case than resuscitating traditional apologetics or rehearsing foundationalist attempts of providing the ultimate explanation of existence and

49. *Op. cit.*, p. 30.
50. In his 1992 Stanton Lectures *Religions, Reasons and Gods*.
51. Clayton, *op..cit.*
52. Cf. Chr. Schwöbel, After 'Post-Theism' in this volume.

order of the world, and/or of the certainty and reliability of our knowledge of the world. The first is, if at all, a task of theology, not philosophy. The second, as we have come to see more clearly in recent years, is not something we require in order to be able to live and act successfully and responsibly in our world. Thus it is not the answers theism gave but (some of) the questions it asked and (some of) the problems to which it responded that will continue to engage philosophy of religion. Whatever its answers will, they will have to be very different from classical theism, more so, in any case, than neoclassical panentheism. Philosophical 'theism' of this nondogmatic but grammatical type could serve a continuous and vital function as the public criticism of religious ideas and doctrines of God, as a common medium of reasonable argument and debate between opposing religious views and convictions, as a shared discourse for comparing and distinguishing the similarities and differences between religious claims and positions, and as the realm of mutual interpretation and translatability between different religious perspectives on God, ourselves, and our world.[53] And this not with an eye to replacing these religious perspectives by a philosophical perspective which provides a better, more comprehensive, more general, or at least less idiosyncratic view or conception of God, but in order to enable religious individuals and individual religions to develop towards greater clarity, truth and humanity by clarifying their own concepts, doctrines, and images of God in the light of and through dialogue with others.

53. Cf. I.U. Dalferth, *Theology and Philosophy*, Oxford 1988, pp. 147f.

The Historical Roots of Anti-Theism

Jan Van der Veken

Introduction

The problem of the historical roots of anti-theism belongs to the discipline commonly called 'history of ideas'.

Our initial question comes down to this:

Why is it that a-'theism' which started as a minority position only in the seventeenth or eighteenth century, has taken over almost completely the intellectual scene? What has gone wrong with 'theism', once so widely accepted so that only the fool in his heart could say 'there is no God'? How and why is it that the christian God understood theistically has become incredible? As an historical fact the existence of atheism has to be accounted for in terms of the ideas which preceded it.

What is the form of 'theism' which was rejected by atheism, when this position became an intellectual possibility in the seventeenth century? It certainly is a problem of the history of ideas to ask the question why and how so many people have started to see the traditional belief in God as theoretically inadequate and no longer liberating on the practical (political and social) level.

It is my contention, however, that in the philosophy of religion we cannot limit ourselves to the mere record of what has been thought. As philosophers of religion, we also have to tackle the question whether that what in fact was thought in the past can and should be thought by us today. Is atheism to be understood as a mere rejection of theism, or is it rather the denial of any belief in God? With other words: does a-'theism' necessarily imply unbelief or rejection of any belief in God? Or are there alternative ways to conceive of God and of the God-world relationship, so that a-'theism' must be interpreted in a rather stricter sense, as the criticism of 'theism', which as such does not imply a rejection of God at all? In this respect atheism is more than a question of the history of ideas. How should this intellectual evolution from (the) 'God'-of-theism-affirmed to God-denied be evaluated? Do we just have to accept 'that the supersensible world has lost its reality' (Nietzsche in *Die Fröhliche Wissenschaft*)? Do we realise what the consequences of this major cultural event are for any belief today? (The madman's question).

The overall thesis of this paper is that at least one of the reasons for the cultural success of atheism is that the first apologetics were unable to see that serious conceptual changes were at hand. They proposed — unsuccesfully — traditional theism as an answer to questions which had already been asked in a different context. Instead of looking for new and more suitable ways of talking about God, they rejected the 'heretical' attempts of such people as Giordano Bruno and Spinoza, and failed to renew their own way of talking about God and the world. The absence of real cultural interchange between believers and those who understood the implications of the collapse of the Aristotelian world-view has been one of the major reasons why Western philosophy, with Nietzsche, ended up in nihilism.

Michael Buckley, in his authorative book *At the Origins of Modern Atheism*[1] suggests that the basic mistake of the early apologetics such as Leonard Lessius and Marin Mersenne was that they turned the question of atheism into a philosophical issue, leaving out any reference to Jesus and to historical revelation. To my understanding, however, the problem with these early apologetics is not that they were looking for philosophical arguments to counter nascent skepticism. My position is that they had very good reasons to look to philosophy to answer the objections of incipient skepticism. A religion which had given rise to intolerance, persecution and religious wars was, in the eyes of early free-thinkers, hardly better than superstition. Plutarch pointed out that the atheist thinks that there are no gods; superstition is the cause of the rise of atheism, and afterwards it is its justification.

They saw that the sole arbiter between skepticism, atheism and 'superstition' must be reason. An appeal to revelation would have made the whole discussion suspect. The problem was that, as the 16th and 17th centuries wore on, any appeal to revelation appeared less and less acceptable to intellectuals. That is the reason why, in those times of religious turmoil, an appeal to 'the God of Pascal' or to religious experience would have seemed strangely unconvincing.

It was exactly this climate of religious rivalry and intolerance which

1. Michael J. Buckley, *At the Origins of Modern Atheism*, New Haven 1987.

turned thinking people away from revealed religion. The problem was not that Lessius and Mersenne brought the discussion before the tribunal of reason, but rather that they tried to answer new questions within the framework of a conceptuality which was no longer fit to account for the complexity of the world as it was known at the beginning of modern science.

The meaning of anti-theism and of a-theism

The term anti-theism goes back to Proudhon, who described himself as 'an enemy of God'. Anti-theism seems to make a stronger claim than atheism, which merely implies a non-acceptance or a negation. Anti-theism seems to be atheism with a vengeance. But are we not involving ourselves in a contradiction here? How can a non-believer call himself an enemy of God? Is this not a contradiction in terms or worse, a case of a Luciferian 'revolt' against God? A revolt against God makes no sense unless God exists. Such authors as H. De Lubac[2] and A. Etcheverry[3] have pointed out what has been called 'les antinomies de la revolte' (a chapter in Etcheverry's book). Also, according to De Lubac, modern atheism is far more than a-theism; it is an 'antitheism' or even an 'anti-Christianism'. The reason of this revolt against God is the passionate affirmation of the 'humanum'. And here, according to De Lubac, we are confronted with a tragic misunderstanding: whereas the modern atheists (Feuerbach, Marx, Nietzsche) are atheists because they are humanists, it is in fact only belief in God which can make us truly human. Why, then, are atheists so strongly 'against' God ? It must be said that many atheists deny God because they have a grossly deformed image of God. But if they refuse a false 'image' of God, can they still be called a-theists?

Anti-theism should not be conceived, it seems to us, as an active revolt against God, whose existence is implicitly accepted. Anti-theism is rather to be understood as the rejection of 'theism', i.e. of a certain way of believing in God. Anti-theism as well as atheism are truly relational terms. 'On est toujours l'athée de quelqu'un', says the French author Henry Duméry. The first Christians, such as Justin the martyr, called themselves atheists with regard to the pagan 'gods'. Anti-theism and theism can be truly understood and evaluated only if the 'theism' that it rejects is well circumscribed. Anti-'theism' does not make one necessarily an a-'theos'. A-'theism' can be — but is not necessarily — a way to a more adequate conception of God. Hence,

---

2. H. De Lubac, *Le drame de l'humanisme athée*, 4th ed., Paris 1950.
3. A. Etcheverry, *Le conflit actuel des Humanismes*, Paris 1955.

anti-theism should not be understood (as has sometimes been the case) as a 'refus de Dieu, combat contre Dieu, défi à Dieu', but as the rejection of 'theism' as an historical doctrine in which the belief in God has been formed.

So we first have to turn to the understanding of God in traditional or classical theism, and to find out why it came under attack. In a second move, we have to make clear that the rejection of 'theism' does not imply a denial of the reality of God altogether. The expression anti-theism makes it clear that the position which is rejected is 'theism' as it is traditionally understood. In this sense antitheism is somewhat less ambiguous than the more common term atheism. Anti-theism takes a clear stand against a certain form of theism. In this paper, anti-theism and the more neutral term atheism have to be understood in relation to the 'theism' which they reject. Because this meaning comes out more clearly in the term anti-theism, I choose to include this term in the title of my paper. For the purpose of discussion, however, it is more elegant to use the more common term atheism, whenever adequate. Sometimes the distinction has its importance: not all anti-'theists' are atheists!

Some anti-theists reject the very idea of God, and in this sense they are truly 'a-theoi'; others on the contrary reject 'theism' as a theological mistake (Tillich, e.g.) and claim that the rejection of a certain 'theism' is a necessary step to 'a more divine God' (Heidegger). So not all anti-theists are truly 'without God' (a-theoi).

Some atheists (as Nietzsche and Proudhon) cherish (implicitly or explicitly) the term 'antitheists', because they hate the God of the believers. According to their understanding, this pseudo-idea is a source of alienation and fear.

In antiquity, very few atheists were to be found: Democritos and Leucippos, and probably also Lucretius, can be seen as true atheists. In fact, they are pure and simple materialists.

In modern times, Ludwig Feuerbach, Karl Marx, C. Vogt, Jules Molescott, Ludwig Büchner, Ernst Haeckel, Felix le Dantec (sometimes called the French Haeckel) and J. Proudhon can truly be called atheists (although some qualifications should be made: is Feuerbach not rather an anthropotheist than an atheist? And sometimes Ernst Haeckel comes very close to monistic pantheism).

Amongst those who reject traditional or classical 'theism', one finds Giordano Bruno, Baruch de Spinoza, Hegel and on a more general level, all German idealist philosophers; also theologians such as D. Bonhoeffer, P. Tillich, John T. Robinson, J. Macquarrie and others. Some will call those authors atheists as well. It is a debatable issue whether e.g. Spinoza can truly be called an atheist. Some have had no doubts about it. Yet, Spinoza himself uses the term God with remarkable ease, and Novalis has characterized him as a 'Gottestrünkener Mensch'. Some have called Spinoza a 'panentheist'. It is difficult, however, to conceive of Bonhoeffer, Tillich or Macquarrie as atheists. To make my point, it is enough to state that certainly not all those in this list who reject theism can be called atheists.

Jules Lagneau has pointed out that atheism is always a correlate of a certain conception of God. This has brought him to the controversial position that atheism might not exist. If no conception of God is fully adequate, no rejection of it excludes God in a definitive way. I think that this is pushing an acceptable position too far. It is possible that in refusing a certain conception of God, in fact the very idea of God is rejected. Otherwise, true belief would not be possible either. The same reasoning (but in a converse sense) applies to the act of faith. It is possible to be a true believer, even if one's concept of God is rather inadequate. According to Aquinas faith 'non terminatur ad enuntiatum sed ad rem'. A distinction between the representation and that which is intended ('la visée') should be introduced.

Atheism depends upon theism for its vocabulary, its meaning and its adversary (Buckley). The meaning of atheism is spelled out by the intellectual process of a transition from the God of traditional or classical theism affirmed to 'God' denied. If atheism depends upon theism for its very existence, does theism not only shape, but generate, its corresponding atheism? Karl Rahner says: 'The philosophical criticism of atheism must always be at the same time a criticism of existing popular and philosophical theism, because atheism lives essentially out of a wrong understanding of God.'

Traditional theism
So, if atheism is parasitic on theism for its name, its meaning and adversary, it becomes urgent to understand exactly what it is in traditional theism that is no longer credible, and to ask what has made the transition from self-evident theism to atheism possible.

Since in this paper I understand anti-theism and less clearly also atheism in a limited way — as the rejection of theism — we first have to circumscribe the meaning of theism.

By traditional or Aristotelian theism I understand the concept which represents God as the Highest Substance or Highest Being, the Unmoved Mover, wholly separate from matter (choristos) and unchanging.

By traditional Christian or classical theism I understand Aristotelian theism as qualified by the Judaeo-Christian doctrine of God as creator and sustainer of the world. That mediaeval writers such as Aquinas do not shun the term 'Unmoved Mover' when talking about God shows the lasting influence of Aristotelian theism whithin the Christian framework.

I conceive traditional or classical theism as the result of the conflation between Aristotelian theism and the Judaeo-Christian doctrine of the Creator-God.

For Aristotle, there are three basic realms or kinds of substances:

There is, to begin with, the sublunar world, which is both perishable and material. It is the world of coming into being and passing away of individual beings, such as horses, cows, and human beings. The kinds itself (the species) are as eternal as planet earth itself.

Secondly, there are the heavenly bodies. They are both linked to matter and moving, but their movement is along circular (or perfect) trajectories. They have always existed. Hence the problem of creation does not even arise.

'Are the physical entities and the heavenly bodies all there is?' This is a question asked by Aristotle himself, when he investigates the subject-matter of his 'first philosophy'. If material and perishable entities are all there is, then the study of those material and movable substances would be 'first philosophy' or the most general science. However, if there are substances (or a Substance) which is both separate from matter and unmovable, then that Substance would be the most perfect one or the divine substance. The study of this Substance is the study of substantiality as such. Hence, it is the subject-matter of first philosophy. So we can understand why the most general study (the study of being or substantiality as such) is at the same time called 'theologike'. Aristotle's metaphysics is a clear instance of what Heidegger has called onto-theology. For Aristotle, metaphysics is at the same time the study of being in general (*to on*) and of the Highest Substance or Being (*Theos*).

Thomas Aquinas takes over much of the conceptuality framed by Aristotle. First, to him, philosophy or metaphysics are also at the same time the study of being as such and the study of 'transphysica' or 'res divinae'. God is understood as separate from matter, and unmovable, as pure form or pure action. Aquinas makes, however, two important qualifications: the relationship between God and the other substances is not just a relationship of motion, but a relationship of bringing into being, of creation. The world has not always existed. So God is somehow Subsistent being, *Ipsum esse subsistens*. An important conceptual change has occured: because the world is wholly dependent upon God, God is conceived as *Ipsum esse subsistens*. Aquinas and many neo-Thomists connect this understanding of God to the communication of the divine name in Exodus 3, *'sum qui sum'*. All exegetes today agree that this is a poor translation of the Exodus text. Yet, this 'metaphysics of Exodus' has been widely accepted even by neo-Thomists such as E. Gilson and D. Mercier. God does not really require the world in order to be Himself. Between God and the world there is no real relationship; only a relationship for reason (*relatio rationis*).

Although far more can be said about Aquinas' doctrine of God, the main features of classical theism have already been mentioned:

> God is Subsistent Being, not really requiring the world in order to be Himself. God is both separate from matter and unmovable. If the world exists, it is due not to any necessity whatsoever, but to a gratuitous creative decision.

> God does not require anything else in order to exist. The world requires God. The existence of the world does not add anything real to God; it adds only to His external glory.

> God is conceived as completely outside of time and outside of the material world; he is purely spiritual and unmovable. He knows however the world and can act in the world.

Aquinas' theism contains the paradox of a completely spiritual and atemporal god who creates a completely material world in time (or who creates time together with the world). How can this happen? Do we have any experience of a spiritual reality 'separate' from matter?

The world needs no further reason than God. God owes nothing 'ontological' to the world. Creation does not add anything real to God. The paradox is: wouldn't it be more logical to say that God and the world are 'more' than just God by Himself? Hence, shouldn't we say that God-and-the-world together deserve to be called the Absolute? There can be only one all-inclusive Reality: God and the world qualify better than just God by himself.

The classical answer to the paradox that the world does not add anything to God is as follows: when God creates the world, there are more beings, not more being: *'dantur plura entia, non datur plus entis'*. But how can that be conceived? Is this meaningful talk? Is the price to pay not too high? Is the world not becoming totally irrelevant?

Another paradox is the question of the asymmetrical relationship between God and the world. If God is not really related to the world, how then can He still be the Creator? And how can God know from all eternity that which will happen only contingently?

The main problem, however, which is the rock on which all forms of classical theism and deism have foundered, is the problem of evil: if God is almighty and all-good, why then is the world no better than it is? It became more and more evident that from an imperfect world one cannot deduce a perfect God (Hume's difficulty).

This unsolved paradox of classical theism contains the seeds of atheism. The objections of the first atheists are nothing else than a long meditation upon the intrinsic difficulties of traditional theism. First, these objections were phrased very hesitantly. The first atheists were skeptics rather than non-believers. We know them only indirectly, mainly through the works of the apologetics. After a long intellectual search, Denis Diderot, who once considered becoming a Jesuit and wrote his first work 'about God', voices the objections more forcefully, and proposes an alternative. In the end the objections are uttered in an almost triumphant tone by Baron d'Holbach.

How did the first apologetics try to answer the objections of those skeptics which bit by bit eroded the traditional proofs of the existence of God?

This in itself is a most interesting story. People like Leonard Lessius of Leuven and Marin Mersenne of Paris were in fact convinced that philosophical challenges should be answered philosophically. Taking into account the rivalries between the different interpretations of e.g. catholicism and protestantism, an appeal to biblical insights would have created more controversies than it would have solved. An additional consideration is that the arguments had to be valid even for those faraway peoples who had never heard of Christianity and who had to be convinced by rational arguments. The work of Lessius, 'De providentia numinis'[4] was published in 1613 and generated sufficient enthusiasm to be printed in a Chinese edition.

And who were those free spirits, who hesitated to call themselves

---

4. Leonard Lessius, De providentia numinis et animi immortalitate. Libri duo adversus atheos et politicos, in Opuscula Leon. Lessii, S.J., Paris 1880. Reference in Buckley, Op.cit., p. 377.

atheists, and who only gradually moved further and further away from the received doctrines? They are not famous. We know them thanks to the apologetic works which tried to refute their skepticism. They were by no means fully fledged atheists right from the beginning. The question at stake was not whether there is some first principle, but whether it can be conceived as completely separate from the creation. The proofs of the existence of God were not rejected out of hand; but bit by bit it became obvious that those proofs were no longer arguments for the God of traditional theism. Other conceptions started to emerge. Maybe a creative force at work within the world itself? How can a totally spiritual and a-cosmic God intervene in a totally material world? Isn't it more reasonable to assert that spirit and matter are not separate from one another (in fact, who ever met a disembodied spirit?); that instead, they are intermingled (maybe in different proportions) in all realities? With Denis Diderot an important step is taken. Taking into account the obvious creativity of the life process itself and its equally obvious shortcomings, Diderot attributed 'eternal' and 'creative' qualities to dynamic matter itself. He did not (yet) dispense with the idea of some necessary substrate of being, but he conceived it as dynamic matter. Diderot was the first to voice the alternative stance of 'dynamic matter'. He did it in a crude way, which left many problems unsolved, even to his own eyes. But he thought that it was more reasonable to leave unsolved that which we could not understand, than to accept metaphysical solutions which more and more came to resemble gratuitous affirmations. The spectacle of the world in which we live seems to require some dynamic force and even some teleology at work in nature itself, probably pushing ongoing creation towards higher stages of complexity, so that at a certain moment consciousness itself may arise. But this dynamic creative force does not seem to be controlled by an omnipotent and all-good God. On the contrary, the imperfection of the world, the fact that there are blind people (Diderot's *Lettre sur les aveugles*, where he reports on Saunderson, a blind mathematical genius), that the upward trend in evolution is not stable, that there are also degradations and misfits: all that may more easily be explained by the anonymous force of Dynamic Matter itself.

These are the standard arguments — somewhat rephrased — of the early atheists. In fact, they repeat the age-old objections against the belief in God or in the gods. It is by no means a question of chance that the early apologetics such as the Louvain Jesuit Lessius fell back on Cicero's *De Natura Deorum* to deal with the very same objections. The protagonists of the discussion are Balbus, the Stoic, believing in an immanent *logos* which is clearly present in the course of things; there is Velleius, the Epicurean, for whom 'chance and necessity' and the random circulation of bits of matter, endlessly, meaninglessly is 'all there is'; there is Cotta, the Academic, who encourages the discussion, and who is very tolerant, except towards Balbus (who might offer such a powerful argument that he, Cotta, might be forced to give up his skeptic neutrality). There is much analogy between the position taken by Balbus (in Cicero's *De Natura Deorum*) and that of Lessius himself. The arguments are the same: the beauty of nature, the evident purposiveness, visible in all living organisms. Yet, there is an important difference: Lessius borrows the arguments from Balbus, pointing to the beauty and the intricate nature of all that exists; he accepts this as clear evidence of a creative *logos* at work in creation; but Lessius connects the premises of the argument for an immanent logos at work in creation itself with the idea of a wholly transcendent Creator, the God of his own Judaeo-Christian tradition. Because Lessius was using the argumentative line, followed by Balbus, the Stoic, to prove his own theistic position, the argument became less strong than it would have been if he had attempted to prove less. In short, the evident teleology of the universe was understood theologically. That, in the long run, made the whole argument suspect, as the whole debate about physicotheology will show. If the design which is clearly present in nature is an unambiguous indication of the 'telos' of an almighty and all-good God, why then is that *telos* not accomplished in all instances? Why is there so much decay? Why monsters and misfits? Why blind people? (Diderot's question).

Bit by bit, it becomes clear that the arguments for the existence of God — before all the argument from design — indeed do prove something (even Hume and Kant admitted that it is the most powerful argument) but the argument from design is flawed in this sense, that it does not prove what it is supposed to prove: the existence of an all-powerful and all-good God, who would be completely outside of creation. Hume has made that point irrefutably in his stimulating *Dialogues on Natural Religion*.

Leonard Lessius, a Jesuit, treats the question of the existence of God in a merely philosophical way. The arguments are borrowed from the universal consent, the impossibility to account for the order in nature by mere chance, as suggested by the renascent Epicurism. Of course, Lessius could appeal to the *Summa Theologiae*, which gives general arguments for the existence of

God, which do not presuppose the specifically Christian revelation.[5]

Marin Mersenne, a Franciscan theologian, stumbled on *Les Quatrains de Deists ou l'Antibigot*, a pamphlet which was widely circulated throughout France by 1622, hammering away at Christianity (whether Huguenot or Catholic) as a superstition, arguing for an impersonal god, one as indifferent to human acts as unaffected by human prayers. In 1624, Mersenne published *L'Impiété des Déistes, Athées, et Libertins de ce temps*. The subtitle of the work indicates which atheists he has especially in mind: 'la refutation des Dialogues de Iordan Brun, dans lequel il a voulu establir une infinité de mondes, et l'ame universelle de l'Univers'.[6] Giordano Bruno, the turbulent and tragic figure of early modern Europe, had invented (according to Mersenne) 'une nouvelle facon de philosopher' for his battle against Christianity. Bruno had brought back to Europe the underlying god of the Stoics, god as an immanent principle of the universe. In other attempts to talk about God, such as those of the skeptic and fideist Charron, Mersenne could see only a sub-species of that atheism against which he wrote his dialogue, *L'Impiété*. As with Lessius some ten years before, Mersenne's protagonists can be found modeled with remarkable likeness in Cicero's *De natura deorum*. Again, Mersenne seeks not to adapt these philosophical schools, but to refute them. Completely in the line of traditional theism, Mersenne proves 'le grand moteur de l'univers pour createur de toutes choses'.

Leonard Lessius and Marin Mersenne were two of the most influential theologians of their time, and amongst the first to write against the early awakenings of atheism. They deal with it as with a philosophical problem.

Descartes follows the same line: 'I have always been of the opinion that the two questions — those dealing with God and with the soul — were among the principal ones which should be demonstrated by philosophy rather than by theology'.[7]

Descartes agrees that the issue of the divine existence is more in the realm of philosophy than of theology, but he reverses the procedure of philosophy totally. The starting point is now consciousness itself, not nature. It is not the

5. In the *Summa theologiae*, Christ makes a central appearance only in the third part, after the doctrines of God, providence, the nature of the human person, creation, and human finality have already been defined.
6. Michael J. Buckley, *Op.cit.*, p. 58.
7. Michael J. Buckley, *Op.cit.*, p. 75: 'Quae Philosophia potius quan Theologia ope sunt demonstrandae'.

sensual universe that is evidence for God, but the nature of God that is the warrant for the sensual universe. So Descartes still thinks that there is a firm foundation for belief in God and in the immortality of the soul. But at what a cost: Descartes removed final causes from the universe and left the world godless: a mechanical system, with no intrinsic aim, no inherent *logos*, no creativity of its own. The world becomes the field of mechanics, and can prove nothing about God's existence. In a philosophy that must use God to prove the world, the world does not assert or witness the existence of God. Descartes has paved the way for deism, which conceives God as the great architect, who remains, however, completely exterior to his handiwork. The dualism between matter and spirit is total, and cannot be bridged. Newton has taken up the basic assumptions of Descartes: his *Pantokrator* is an almost a-cosmic God (who, however, has the world as his sensorium), and a godless world, governed by imposed law. This opens up a new chapter in the history of ideas: we are at the brink of one of the most powerful periods of natural theology, which, however, already contains the seeds of its decline, because we are confronted with all sorts of dualism: between God and world, between matter and spirit, between time and eternity.

Spinoza has seen the difficulties of the unsurpassable dualism between mind and matter. He has endeavored to see the relationship between the Infinite and the finite in a radical new way. There is much to say about Spinoza's attempt. The modes follow from Substance with necessity. Hence, there is no place for any creativity left to the modes itself. And the problem of evil, too, tends to disappear if everything happens exactly the way it should happen. Yet, Spinoza has demonstrated the fallacy of any attempt to think the Infinite and the finite in separation. According to Hegel, philosophy has to start with Spinoza. This is his way of saying that it must be post-'theistic'.

It is the contention of this paper that the pitiful situation in which 'theism' finds itself today is mainly due to the fact that the most prominent theologians of the Enlightenment period were not able to make the necessary conceptual shifts when it might have still been time to do so. There have been all kinds of attempts, demonstrating of the continuing vigour of religious thinking in a secular culture. John Macquarrie in his stimulating book *In Search of Deity*[8] shows that throughout history, there has been an undercurrent of philosophers and theologians who have stressed the dialectical

---

8. *In Search of Deity. An Essay in Dialectical Theism.* London 1984.

relationship beteen God and the world far more than has been done in traditional theism. His impressive list of 'allies' belonging to the alternative
tradition includes people like Dionysius, Eriugena, Cusanus, Hegel, Whitehead and even Heidegger. Mystics, avoiding Greek categories, have found
God present in the soul and in nature. Hegel has seen God not as separate
from nature and history, but as the unfolding Absolute. God has been
discovered as revealing Himself in the great value systems and religions of
history. But all in all, those philosophical endeavors to think differently about
God have had little influence upon mainstream natural theology. Even to
believers themselves traditional natural theology, which is still mainly
'theist', has become unbelievable. That may be the reason why such a strong
reaction against any form of natural or philosophical theology is fashionable
in some theological circles.

We have to face the question: was it a good or a bad thing that an
independent natural theology began to emerge? It is at least a puzzling fact
that arguments for the existence of God are borrowed from antiquity, a world
to which theology itself has little contribution to make. The preamble to the
most basic Christian conviction does not include Christ. But it is also a
puzzling fact that for many centuries some assumptions about the very
nature of God have been borrowed from Aristotle and from Greek cosmology, even when it is hard to see how they can be reconciled with some
insights of the Judaeo-Christian tradition, such as the very idea of the
covenant between God and man.

Looking at that chapter of intellectual history in the West, where
traditional ways to think about God gradually lost their hold upon the
intellectual life of the time, two positions are possible.

Michael Buckley talks about a self-alienation of religion. The first
apologists addressed themselves to the atheists using only philosophical
arguments, and leaving out completely 'the witness of faith'. Of course, there
are reasons which make this move towards natural theology understandable.

First, 'for Lessius and Mersenne to have appealed to the witness of Christ
or to Judaeo-Christian religious experience would have seemed to be lining
up with the skeptics, those who pushed revelation at the cost of the
soundness of reason, and neither man would content himself with this'.[9]

The second factor is the doctrine of the one God to be found in the
Summa Theologiae. The early questions inquire into the intelligibility and

---

9. Michael J. Buckley, *Op.cit.*, p. 66.

validity of the existence and attributes of God: they would and could be demonstrated through philosophy from the evidence available to anyone.

Buckley seems to resent that the early apologetics were not drawing upon the own resources of Christian theology, 'as if Christianity did not possess in the person of Jesus a unique witness to confront the denial of God or as if one already had to believe in order to have this confrontation take place'.[10]

My own interpretation of the situation is not that theology would have been better of if it had refused to be natural theology. I think that Lessius, Mersenne and Descartes like so many others saw that the main tenet of Christian theology, the belief in God, should be open to rational discussion. The problem is that their natural theology was not keeping up with the important conceptual changes which occurred when the basically dualistic traditional Greek world-view had to give way to a more monistic approach to reality as a whole. It is not my contention that any of the new attepts to think God and the world together were religously acceptable. They were far too tentative at that time, and had not yet matured. But the fact that theology did not engage in a serious dialogue with those new ways of seeing the world is — according to my understanding — the basic reason why theology which was once the queen of the sciences lost almost all credibility. Any science has to face radical conceptual changes. Theology will regain its intellectual vigour only when it learns to face change in the same way as science does. And the first and most urgently required conceptual change is a change in our very concept of God.

It is not my task in this paper to point the way to alternative models for classical theism. Having mentioned already John Macquarrie's 'dialectical theism', it is clear that he wants to adopt a view of God which stresses the divine immanence far more than classical theism. For him, God is not an entity, absent from the world, and reached by inference. He finds himself in agreement with Keith Ward when he says: '[God] is not an object apart from the universe, of which we can only detect faint traces. On the contrary, he is the mind and heart of the universe itself.'[11] The relationship between God and the world is clearly the main problem of Macquarries's *Dialectical Theism*. The title of Chapter 10 is also telling: 'God and the World: Two Realities or One?'. He feels that he is in agreement with Lord Gifford himself, when he

10. *Ibid*.
11. John Macquarrie, *Op.cit.*, p. 11.

says that 'natural theology is the science of infinite being'. It is crystal clear that for Macquarrie, the object of natural theology (or the referent of the word God) is not a being called 'God', an item within the world or above the world. For him, the concept of God is an interpretative concept: it is 'meant to give us a way of understanding and relating to reality as a whole'.[12]

One thing I hold for certain: God cannot be thought about in isolation. The word God functions as a syncategorematic word. It functions as a qualification of all other meanings, and most of all of the most basic ones, such as existence, value, life and death. God and His Kingdom cannot be thought of in separation. 'Separation' is a key word in Aristotelian theism. It is meaningful only from the point of view of the presuppositions of Aristotelian cosmology. I think it cannot be reconciled with a theology of incarnation, whose key word is relation.

---

12. John Macquarrie, *Op.cit.*, p. 29.

A Defence of Metaphysical Theism

Keith Ward

Some philosophers think that metaphysics, in the sense of an attempt to state objective truths about the general nature of reality, is impossible. At the same time, however, there has been a marked recovery of metaphysical confidence. It began, in Britain, with P.F. Strawson's 'Individuals' and Anthony Quinton's 'The Nature of Things', and has continued with an increasing flow of publications. As one who belongs to the latter class of philosophers, I have a special interest in defending the coherence of a metaphysical notion of God, that is, a notion of God as an objective existent reality. Richard Swinburne and Thomas Morris have done it excellently; but I will briefly attempt a slightly different approach, from a rather more theological angle. My view is that there are great difficulties in some traditional concepts of God, but that there is a coherent concept of God which is also the foundation of a plausible metaphysical understanding of reality. It is only the coherence of the concept that I have time to defend in this paper. I shall do so by examining Anselm's definition of God as 'Aliquid quo majus nihil cogitari possit'[1] which is a particularly elegant definition that all orthodox theists would accept. The idea of a greatest conceivable being may seem to be utterly abstract and vague, to be without content. John Hick regards it as a 'purely formal' concept.[2] After all, may people not have totally different ideas of what a 'great being' is, and conceive of very different beings as the greatest they can think of?

It is unlikely, however, that there would be no agreement on at least some of the properties which are 'great-making', which it is better to possess than not to possess. An obvious example would be power, in the sense of capacity to do what one wants. Would any rational person hold that it is not better to be able to do what one wants than to lack such ability?

It may be said that some people would rather do what they are told, so that they would not have to make their own decisions. But if they are

---

1. Anselm, *Proslogion* 2, London 1979, p. 116.
2. John Hick, *An Interpretation of Religion*, London 1989, p. 246.

oppressed and enslaved, tortured and manipulated, they could not desire their situation. This shows that one can only rationally wish to be obedient to a being which is fundamentally benevolent. The best being to obey would be one with knowledge, power and goodness, so that obedience will not bring great suffering, but will bring many things one wants. Even if one does not want power or autonomous freedom of decision oneself, one must think that it would be good if some being with great knowledge, wisdom, goodness and power existed, which could plan one's life for one. Even timid, other-directed and subservient people, when they think it through, will have to admit that it is better for some being to possess power to do what it wants than not. An important qualification is that such power must be associated with knowledge and goodness. So the appropriate great-making property is a complex property of knowledge-goodness-power. With this qualification, all would, I think, have to agree that such a property is one that a greatest conceivable being would have to possess. So the idea of a greatest conceivable being is not vacuous or wildly different from one person to another. Given a little reflection, the idea has a definite content and would be accepted by any rational person, at least at this basic level.

Another possible objection to this argument is that, as Lord Acton said, power corrupts and absolute power corrupts absolutely. Might it not be better, then, if no absolute power existed? This objection is answered, however, by reiterating that the property in question is not brute power, which may go along with selfish passion or ignorance; but 'knowledge-goodness-power'. Only such a power is incorruptible, since it would only be exercised in bringing about states which are known to be good and which are willed for the sake of their goodness. As I have already suggested, the idea of supreme power implicitly contains the more complex property of supreme value, of perfect being. That point will be argued more fully, but all one needs for the moment is that some definite complex property is entailed in the very idea of a greatest conceivable being.

If power is a perfection — a property it is better for a perfect being to have than not to have — then it seems clear that the more power such a being has the better. There may not be a maximal degree of power, in the sense that there are a definite number of capacities which could not logically be any greater. But one can think of a being which is the source of all other powers there are or could ever be, which is actually greater than any other powers there are, and will always be greater than any other powers there could ever be. The greatest possible power cannot be limited in any way by anything other than itself, and its own power must be greater than any other conceivable power. Such a being will be a creator of everything other than itself. It will have total power over all actual and possible created things. It will be, in Peter Geach's term, 'Almighty'.

Some views of God deny that omnipotence, construed in this sense, is possible. Some Process theologians claim that no being, not even God, can be the source of all power. For, they argue, existence itself is a power, and if anything exists other than God, it must have a power other than God's. Thus David Griffin holds that many natural powers exist which are not capable of being wholly determined by God, though God may have various sorts of influence upon them.[3] Griffin picks out what he calls the 'omnipotence fallacy', as one which has misled many philosophers and theologians. This is the fallacy of moving from the assertion that a state of affairs, S, is logically possible, to the assertion that, necessarily, God can create S. He is surely correct in taking this move to be fallacious. It is logically possible for a world of irredeemable evil to exist, but God cannot create it. This is because God is necessarily good, so that such a world, though conceivable in itself, is not conceivable as creatable by a perfectly good being.

One might put this by saying that any creatable world must be compatible with the nature of the creator. Any creatable world must also be compatible with the purposes of the creator in creating it. Thus if God wills to create a world of free, partly self-determining, moral agents, then even God cannot wholly determine their actions. Divine power is limited — though not in any bad or avoidable way — by the Divine nature and the Divine purposes. Griffin wants to make the point rather more strongly than this, however. He holds that it is a metaphysically necessary truth that all actual beings must be self-determining to some extent. If that is true, then God cannot wholly determine any creatable universe. It is hard to see how such a very strong metaphysical necessity could be established. I may wholly determine something, like a piece of music, which actually exists, though it has no determining power of its own. Indeed, the important sorts of self-determination with which moralists are concerned seem to belong only to higher animals. As Griffin points out, theologians like Augustine and Aquinas held that even free human acts are in fact wholly determined by God to be what they are, since freedom and determination are compatible. Such a view is a logically possible one, on a particular interpretation of

3. David Griffin, *God, Power and Evil*, Philadelphia 1975, p. 264 ff.

freedom, even if it is rejected. So, while I accept Griffin's point that God cannot wholly determine what he wills to be self-determining, I am unconvinced by his wider assertion that all beings are self-determining to some degree, simply by existing.

It is coherent to hold that God is capable of determining all beings, though he may not wish to do so. Further, all powers can derive from God, even though they may then, by Divine will, have a limited power of self-determination. God must uphold that power and permit its exercise, and is thus omnipotent in the sense that he could determine everything, and if he does not do so, it is by his own decision. As creator, it is within God's power of free decision to create a universe containing partly self-determining beings or not. For Griffin, on the other hand, God must create some universe of self-determining beings, and then cannot wholly determine what shall happen to them, since that is ultimately up to them. I can see no compelling reason, however, to posit these beliefs as necessary truths.

On the Biblical view, God freely bring to be things other than himself. But why should such a being bring anything to be? The suggestion that there is no reason would reduce the universe to just the sort of arbitrariness that atheists posit. But what sort of reason could there be for creating anything? The simplest answer to this question, in the case of any finite mind, is that one will act for the sake of good; that is, for the sake of bringing about a state which realises some desire. Desires are not within conscious control. The fact that one has certain desires is just a given fact of one's nature, which one does not choose — even if one can choose whether or not to pursue a given desire. Is it the same for God? Is the universe the product of Divine desire, which God does not choose to have? If so, it might have a sort of necessity, as resulting from desires which God necessarily has, and which naturally express themselves in creation.

God must have a given nature, which is not chosen, but which he possesses of necessity. It does not make sense to suppose that God chooses his own nature completely, since there must already be a choosing nature in existence to make such a choice. For any choice to be made, there must already be knowledge of what could be chosen, power to choose, and some rational criteria of choice. There must therefore already exist a being with knowledge, power and standards of choice. The Divine nature cannot be caused by any other being, since then the creator would not be the creator of everything other than itself. And it cannot come into being out of nothing, since that would make it purely arbitrary and random. The Divine nature is not only uncaused. It is uncausable, in that nothing is able to bring it about. It is not the sort of being which could be brought about. It is not capable of coming into being or passing away. In that sense it is immutable. Thus it seems that there is a given, immutable, uncreatable Divine nature, which conceives possible states of affairs, has the ability to bring a universe into being, and has certain desires, or conceptions of and inclinations to produce states which are pleasurable or in some other way worthy of rational choice. God is essentially knowing, powerful and wise, and cannot either create or destroy or change his possession of these basic properties, which constitute the Divine nature.

To some theologians and philosophers, it is a restriction on God's power to possess a nature which he is unable to change. They accordingly think of God's creativity as including the capability of creating his own nature. Thomas Morris proposes that God might be thought of as the cause of his own properties[4] — 'It just seems to me that there is nothing logically or metaphysically objectionable about God's creating his own nature', he says. What is wrong with the idea of Divine self-creation is that, for x to be a creator, x must have thoughts, intentions and the power to realise them. These are logically necessary preconditions of x creating anything. They are thus logically necessary preconditions of x creating his own properties. Such properties, at least, cannot be created, since they are presupposed to all acts of creation. Creation is causing to be what would otherwise not exist. Even if creation is thought of as a possibly timeless activity, what is created depends causally upon the act of the creator. Thus, if anything is created, there must exist, in a causally prior way, an intending powerful being. It follows that God cannot create those very intentions and powers which are causally prior to his act of creation.

Morris holds that God's nature causally depends upon God; but what is this God without a nature? In speaking of causal dependence, one is ascribing power to it; but such power is part of a nature, and so it, at least, cannot causally depend upon God. The Divine nature is uncreated, even by God, since it is presupposed to all creation. Morris offers an admittedly weak analogy, but it is too weak to do any work at all. He supposes a materialisation machine which materialises itself as it ceases to exist; so in the end, it can be described as self-created. The inescapable truth, however, is that some original version of the machine must have existed to get the process started.

4. Thomas Morris, *Anselmian Explorations*, Notre Dame 1987, p. 172 ff.

Somewhere, there is an uncreated nature, and that must be regarded as inescapably given.

Karl Barth, too, suggests that God may choose his own being. 'God's being is...his willed decision'[5] he writes. And again, 'There is no moment in the ways of God which is over and above this act and decision'. But it is a logical truth that the making of a decision presupposes the existence of a being which has the power to decide. Such a being must have knowledge of what it might decide and the power to decide. It cannot decide to have such knowledge and power, as though it was a blank nothingness which could decide to become wise and powerful. The Divine knowledge and power are presupposed to any decisions God might make; and this is a moment in the being of God which is over and above his free decision.

It is possible that Barth may be misusing language slightly in a rhetorical way, and that what he means is that God *freely assents to* the nature which he has and affirms it. That is a rather different matter, and there is every reason to think it is true. God's nature is just as he desires it, and he chooses its continuance, just as it is. Nevertheless, the existence of that nature cannot properly be spoken of as chosen. It necessarily is what it is. Perhaps Barth is concerned to affirm that nothing compels God to be as he is, that he owes his existence to no other being. That also is true. God's necessity is *a se*; it derives from no other and is constrained by no other. If one thinks of freedom as affirmation of one's nature — 'Freedom means to... be determined and moved by oneself'[6] — then God is indeed supremely free. Such freedom is quite compatible with Divine necessity, but it does not involve any possibility of alternative choice in God.

Paul Fiddes also stresses an element of choice in the Divine nature. He writes in a context of struggling with the idea that 'the world is in some way necessary for the being of God'.[7] He wishes to hold that God chooses to suffer for the sake of love, and this leads him to hold that creation is 'necessary in some sense to him', since it enables him to express and even fulfil his being in love. Wishing to affirm this, and yet to mitigate the sense of placing God under any sort of necessity, Fiddes proposes that 'God is free to be what he chooses to be'. God can thus choose 'whether to be con-

5. Karl Barth, *Church Dogmatics* 2,1,6, Edinburgh 1975, p. 271f.
6. Barth, *op.cit.*, p. 301.
7. Paul Fiddes, *The Creative Suffering of God*, Oxford 1988, p. 57.

ditioned or not', and he can 'choose that the world should be necessary to him'.[8]

This notion of God choosing that something should be necessary to him is incoherent in the same way as the notion of God choosing to be whatever he is. God may choose to limit himself by creating beings who have some degree of autonomy. But even God cannot *choose* that his own being should be such that he *must* create.

Fiddes finds it unsatisfactory to suppose that God needs the world 'in the sense that there is some intrinsic necessity in his nature, binding his free choice'.[9] Thus he objects to the view of many Process theologians that creativity is a necessary property of God, on the ground that it 'subordinates God to a principle of creativity which is beyond his decision'.[10] Why does he object to necessity in God? It can only be because he finds this to be some sort of constraint on God. However, I have already argued that the notion of a wholly self-decided God is incoherent. God must have a nature. But nothing other than God determines what this nature is. There is no independent principle of creativity which forces God to conform to it, even though Whitehead at least once carelessly spoke of God as 'the first creature of creativity'. In saying that God is necessarily omniscient, one is not saying that there is a principle of omniscience that God must conform to. It is better to be omniscient than not. And it is better to be necessarily omniscient than to be contingently omniscient. For contingency implies the possibility of failing to be omniscient and of perhaps never having been omniscient. If omniscience is good, it is better to be unable to gain or lose it. Process philosophers argue that it is in a similar way better to be creative than not. If this is so, then it is better to be necessarily creative than to be contingently creative.

Does it make sense to speak of God as constrained by his own perfection? Would it be better for God to be able to be imperfect, evil, malevolent, weak or ignorant? Surely not. Perhaps what worries Fiddes is that, if God is necessarily good, it would make no sense to praise him for his goodness. After all, he has no alternative, and one does not praise someone for what they cannot help. On further reflection, however, there is surely something odd about praising God for being good, realising that he might decide not

8. Fiddes, *op.cit.*, p. 67 f.
9. Fiddes, *op.cit.*, p. 74.
10. Fiddes, *op.cit.*, p. 135.

to be good — why should he be constrained by immutability? — so that we may find ourselves one day blaming him for his badness. To praise God is to revere and admire his perfection, not to congratulate him on his decisions.

Thus the reply to Fiddes' unease is that necessary goodness is no constraint upon God, but a property necessarily possessed by any perfect being. Fiddes speaks of Divine choice of goodness, yet he is using a Pickwickian notion of choice here, since he also says that 'there can be no meaning in the phrase, 'he need not have done so'.[11] The Divine choice is such that it is necessarily what it is. Barth holds that God necessarily chooses to constitute himself as loving, in the Trinitarian relation; but he chooses to create, when he need not have done so. Fiddes extends the idea of God's necessary choice to include creation, since 'a desire for relationship and fellowship is certainly essential to love', and God essentially constitutes himself as loving. 'There can be no question of God's not longing for our love', for God 'has freely chosen to be in need'. What force remains to the idea of choice, however, when it makes no sense to say that it could have been otherwise? There may be an important distinction to be made between Divine necessity and Divine freedom, but it is not helpful to deny necessity altogether of God, on behalf of an argument for total Divine freedom.

John Zizioulas[12] in a similar way makes a contrast between ancient Greek thought and Christian thought. The Greeks, he holds, saw being as constrained by necessity, and human personhood as harmonising with this rational necessity. The person, however, is a 'free, unique and unrepeatable entity'. Christians, he holds, found the being of the Trinity itself in the person of the Father. The Father is the ultimate cause of the Trinity, and in this sense the person is the cause and the constitutive element of the substance or nature, not the other way around. Persons are not bound by 'ontological necessity', but act in freedom. Thus 'the Father out of love — that is, freely — begets the Son and brings forth the Spirit'. Zizioulas concludes that 'that which makes a thing to exist is not the substance or nature but the person or hypostasis'

This claim seems to express the same sort of incoherence as those of Barth and Fiddes. For if the person is a cause, then it must have properties in virtue of which it is a cause. Indeed, Zizioulas stresses that it is a free cause, one which acts out of love. Presumably this entails that it acts out of

11. Fiddes, *op.cit.*, p. 74.
12. John Zizioulas, *Being as Communion*, London 1985, p. 33ff.

knowledge and by intention. So the person must have a nature, which it does not freely choose.

I think the clue to what is going on here is a distinction which Anselm makes between 'necessity' and 'will'. In *Cur Deus Homo*, Anselm argues that 'necessity is always either compulsion or restraint'.[13] In this sense, no necessity precedes or compels the will of God. If necessity is conceived as a blind force of compulsion, then God is not necessary. But it is still a fact that not everything about the nature of God can be chosen, and that the Divine nature cannot be either arbitrary or wholly contingent (*i.e.* existing for no good reason). God consents to his nature, in the sense that it is what any perfectly rational and good being would choose. His being is of supreme and usurpassable value. There is no constraint or compulsion in it that God does not freely choose. If this is so, the point all these theologians are making is that God is not some sort of impersonal substance from which the universe arises by a natural and inevitable and unwilled emanation — the Neo-Platonic emanation of the many from the primal One. God is a personal being of love and freedom, who affirms his own existence as of supreme value and in that sense wills it to be. In a carefully expressed sense, however, for which necessity is clearly distinguished from constraint and compulsion, it is no restriction on God to say that there are necessities in the Divine nature. The suggestion has been that these necessities must be such that they would be chosen as of supreme value by any being of sufficient power and knowledge to do so. But can one say what an omnipotent and omniscient being would choose?

I think that to some extent one can, and one can begin by seeing that there is a conceptual connection between goodness and desire. What any rational being — and an omnipotent, omniscient being will certainly be rational — desires is, as such, good. Aristotle even defined goodness in terms of rational desirability. It is a plausible view that the existence of any good depends upon the existence of some consciousness which values it as good. It is not very plausible to think that one state of the universe would be better than another if no being was conscious of the difference. It is hard to see what 'betterness' would come to in such a case. The philosopher G. E. Moore once held that a beautiful universe, unseen by anyone, was better than an ugly universe.[14] But it seems to me that without being appreciated or dis-

13. Anselm, *Cur Deus Homo?*, translated by S.N. Deane, La Salle, Ill., 1982, p. 288.
14. G.E. Moore, *Principia Ethica*, Cambridge 1951, p. 83f.

liked, no state of the universe would really be of greater value than any other. If that is so, value must consist in appreciation by some consciousness.

What is good is what is valued, approved of or desired by some mind. Some goods can be better than others, in the sense that some mind can prefer them. Moreover, it will be reasonable to prefer some goods to others. For example, it is rational to prefer a good which is longer lasting, more intense, and which holds more potential for interest and so is fairly complex. It is clear, however, that different minds will prefer different goods, and that there will be a huge number of different sorts of valued states, not all of them being directly comparable to one another. How, for example, could one compare the good of hearing a Beethoven symphony with the good of an exhilarating country walk? Both are good and desirable. Yet not everyone may desire them, and there is no obvious common scale of values on which they could be placed. Much will depend on the context of such experiences, and perhaps one would choose to have both, without trying to rank them in comparative value.

If God is thought of as a being of supreme value, will he include all possible values in his own being, to the highest degree where that is applicable? That is almost certainly an incoherent idea, since many goods are incompatible with one another. For example, many people would find good, would prefer and choose, a state of trying to attain some object with difficulty but with some hope of success, even though there is a risk of failure. The risk increases the value of the process, for many people. But such a value, of disciplined and difficult effort, is incompatible with the good of instant attainment, of pleasure without effort, which others would prefer. One can have both these goods, one after the other, restful pleasure after disciplined effort perhaps. But one cannot have a state in which both exist at the same time, in one state of consciousness. Indeed, many sorts of rest are valued precisely because they are the result of striving and anticipation, and would lose their value without such a preceding state. In that sense, many goods are essentially temporal. They would lose their distinctive character if one tried to unite them in one conscious state.

Bearing this in mind, one can see how the present absence, together with the future anticipation of good, is essentially involved in certain good states. The anticipation, the envisaging and deliberation, the planning and gradual execution, are often in themselves pleasurable states. If one is engaged in a creative process, it is essential that there should be some good yet to be realised. The encounter with various problems in the way of realisation and their creative resolution is a very great good, for most creative people. Such a good may also involve frustration, the possibility of at least relative failure, and many periods of unproductive torpor. Yet without them, the creative process would be too easy, not so valuable, and not so valued when it gets going.

If one is speaking of God, one cannot speak of such things as failure, torpor and frustration by recalcitrant materials. But one may wish to speak of the imaginative and creative realisation of goods as itself a great good, and one that involves something analogous to desire, desire for the existence of such goods, in God. It is often said that the existence of a desire entails some lack in God. A desire is for the existence of some good, so its present lack of being is a privation of good. For this reason, theologians have been reluctant to ascribe desire to God, if that means that God must lack some good, and thus be less good than he might be. If God is primarily known as the creator, however, then it may be that Divine desire is a good, the good of creative activity itself, in which the creator realises new and imaginative forms of beauty and intellectual complexity. If such creative activity is good, then it entails some unrealised desire in God; namely, particular aims which God realises in the creative process, but which cannot be instantaneously and effortlessly wholly realised without destroying the good of the process itself.

The existence of such desires in God does not mean that God is perpetually frustrated, in not having what he wants. It is not that God wants something which he does not have, and frets because he has not got it. On the contrary, God wants to have the desires he has, desires for future goods in some universe. He does not fret or feel frustrated or incomplete in not having them already realised. It is a good thing that there are many goods which may be realised if he wishes, and it would be contradictory to wish to have them already realised without creative action. What is required here is a clear distinction between 'desire' in the sense of a frustrated wish, and 'desire' in the sense of a calm and creative realising of new forms of goodness. To have desire in the former sense is an imperfection; but to have desire in the latter sense is a perfection, for it is a condition of creative action, which is itself good.

It may well be, even though it sounds paradoxical at first sight, that the most perfect possible being is one that does not possess every good property, nor even an unchanging state consisting of a large set of compossible properties. For the possession of the great good of creativity entails the non-possession of many goods yet to be creatively realised, and the existence of desire for their realisation. So one arrives at the idea of God as desiring to realise creatively many sorts of good.

It looks as if, however one thinks about it, one cannot assert that God actually possesses all possible goods. For if all the goods God possesses are actualised in one state, then the being of God must exclude all temporal goods, all the goods of creativity and imagination. God, so conceived, will lack an indeterminately large number of goods altogether. On the other hand, if God is to possess such temporal goods, then God cannot actually possess them all at once, which would contradict their nature. One will have to think of something like an infinite realisation, without beginning or end, of an endless series of goods. God will be inexhaustibly creative of good, but will not actually possess all possible goods immutably and timelessly.

This does not mean that God is in a condition of total changeability. A condition of such everlasting creativity in God is that he should immutably possess those properties which are necessary conditions of being an inexhaustible creator of good. God must be a source of dynamic and imaginative creativity. He must possess knowledge of all good things that might be created, and of the best way that they might be realised. He must possess unlimited power, which can continually produce new goods. He must know what things are good and desirable, being sensitive to and appreciative of beauty of all sorts. He must find supreme happiness in the contemplation of what is thus produced. He must be incapable of being brought into being or of being destroyed. Thus God must possess those properties which Anselm himself specified: 'This Being must be living, wise, powerful and all-powerful, true, just, blessed, eternal and whatever, in like manner, is absolutely better than what is not it'.[15]

These properties are essential to the Divine nature; and though God would freely choose them for himself, in fact they can neither come into being or pass away or be changed in any way, either by God or by anything else whatever. God therefore possesses a number of essential or necessary and unchanging, properties and a number of contingent and changing properties. Broadly speaking, the set of essential properties consists of what may be called dispositional properties. God's happiness is his disposition to take delight in the things that he does and knows. God's wisdom is his disposition to order all things to their proper fulfilment. God's power is his disposition to bring states into being. God's goodness is his disposition to

15. Anselm, *Monologion*, translated by S.N. Deane, La Salle, Ill., 1982, p. 110.

make those states desirable. God's knowledge is his disposition to be fully aware of the natures of all things. The set of contingent properties consists of all those particular states of the Divine being which form the particular content of the Divine knowledge and power, and the objects of Divine happiness and wisdom. The dispositional properties are immutable; the occurrent properties are in continual change, as the Divine awareness lives in a process of everlastingly self-expressive dynamic creativity.

It may be suggested that, even if God cannot contain all possible goods in one unchanging state, he may be able to possess a maximal set of good states which are compossible. This would be a very mitigated doctrine of perfection as Divine actuality, but it might preserve a sense of the strict immutability of God. Normal Kretzmann writes, 'A perfect being ... must possess the sum total of all logically compossible attributes which could be reasonably conceived as bestowing value on their bearer'.[16] There are certainly many value-bestowing attributes; equally certainly, they are not all compossible. So what is meant by the 'sum total of all compossible attributes'? One may have a number of sets of compossible attributes; but there will not be a sum total of them all, since the sets are not compossible with each other. May one say, then, that there is one largest, or greatest, set of compossible attributes? One may have conflicts here between, for example, an extensive set of reasonably good attributes, and a smaller set of extremely good attributes. It is not obvious that there will be just one maximal set. Moreover, many good properties have no maximal term, so that no being can, as a matter of logic, exhibit them maximally. Happiness is such a property. One could always be happier than one is, however happy one is. It is good for God to be happy, and to be happier than any other actual being. But it is, in whatever state God is in, always logically possible to be happier. If this is so, even in a perfect being not all change would be for the worse (as Aristotle held it would be, in *Metaphysics* 1074b). It would always be possible to increase in non-maximisable perfections. Yet doing so would not render the previous state of the Divine being less than perfect, since it would still be the greatest actual degree of happiness at that time, and there simply is no maximum possible degree. Charles Harshorne developed the 'principle of dual transcendence', that God's happiness, or similar intensive properties, may be unsurpassed by any actual being at a given time, and

16. Normal Kretzmann, Omniscience and Immutability, *Journal of Philosophy* vol. 63, 1966, 409-21.

unsurpassable by any other being at any time, but surpassable by itself at some future time.[17] This seems an intelligible construal of a notion of perfection for any property which does not have a maximal degree, and it helps to deprive one argument for the strict immutability of God of force.

Even properties like power may not have a maximal term. It is easy to construct a verbal maximum, just by saying that God is omnipotent. But it is much harder to spell out just what is involved in this notion. If power is construed as capacity, does it make sense to say that there is a number of capacities such that no number could be greater? If there is an infinite number of possible capacities, to say that God possesses all possible capacities is to say that he possesses no definite assignable number. That may well be true, and indeed I think it is implied by the Biblical notion of supreme Divine power. God may have numberless capacities; he may be wholly unrestricted in power. But is that to say that he is actually in an unchanging state of possessing maximal power? Or is it not rather to say that there is literally no end to the number of ways in which he may exercise power?

What is happening here is a capitulation to the basic metaphysical temptation to turn dispositions into states, to deny time, potentiality and change by somehow subsuming them under changeless actuality. One can say that God has maximal power; but one is not thereby saying that some actual state that God is in constitutes the complete actualisation of such power. One is saying that God has inexhaustible capacities, that there is no end to the number of things he can do, and that all other powers depend upon his. To possess perfect power is not to be in some state such that all possible powers are exercised at the same time by the same being — a dubiously coherent idea. It is to be able to exercise an innumerable set of powers limitlessly, without restriction or limitation. Maximal power is, after all, maximal potency, not maximal actuality. It is more like a potency for infinite realisation than the possession of some occurrent property of 'being powerful'.

If one asks whether God is as good as he can possibly be, the reply is accordingly rather complex. He is as good as he can possibly be, he is the greatest conceivable being, and greater than anything we can conceive, in

17. Charles Hartshorne, *Creative Synthesis and Philosophic Method*, London 1970, p. 227ff.

that no being can possess more actual happiness or power or greater potential for action and happiness. But he is not as good as he can possibly be, in that there is no actual maximal state of unsurpassably exercised power and happiness. Whatever actual power is exercised, just a little more could be exercised; and whatever actual happiness he has, just a little more could be experienced. That, after all, is exactly what the possession of infinite power and happiness means. What the logic of maximal perfection requires, therefore, is that the perfect being is unsurpassable in power and happiness at any time, but that at every time he possesses infinite potential for more, or different kinds of, happiness and the exercise of creative power.

With regard to the Divine possession of a maximal set of great-making properties, one can say that a perfect being must possess a set of logically compossible attributes which is not smaller or less valuable, overall, than any other actual set, which is not less great than any other possible set which could be measured on some comon value scale, and which, though it might change, could never at any time be surpassed by any other actual set. Thus an omnipotent, omniscient and perfectly wise being will be necessarily good, in the sense that it will maximise in its own being a great number of compossible intrinsically desirable states. God will be good, as the supreme object of rational desire, whose being is fulfilled in the contemplation of its own supreme goodness.

Some theologians have found difficulty with the idea that God may both be immutable and mutable. H.P. Owen, for example, bluntly says that the idea is self-contradictory.[18] The appearance of contradiction disappears entirely when one construes this as saying that God possesses both immutable and mutable properties, the former being necessary to God and the latter being contingent. There is no contradiction at all in that claim, since one is not saying that God is both immutable and mutable at the same time and in the same respect. One is saying that God is immutable in his 'absolute perfections' and mutable in those perfections which do not admit of absoluteness, non-temporality or total compossibility.

This should not be a very surprising notion of a God who is, after all, seen in the Biblical tradition primarily as creator. But what is being suggested is that, even in the realisation of the supreme value in the Divine Being itself, one cannot coherently think of all values somehow summarised into one timeless actual state. One must think of God as bringing into being, within

18. H.P. Owen, *The Christian Knowledge of God*, London 1969, p. 105.

his own Divine Life, a series of goods or desirable states, without beginning or end. Perfection is not the actual possession of every possible sort of goodness, which is a logical impossibility. It is the possession of a form of goodness which by nature creatively expands itself into relation with other forms of created goodness.

The idea of causal relations within the Divine being is one that Christians are committed to, in any case, by the doctrine that the Father eternally 'begets', or causes the Word to be. Indeed, one can discern a threefoldness in the idea of God that has been sketched here that is already one embryonic form of a Trinitarian doctrine, and that can be articulated with the aid of concepts drawn from Christian revelation. There is an abysmal potency in God, containing the dispositions for infinite actualisations. There is the manifestive creativity of God, actualising these dispositions in endless names and forms. And there is the Divine experience of those forms, as united into one ever-extending awareness of actualised value, held forever in the Divine mind. One might say that an endless series of 'forms' or images of God (which, taken as one unitary totality, one might metaphorically call the uttered 'Word' of God) is begotten from the abysmal ground of being (the 'Father') through the creative Spirit, and thus that there is a causal generation within the being of God itself.

God, as that than which no greater being can be conceived, will possess an essential nature. He will necessarily exist, as omnipotent, omniscient, supremely happy, wise and perfectly good. He will be of unsurpassable goodness (rational desirability), and will, without beginning or end, create new realisations of value within his own being, which will be included in one ever-extending and perfectly appreciated experience of actualised value. Such a God will be truly a living, active God, everlastingly creative and inexhaustible in apprehended value, the source and final realisation of all possible goodness. That, it seems to me, is a coherent concept of God which fits well with Biblical and Trinitarian beliefs about God, and avoids many objections that can be brought against the more Platonic classical view. If this claim is reasonable, that in itself is sufficient proof that metaphysics is possible. Whether it is plausible, of course, is another question.

Is the Theistic Conceptual Model Tenable?

Klaus-M. Kodalle

I   Observations

1.   Preliminary Remarks

a) The concept 'theism' first became prominent in the seventeenth century. One can, no doubt, also quite plausibly make use of Thomas Aquinas in order to elucidate theistic lines of argument. But in view of the typically modern turn to self-reflexive subjectivity — which involves the refraction of an objectivistic (realistic) ontology — it seems to me advisable to supplement Thomist considerations with those that take the Descartes-Leibniz constellation as their starting point.

b) In the lexicon *Die Religion in Geschichte und Gegenwart*, one finds the following definition under the entry 'theism': 'In contradistinction to deism, theism maintains not only the bare preservation of creatures by God, but also his active participation in all of their doings, as well as a positive revelation and *the possibility of sovereign interventions in world events*'.[1] I have emphasized this last point because it is particularly connected with the theistic idea of a personal, self-conscious and planfully active God above and beyond the world. The critique of this idea is a steady reference point in the following exposition.

c) 'Philosophy of religion' can be understood as the attempt to *reconstruct*, on the basis of a coherent model, the historically given *religious notions* of Christian dogmatics. On this view the truth claim on the part of tradition is granted a quasi *a priori* credence; the contribution of the philosophy of religion consists in clarifications and supporting arguments. This type of philosophy of religion is — as far as I understand — exemplified by Keith Ward's paper.

---

1. *Die Religion in Geschichte und Gegenwart*, 3rd ed., vol. VI, p. 734 — my italics.

But the type of philosophy which, while remaining *receptive* to the truth claims of religion in general and of the Christian faith in particular, retains an awareness of the specifically modern *distance* or difference between philosophy and theology will take pains to keep in mind the strengths of the finite ratio and will explore the extent to which this finite reason by virtue of its *own* depth and complexity touches upon a godly 'ground' that it attempts, with caution and due scepticism, to articulate. It might turn out that there are not only certain *correlations* between this type of philosophical self-reflection and the tradition of Christian doctrine, but also certain *reflections* [Spiegelungen] (of the holy in the profane); however, if a philosophy of religion wishes to remain within the context of contemporary philosophical discourse, it cannot accept the role of *handmaiden* to theology, as simply an instance for strengthening plausibility, as it were.

I understand the following observations as belonging to this second type. It is perhaps helpful at this point to bring to mind some distinctions made by Kant: Since the question of the tenability of theism cannot be decided definitively by speculative reason, Kant moved the problem to the domain of ethics; the concept of God which he postulated at this level most certainly does retain at least places of theistic arguments. At the level of *knowledge*, however, the decisive point with respect to the intelligence of a 'supreme and all-sufficient being' is 'accurately to determine this concept on its transcendental side ... to free it from whatever, as belonging to mere appearance (anthropomorphism in its wider sense), is out of keeping with the supreme reality, and at the same to dispose of all counter-assertions, whether *atheistic, deistic,* or *anthropomorphic.*'[2] As far as the *existence* of this supreme being is concerned, Kant, as we know, makes a case for the possibility of an *existential decision*; in spite of the epistemological plausibility of scepticism, we may allow ourselves this leap, for it is not contrary to reason but simply beyond it: 'Should we seek to make good this lack of determination in our concept by means of a mere idea of [a being that possesses] the highest perfection and original necessity, this may indeed be granted as a favour: it cannot be demanded as a right on the strength of an incontrovertible proof.'[3] Why should we hesitate to avail ourselves of this *favour*? It might even be possible to take this weak form of rationality as a gain in freedom. At any rate, Kant remains a 'thorn in the flesh' of theological speculation: A modus operandi

---

2. *Kritik der reinen Vernunft,* B 668.
3. *Ibid.,* B 665.

for which 'anything goes' cannot be justified by an appeal to Kant; on the contrary, *transcendental* theology in its 'negative usage' remains in place; it is the guideline for critique and the 'constant censor' of all concretions of the notion of God taken from other sources.[4]

2. Creation: A Contingent Act of God's Freedom?

For the theistic model it is quite apparently decisive to conceive of creation not as an *essential* expression of the divinity of God, but rather as a contingent act of freedom. Now with one conclusion reached by K. Ward I definitely am in agreement: the acceptability of the theistic scheme cannot be judged 'by checking it against independent reality', but only 'by an eternal self-critical reflection'. This self-critical reflection leads me to reject the theistic scheme.

In his discussion of Spinoza's solution, Ward holds that this ontological conception excludes creativity and freedom with respect to God or the cosmos. I am not certain that this conclusion is inescapable, for freedom is, after all, *primarily* an act with respect to that which is inwardly held necessary; only in a *secondary* respect is it the ability to make an arbitrary choice with respect to some aim or other! It will help to recall that even Thomas Aquinas viewed creation as an 'emanatio totius a causa universali quae deus est'.[5] Aquinas gave expression to his conviction 'that the first cause could not create a plurality of worlds' ('quod prima causa non posset plures mundos facere'). Keith Ward summarizes this view thus: 'There is, in the divine being, an immutable intention to bring precisely this universe into being'. God's knowledge and will are just as necessary as the being of God itself. In this connection, he comes to the following conclusion — which I would like to retain irrespective of Aquinas: 'God's willing the universe is not something that God came to a new decision about: it is part of the immutable Divine Being from all eternity'. God's knowledge of the temporally existent is itself eternal — in a flash. In God's eternal being temporality is preserved [aufgehoben]. The connection must be examined more closely between this thesis and the thesis that God exists *now*, that He is 'co-present' or 'co-temporal' with everything. Here I would like to raise the following objection: I cannot *think*, let alone *imagine*, a divine 'time' that has nothing to do with our spatio-temporal time. Within the perspective of a time

---

4. *Ibid.*, B 669.
5. *Summa Theologiae* I, q. 45 a.

swallowed up (aufgehoben) in eternity, talk of radical *new decisions* and *new* deeds of God — which Keith Ward wants to retain — in my opinion loses all possible meaning. Is not talk of 'new decisions' of God simply a *projection* of thought patterns that are completely infected by the sequential nature of spatio-temporal existence? Everything that belongs to the future in a temporal-finite sense (namely potentiality) is nonetheless 'necessity' in God. God cannot drop beneath his level, as it were, and make improvements on creation.

Only on the condition that creation is *not* conceived as a purely contingent act does it make sense to honour it, along with Keith Ward, in good Hegelian fashion as the 'visible expression of the mind of God'. But I still have difficulties, as I have indicated, with the thesis that 'discontinous emergent events... prefigure the consummation of value which is the goal of creation...'

The problem of 'many worlds' has to be dealt with at this point. In 1277 the Church (more exactly: the bishop Étienne Tempier of Paris), acting out of concern for the absolute sovereignity of divine freedom, condemned the thesis 'that the first cause could not create many worlds.'[6] Thus we see that it is of paramount importance for the theistic view that God could also have created a specimen of world other than the one in which we live. This is no doubt meant in the sense of a world that could be wholly other than ours in its essence. In what could the otherness of this world consist? It certainly could not be better or worse than the existing one, for this would clash with God's perfection. God is not free to perform at a level beneath his own perfection in the creation of the finite-transitory. I follow Leibniz on this: the inventory of basic truths — logical, mathematical and metaphysical — is a fundamental feature of every possible world, for it is identical with the divine understanding itself. For Leibniz, the most perfect world is that which 'is at the same time the simplest with respect to hypotheses and the richest with respect to phenomena'. Hence the contingency of possible *other* worlds, about whose otherness absolutely nothing can be said, is neither pertinent to nor interesting for our question about God. To my way of thinking the *contingent* character of the created is in keeping with the *necessity* of the act of creation for God. Here I differ from Keith Ward, who — apparently in order to save the divine *liberum arbitrium* — expressly maintains the

---

6. Cf. J. Weischeipel, *Thomas von Aquin. Sein Leben und seine Theologie*, (New York 1974), Graz 1980, pp. 302-9.

contingency of the divine capacity for creation. I content myself with what Ward terms the 'classical view' and see myself in no position to raise the *narrative* 'biblical talk of God' to the normative standard of philosophical discourse. But philosophical discourse can make Biblical discourse the point of reference in order to generate fruitful critical tension.

Here I would like to remark something in passing that will be discussed more fully later on: The semantic correlation necessary/contingent is itself merely a point of orientation for our finite understanding — as are for instance analytic/synthetic or possible/real. There is no objective indication for that which we take to be 'merely' contingent; there is only the possibility of reaching an understanding in the course of debate if we succeed in tracing a problem back to its irreducible, simple, and trivial elements.

3. Enhancement of value?

I am not convinced by the rehabilitation of the teleological proof of the existence of God by means of a theory of the enhancement of value. K. Ward designates God as a being 'of supreme value', 'realizing distinctive values'. What, then, is intrinsically of *supreme* value? What is that supposed to mean? K. Ward himself concedes that we are not able to comprehend 'what values were to be realized', 'the conditions of their realization', 'the nature of God', or 'the way in which God is able to structure events to ensure their final realization'. All that remains for us, therefore, is the simple postulate 'that this universe does exist in order to realize specific [*sic*] values'.

In such a postulate I am not able to see more than wishful thinking. It is in no way possible to set forth the aims that God intentionally pursues in the physical structure of natural laws. The value-enhancement formula is a likely source of self-deception: The gravitation of the value enhancement 'God' becomes the function of the evaluation of the finite subject. Thus for an authoritarian character God's eminent *power* would be decisive; a sensitive, sovereign individual, on the other hand, might well put the emphasis on God's capacity for compassion with the maltreated creature — at the expense of suppressing phantasies of omnipotence (cf., e.g., the god-myth of Hans Jonas).[7] The following train of thought also belongs in the context of the thesis of divine value enhancement: the starting point is an assessment of the deficient nature of the finite, over against which God is then thought of

---

7. Unsterblichkeit und heutige Existenz, in Hans Jonas, *Zwischen Nichts und Ewigkeit. Zur Lehre vom Menschen*, Göttingen 1963, p. 44-62.

primarily as the compensatory instance who, by virtue of the fact that He himself *is* the opposite of these deficits, will rectify these deficits in the present or in the future. All such lines of thought have long since fallen prey to the accusation of projection posed by the critique-of-religion school.

Keith Ward's philosophy of value can presumably be traced back to an underlying *ontological objectivism*. An immediate pointer in this direction is the fact that — in spite of Kant's incisive objections — he treats the 'necessary existence' of God as an attribute, as an objective feature, and not as a highly problematic product of our thinking. Along with omnipotence, goodness and omniscience, 'necessary existence' is counted among the necessary attributes of God.

An ontological objectivism is also suggested by the fact that Keith Ward treats freedom, justice, etc. as 'the objective good of this universe', that is, as if these manifestations of subjective and intersubjective self-determination are 'fulfilments of the natures of the sort of sentient social animals'. Speaking for myself, this sort of metaphysical security has crumbled, *i.e.* the security of being able to proceed on the basis of categorically given determinations of the natural essence of the human. And in view of the condition of this world one will hardly expect from the empirical data a confirmation of such an 'objective good'; on an empirical basis there is good reason for positing a deus malignus. K. Ward on the other hand adheres to the view that 'the true human good is to be found in appropriate fulfilment of natural human inclinations: that goodness is rooted in the nature of things'. On the basis of this ontology it is perhaps possible to collect a few arguments in favour of theism, but in this case the overwhelming experience of negativity — in ourselves, in our relationship to others and in our world — must then be pushed off onto the periphery, as exemplified in Ward's text, where the theodicy problem is not even taken as seriously as it is, say, by Leibniz.

This ontological objectivism is certainly connected with the fact that K. Ward deals with concepts such as consciousness, freedom, value, justice and creativity at the level of the abstract natural sciences. But in my opinion there is no longer any likelihood of success in trying to exhibit divine love in the structures of the cosmos as described according to the methods of natural science. And therefore I cannot be convinced by the thesis that theism is to be understood 'as an implication of the scientific attitude itself'.

I do not share Ward's expectations with respect to the synthesizing ability of reason. If 'ultimate' states of affairs are simply given — 'simple' and 'elegant' — what then compels us nevertheless to want to 'explain' them?

Why should it otherwise make us 'unhappy'? Is more than an empty play of words involved in the assertion that these 'ultimate brute facts' are given meaning [aufgehoben] by a theory of 'ultimate values'? Is it not true that in the final analysis talk of 'universal intellegibility' is utterly without foundation? That which *ultimately* can be seen to be totally simple and trivial cannot be something for which one wants to provide reasons. Put otherwise: a good reason is one that is good because it is accepted by reflective natures without question.[8] Of course, even the correlation simple — complex points to a fundamental problem: what are the criteria for simplicity, for complexity? Even the unquestionable validity of the ultimately simple cannot be *ascertained* apart from the context of discourse.

The same primordial ontological confidence is manifested by the combination of teleological and aesthetic argumentation. With reference to the cosmos, Ward repeatedly brings in aesthetic judgments: 'elegant set of boundary conditions'. Analogies from the realm of art must be used with caution, however, and are presumably less appropriate for purposes of illustration than K. Ward believes. He orients himself in terms of a very traditional model of artistic production: Mozart. What he feels able to exclude is just what is precisely characteristic for contemporary art: e.g., computer-generated musical sequences (Stockhausen) and the abandonment of the effort to conclude an open possibility of meaning, i.e. the abandonment of a 'unique and original form of beauty', evidenced for example by the inclusion of completely arbitrary noises taken from everyday life (John Cage).

If my understanding is correct, Ward accords a *higher* value to complex configurations as compared with simple ones. The contrary assumption strikes him as being 'counter-intuitive'. Is that really true? Do we not normally assume nowadays that a work of art effected by few, simple means is more elegant, more authentic than a complex, overloaded one? It is certainly the case that art has gone down the same path as science: the reduction to the simplest, irreducible ultimates, which no longer require an investigation into the 'underlying meaning'.

4. Physics and Divine Teleology

With the help of metaphors and analogies, it is possible to create the impression of a nature-spirit-god unity. However, to me this approach seems to be a sort of a theological 'private language'. For Max Planck, for example,

---

8. Cf. Ludwig Wittgenstein, *Philosophische Untersuchungen*, par. 481 ff.

it was 'self-evident that to an ever-increasing extent the world-view must be purged of all anthropological elements'.[9] In my opinion it is illusory to want to describe a kind of unified science on a synergetic basis. Modes of human, social behavior lose their specific quality if they are integrated into the explanatory framework of natural science. Ontologically understood levels of value that are supposed to express the fact that nature is tending toward a state of perfection — such entities presuppose an objectively real teleology, which is completely uncharacteristic for the methods of physics. I would strongly suggest not to drop behind the differentiations of the modern era by falling under the spell of a synergetic myth. Over and against the temptations of a naturalistic ethic I would for example like to maintain the sharp distinction between 'is' and 'ought'. Perhaps it is the case that the new cosmological search for meaning is only a reflex of the disappearance of the *political* utopias.

What results from such enterprises is 'a scientistic mythology with its characteristic mixture of reductionism and metaphorical overloading of internal scientific results'.[10] Physics is thereby anthropologically over-burdened and the human is physicalistically reduced. In this way a world view is produced that smooths out everything terrifying and reduces anxiety-creating factors in history and nature to a *quantité négligeable*: a harmonizing of nature-culture-sensibility-ethics. The dangers of scientific-technological civilization and the related uncertainties are suspended in a construction of meaning. From the synthesis of theology and natural science a cosmological overview emerges that makes the anxieties of modern civilisation tolerable.[11]

5. The Cooperation Model

At one point, Keith Ward mentions that 'non-arbitrary emergence' is 'the mark of the divine creative act itself'. If I understand correctly, his intention — for the sake of orthodox faith — is to *suppress* the assertion that the universe proceeds from God 'as a deductive entailment of the divine being'. I am puzzled in this context by the statement: 'There is certainly no regular

9. Max Planck, *Vorträge und Erinnerungen*, Stuttgart 1943, p. 223; quoted by Hans Dieter Mutschler, Mythos 'Selbstorganisation', *Theologie und Philosophie*, vol. 67, 1992, pp. 86-108, see p. 98.
10. Mutschler, *op.cit.*, p. 104.
11. Cf. Mutschler, *op.cit.*, p. 104ff.

observable succession between God and the production of universes'. I fail to understand what at this point the reference to observation is supposed to mean; for, after all, none of the theistic speculations about the emergence of 'values' are 'observable' either.

Ward has adopted the idea that human beings are 'subcreators' who in their individual actions cooperate with a God who acts purposively with respect to his own superior aims. To me, the formula of cooperation seems to perform an inadequate job of hiding the fact that by this means a concept of God that has the tendency to eliminate human freedom is supposed to be rescued. Ward considers theological reflections that are critical of an abstract conception of omnipotence to be superfluous because it is possible to assume that although God has complete power to determine all things he nevertheless holds himself in check 'in contingent decision!' — God does not make use of his omnipotence all the time, 'so that human beings can decide a few things for themselves...'. But of course God is under no obligation to permit himself to be constantly frustrated by the human abuse of freedom.

This line of thinking seems to be somewhat off track, for it fails to do justice to the dignity of beings created for freedom: God is the supreme patriarch and controlling agent, as it were, who is in possession of the power to intervene in the context of human action and communication whenever necessary and stop the proceedings. Keith Ward apparently would like to eliminate the possibility that God, out of love for human beings, could be exposed to suffering for the sake of *their* freedom. But just this readiness and capacity for suffering is what constitutes a true loving relationship — as opposed to a paternalistic or infantile one.

On June 29, 1941 — a week after the commencement of the German campaign against Russia — Pius XII declared in a radio address: 'Regardless of how brutal the hand of the divine surgeon may appear when it forces its way with iron into living flesh, it is always love that guides it...'[12] The response to such perverse adaptations of the theistic model, for which one could easily find Protestant parallels from the same period, is inadequate if one simply distances oneself from them as aberrations; the theological conceptions underlying such primitive convictions must themselves be repudiated as obsolete.

Our German chairman Ingolf Dalferth has stated that God makes himself manifest 'by freely choosing to let historical events become the place of his

12. Quoted in *Die Zeit*, no. 14, 27 March 1992, p. 42.

experienced presence in our world, thereby hallowing them'.[13] Of course, Dalferth does not have those historical adaptations in mind. But what then urgently requires explanation is the meaning of God's 'free choice'.

We can assume an absolute contingency of divine intervention — with the tendency to speak of the *deus absconditus* as the obscure, arbitrary dimension of the will of God. That would be precisely the leap suggested by the theistic model. From the perspective of reaching a philosophical understanding that must appear too precipitate. Philosophical discourse should take the fullest advantage of the available means of expression of finite-sceptical reason. Thereupon it would indeed be quite possible to interpret the experience that understanding takes place, that a historical configuration strikes me as significant, or possibly even becomes the key experience of my entire life, as the presence of the spirit, that is: as revelation — this revelation, however, is certainly not the arbitrary dispensation of a merciful God who restricts me to receptive passivity, but rather the expression of a felicitious outcome in which one's own erring, easily corruptible existence — which distorts the permanent presence of the divine ground as a result of its obtuse, overbearing insistence on self-realization — breaks through to a salutory inside: it then becomes manifest that that which maintains existence in being always has been the divine ground. And it is a sign of the overabundant gratitude for this experience that the self remains in the background while giving expression solely to the constitutive power of the spirit. But it is a misleading impression to think that the finite self is here least involved. It is precisely in such concretions that it attains its authentic self because (and to the extent to which) it attains the lightning flash of insight into the self-constituting unity with God.

II Our own Proposal

What prompted us to raise the question of the tenability of the 'theistic' model in the first place? If we apply an abstract typology of religion to the narrative descriptions of the Bible, theism makes a first-rate showing as an abstract configuration over against pantheism or deism. Nonetheless, here we are raising the question of the tenability of the theistic scheme. Even if the various constructions appear at first to be smooth and consistent, there still remains a problem. A certain uneasiness creeps in despite the logic of the

---

13. Ingolf Dalferth, *Kombinatorische Theologie*, Freiburg 1991, p. 129.

thousand articles concerning God's ability to create a stone that he himself is not able to budge.

I begin with the assumption that we have lost our onto-theological innocence. We do not have to be mesmerized by the aesthetic arbitrariness of post-modernity in order to concede that a *post-metaphysical* inquiry into God's reality is challenging and fruitful for us. If we abandon the onto-theological suggestion that God *must* be thought of as the supreme being, and if we suspend the projection of God as the highest principle of knowledge, then the finitude, provisionality and accidental nature of our theological self assurances emerge more clearly; for it becomes evident how unsure and uncertain we are of our own selves.[14]

In a previous section, I made a case for keeping in mind the differing scopes of various theories and for resisting the holistic-synthetic temptation of drafting theistically inspired views of totality. After all, it cannot be denied that there is such a thing as a hermeneutic desire for mastery, or will to power, which cannot tolerate the resistance of that which is foreign. The 'rage of understanding'[15] is supposed to ward off the anxiety generated by foreignness. The striving for security, the search for an assurance of shelter, is an urge that possibly can never be entirely overcome: It is reassuring to feel free to see the providence of God at work in all things — even the diaries of a person such as Dietrich Bonhoeffer provide an eloquent testimony of this.[16] Over against this narrow-minded religious craving for certainty I would recommend an *asceticism of interpretation*, in other words: a scepticism over against the promise of the great scientific-theological-aesthetic synthesis. What is required, on the contrary, is to make room in the self-world relationship for primordial encounters, for the *unknown* god, as well as for revolutionary, unexpected challenges that block off the craving for a totalising understanding of meaning.

Those who can understand themselves in this fashion — as God's tight-rope dancers[17] — are 'good for a surprise' with respect to others as well. The perspective that the absolute as free and sovereign manifests itself in the

---

14. Cf. Friedrich Nietzsche, *Beyond Good and Evil*, par. 17, also par. 16.
15. Jochen Hörisch, *Die Wut des Verstehens*, Frankfurt 1988.
16. Cf. Klaus-M. Kodalle, *Dietrich Bonhoeffer. Zur Kritik seiner Theologie*, Gütersloh 1991, p. 97ff.
17. L. Wittgenstein, *Über Gewißheit*, p. 554: 'Der ehrliche religiöse Denker ist wie ein Seiltänzer. Er geht, dem Anschein nach, beinahe nur auf der Luft.'

overabundant dimension of existence, decisively enhances the value of existence as an end in itself. Only the person who refrains from every tendency to manipulate the divine will have the understanding necessary to safeguard against the total instrumentalizing of the living in the finite realm.

The religious mania for seeing the operations of divine powers in and behind all events, on the other hand, sacrifices freedom out of metaphysical anxiety. For those who are free it makes sense to become involved with 'God' as the ground of reality that breaks into our existence as the constant provocation that compels us to the realization that we can attain the fullness of life only if we have no fear of self-surrender and the renunciation of pseudo-rational suggestions of security. Only surrendering to this 'unknown' god — superfluous by the standard of the scientific concept of rationality — provides life with the vigour and the courage necessary to transcend the limits of daily life under the fascination of the enigmatic and to stride ahead in light spirits.

To use a less enthusiastic and philosophically stricter formulation: we take seriously the modern demolition of an onto-theological philosophy based on first principles and no longer take our point of departure from supposedly absolutely valid, objective, ontological statements or principles. We are, for example, no longer certain whether the human being is essentially a *zoon logon echon* or a *zoon politikon*. On the contrary: we are beset by our experiences and unsolved problems. In the experiment of existence we are now looking for theoretical-instrumental solutions to problems by mobilizing our imagination. And then it *can* happen, unexpectedly, that a fitting inspiration announces itself. We were looking for something — but quite possibly we had not been looking for just that. We would say: in a particular context the logos was present; or: it 'came' to us — an inspiration of the absolute, the truth, which according to Walter Benjamin is never the correlate of an intention.

The 'mystical' experience of immediate, absolute confirmation of that which has been discursively developed has been written about by philosophers time and again. As we know, even Descartes had his 'disclosures' in dreams, which provided him with final certainty. And Wittgenstein — in his Lecture on Ethics, 1930 — speaks of the primordial experience of viewing the existence of the world as an occasion for wonder — which is of course 'really' nonsense, 'because I cannot think of myself as not existing'. The existence of language itself refers accordingly to something that could be called 'the absolute good' and that within the limits of language can only be brought to expression in a 'nonsensical' manner. Such experiences have of course no immediate and direct argumentative value; for each individual must make the discovery of the spiritual foundation of his existence in his own unique way. This insight led Kierkegaard to formulate his theory and strategy of indirect communication. In the same sense, by mentioning his primordial experience Wittgenstein in this lecture wanted to prompt his reader to stop and think if he had not had a similar experience: 'so that... we then have something in common for our investigation'.

This reference to 'evidence' strikes us as significant. If that which has been brought to speech in such a way has a meaning for others, then 'truth' has occured. Even the question whether this truth is *the same* for all discourse-participants must remain open. The concept of such an identity would, according to Descartes, itself be unclear. The experience that a theoretical attempt at finding a solution to a problem impresses not only *me* as being helpful and significant but also *us*: by virtue of this experience we participate in an identity that remains precarious, regardless of how pleased we might be about the fact that it stabilized in reciprocal understanding. In the concrete situation of the use of language, meaning manifests itself anew at each occurence. Whether the thesis that the human being is a *zoon logon echon* is true or whether it is an empty phrase — this cannot be determined *in abstracto* but must rather be demonstrated in the linguistic communication processes of human beings concerning their nature; and that cannot be decided once and for all but is rather evidenced by the factual success in reaching an understanding, in which process meaning accrues to the formula. At the same time, it always remains in doubt, as we said, whether those to whom this 'definition' expresses something meaningful really understand it to mean the same thing. By raising the issue of this questionability we are pointing to the fact that for us a discrepancy has emerged between the claim to meaning implied by every use of language on the one hand and the objective 'what' of meaning on the other hand. This discrepancy has to be coped with in discourse, in complicated 'translation steps' — until the questionability of the objective 'what' disappears in a provisionally satisfactory answer to the problem. As a result of the constantly changing problem-constellations on the one hand and of our constitutional imperfection — that is to say: historicity — on the other, the orientation process is open-ended. In view of the unceasing challenges facing us it might be possible to agree on the designation of the human being as a *zoon problemata echon*.

In order to provide a philosophical-historical framework for this fundamental, modern difficulty, Keith Ward suggests looking to Thomas Aquinas. This proposal does not strike me as being particularly helpful. I would prefer Descartes. This choice will probably give rise to some puzzlement, inasmuch as Descartes is considered to be a 'rationalist' and virtually at the antipodes of a philosophy of historicity. However, all such characteristics recede into the background if we take a closer look at the way Descartes grasps the God-relationship — for this is precisely the point at issue here. Here we find a fundamentally new approach over against all forms of scholastic, ontological argumentation.[18]

Above, I have employed the expression 'constitutional imperfection'. Assuming that this characterization meets with the agreement of the sympathetic reader, the following question poses itself: How is an idea of a perfect being, which we call God, possible in the first place? Can a being that understands itself as imperfect be in possession of clear ideas at all? Descartes looked for a solution by means of the 'necessary connections' which constitute an organized whole in our finite reason. He calls these necessary connections 'innate': 'First seeds of useful ideas'.[19] They are 'given', inasmuch as they are 'somehow' immune against the freedom to doubt. Hence we definitely do not know all that is implied by saying that we have some — to this extent: unclear — idea of a perfect being. But, then, do we have a clear idea of all the implications of saying that we are 'imperfect'? That can mean a number of things. But the inseparable, and to this extent trivial, 'necessary' connection of opposites in the semantic correlation of perfect-imperfect is in its simplicity as evident and easy to follow in the act of speaking as is the opposition, for example, mountain-valley. For Descartes, this was evidence of totally trivial limits of arbitrariness that must be accepted without question — precisely *because* they are trivial. Apparently our language is in possession of the given possibility of attaining clarity or consciousness with respect to imperfection in contrast to a perfect being. And from this starting point it seemed plausible for Descartes to form the correlative idea of a ground different from the subjectivity of our finite thought.

---

18. In the following I am making use — often literally — of ideas developed by Josef Simon, Das neuzeitliche Konzept der Geschichtlichkeit der Wahrheit und der christliche Gottesbegriff, in Klaus-M. Kodalle (ed.), *Gegenwart des Absoluten*, Gütersloh 1984, p. 206-26.
19. R. Descartes, *Regulae* IV, 3.

In other words, on Descartes' view the initial connections of ideas, which make reflexive self-awareness possible, cannot be the invention of this self. Hence if methodical scientific communication succeeds, then it has a *good* ground = *deus benignus*. For, from the point of view of the finite self, the innate ideas, including that of God, i.e. the necessary ideas, are in the mind only by accident. And it is 'noble audacity' to assume that they are given to our mind out of goodness or grace — to our mind, which only by this means gains an awareness of its own imperfection! This, again, is what makes it possible to distinguish 'God' from the projective determinations of our finite ideas concerning how God has to be. Furthermore, these allegedly necessary connections do not necessarily have to be thought by anyone — they are only necessary on the condition that they are thought.

Inasmuch as we are imperfect, our thinking is as well. If we think the thought of perfection then we think it together with that of our own imperfection. Hence we are not in possession of this idea in perfect clarity, but only in the clarity of the opposition, i.e. we have both ideas really only as one idea. That we think this 'connection', that we do think the way we think, is a fact. If we inquire into the reason for this fact, we necessarily also ask how it is possible that we do in fact entertain the idea of a perfect being without being able to think it with perfect clarity. We cannot think this through in perfect clarity. Hence we are in possession of this idea (together with the idea of our own imperfection) as an inspiration. The clarity of our thinking that is respectively attained or attainable depends on this inspiration, which from the viewpoint of doubting, analytic thought is pure coincidence. We form the notion of God as the ground of this coincidence, which makes it possible to gain confidence in the given, respective availability of the logos.

This element that impinges on our thought while continuing to remain obscure conveys meaning to our talk of 'truth'. As beings that can doubt everything we have no inherently true idea whatsoever. But this Absolute or, more metaphorically, this presence conveys to us on the one hand that it is 'its will' to be with us, and provides the guarantee for the truth of our finite and provisional ideas on the other. The existence of this transcendent idea in the human mind indicates of course that to this extent the human being is not *only* a finite being. Human finitude consists in the fact that God remains largely obscure to it apart from the insight that God is perfect and therefore must be thought of as existing and as benevolent. The philosophical concept of an Absolute that remains purely transcendent is therefore dispensed with, as is the concept of a type of thinking that believes it can base itself on principles of thought of a transtemporal nature. In the view presented here, 'God' is not a concept that can be subjected to an isolated exposition in answer to the question of what the concept is supposed to mean. For philosophical thought, the existence of God consists in nothing else than this benevolent effect: in the letting be of the truth of our finitude in the successful occurence of its respective historical facticity. The correlate of this modest concept of the Absolute is the dispensation from a concept of the human self based on first principles. Thus by 'God' we mean rather an Absolute that is at work by assuming finitude and that accords to finite historical consciousness the truth appropriate to it. Forms of a priori self-certainty are thereby abandoned, as well as a god susceptible to explication in terms of philosophical first principles.

It is perhaps the case that a theistic, extra-mundane god is entirely natural for the naïve mind, as natural as not giving a thought to what is involved in the act of saying 'I'. But it can indeed be said to be the task of philosophy to put some motion into these naïveties, or, otherwise expressed, to get our pre-concepts to start dancing. We do not experience ourselves and our thinking as changeable and hence as historical until we have generated a flow in our abstractly absolutized ideas. That is to say that the self must go through the experience of self-abandonment and abandonment by God, i. e. through anxiety. Truth as the joyful occasion of coming to an understanding bursts apart the rigid contours of conceptuality. Put another way: Every such experience magnifies our freedom, for in each case we already had a ready-made concept of our freedom that possibly now, contingently, is burst asunder. Those felicitous moments may be called divine in which objectivity accrues — always provisionally — to our semantic competence.

The Absolute, then, is not understood here as the God of a homogeneous world view, but rather as the God of individuality, that of one's own and that of the other. Accordingly it is no longer necessary or possible to determine what 'God' inherently is as the universal encompassing all human subjectivity. Metaphorically spoken, this universal is present in its concomitant withdrawal, thereby opening up as a subsidiary effect finite perspectives of orientation for human freedom. Divine, therefore, is the state of affairs that the ever-so-fragile human logos does indeed demonstrate — from one felicitous moment to the next — that it is up to its allotted task and that we may rest assured that a divine continuity therein obtains. In the *Phaedo*, Socrates gives an apt portrayal of this status of speech: 'Of course no reasonable man ought to insist that the facts are exactly as I have described them. But that either this or something very like it is a true account of our souls and their future habitations — since we have clear evidence that the soul is immortal — this, I think, is both a reasonable contention and a belief worth risking, for the risk is a noble one. We should use such accounts to inspire ourselves with confidence...'[20] Thus we are confident that at the right time the right word will occur, the word that finds assent and that provides us with the foundation for the indemonstrable conviction that the logos is inherently everlasting — and that it is granted to us to participate in it.

The matter at hand can be expressed in another way: we sketch out a rational theology, a dynamic, coherent whole, and find the rationally motivated assent of others; if this rational teleology fails to meet the test of life, the initial effect is to heighten the consciousness of our own finitude. The discrepancy between theory and practice can lead us to dispair in face of the absurd, or we can understand — with all due caution and modesty — this collapse as the beginning occurence of a meaning unlooked for, an unintended truth with an underlying continuity that can only be reconstructed imperfectly and post facto, knowing at the same time as we do that no concept of totality can be suffcently unequivocal to hold up indefinitely.

It goes without saying that a philosophy of finitude of this sort is indebted to Christian inspiration. For it brings movement into the concept of the Absolute — and, in consequence of this, movement into our abstractly fixed notions of God. God is that which comes to meet us [das Entgegenkommende], that which grants a felicitous outcome to our finite, provisional expositions — an outcome that can neither be anticipated nor made the object of conscious intent. The Absolute is just as much *subject* as it is *substance* (Hegel): as *communicativum sui* (Schelling). Where conceptual effort and divine inspiration convene (Plato, 7th Letter), truth *occurs*. Truth so conceived is no longer understood as static-absolute finality, but rather as self-experience in the movement of consciousness, in which movement God, the Absolute, comes to meet us, as it were. The decisive point is the place of encounter.

The more precise formulation of this relationship, in which God is no longer perceived as an objective-abstract entity but rather as the unconditional correlate of personal self-development, must accord with the

20. Plato, *Phaidon*, 114d ff.

contingent constitution of finitude: i.e. contingency as freedom from all determination must be reflected in the God-relationship. God, too, has His existence only *in* this performance, as the 'integrating factor' of the dynamic self-relationship. 'Man is a relationship that relates itself to itself and is grounded in a relationship that it itself has not posited' (Kierkegaard). God *is* a relationship that relates itself by relating itself to the other of itself (= to autonomous *finite* existence) as a being with sovereign freedom (to use a parallel formulation *à la* Hegel). If a leap is introduced artificially at this point — by virtue of the phantasy that the 'ground' thus brought to light in the process of self-becoming is such that it for its part could inherently also 'be' without the human being and its spiritual activity — then this theistic step is taken without being able to provide grounds for it. Even more precarious is the projection of a personality of God that in an eminent sense is supposed to have at its disposal all essentials of the human spirit independent of the reality of this finite spirit. It is clear that in this way the attempt was made traditionally to safeguard the dignity of the absolute sove-reignity of God; nevertheless, the concept implied here is primitive — the concept namely of a freedom for which the communicative dimension of meaning is only an accidental *addendum*. If out of a somewhat justified concern about the human propensity to make God the object of projections and manipulations one wanted to eliminate everything that conceivably could be understood as a manipulative gesture, then it would not be unreasonable to arrive at Schelling's single predicate for the ground of being *as* ground: the predicate of being devoid of predicates = pure indifference.

I have made an alternative, more concrete proposal:[21] if it is the case — as has been aptly put by Heidegger, for example — that the relationship to the world is characterized by *care* (Sorge, Sich-Sorgen-um), if it is true that in everything, even in the most subtle interpretations of life's meaning a hidden will to power obtains which forces everything into an utilitarian context, then *conversio* would have to be designated as a movement in existence (Dasein) that, under the aegis of a dimension of *authentically* superabundant meaning, projects 'God' as a power in our life that explodes all instrumental logic of the care-ridden intercourse with the world. God can then no longer be put into service for any life goals whatsoever, as if He could be pressed into the scheme of a functional performance. I have used

---

21. Klaus-M. Kodalle, *Die Eroberung des Nutzlosen. Kritik des Wunschdenkens und der Zweckrationalität im Anschluß an Kierkegaard*, Paderborn 1988.

Kierkegaard's formulation in this context: the Absolute is without purpose. Supreme purposelessness is, as every encounter with art teaches us, precisely not meaninglessness but the sign of a supreme meaning that culminates in pure superabundance and finally in the relinquishment of the 'self of care'. 'Theory and practice go together, so that the ultimate criterion of a world view is the form of life it expresses' (Keith Ward). On the other hand, the form of life that we consider appropriate depends on a particular scheme of interpretation. I would not choose to go as far as Ward and call this circle 'metaphysical'. The circle 'functions' in a naïve fashion. An awareness of the fact that the human being is free to examine his interpretive scheme critically, to modify and to revise it — this awareness does not emerge until uncertainties arise, difficult questions come up, and existential pressure increases to the point that the conventional answers provided by the naively accepted frame of reference simply fail. Put differently: not until then does one become conscious of the fact that despite massive doubts the frame of reference that previously had been naïvely reproduced can now be appropriated in a reflexively reflected manner — right up to the point of 'quia absurdum'. Hence freedom and decision are constitutive for this self-understanding: 'Such schemes require commitment; one makes a decision when the view of the world and the form of action it renders appropriate come to seem overwhelmingly illuminating and worthwile. And that happens only when one has already taken up a form of relationship to the experienced world which makes possible such forms of description' (Keith Ward). Of course no one can prevent the subject from deciding for an interpretative scheme within which the dignity of his freedom of decision is void (because, for example, God is phantasized as a puppet-show master behind the world stage). Such a decision is derivative nonetheless, for it can be traced back to a constitutive free decision-making competence of the finite self. For this reason I consider only that God-relationship *radical*, in the sense of going back to the roots, within which freedom remains the *terminus a quo* and the *terminus ad quem*.

In K. Ward's definition of theism as a categorial scheme 'which redescribes all experience as ultimately dependent upon and caused by a self-existent spiritual reality', everything turns on the way in which 'ultimately dependent' and 'caused' are understood within the context of the freedom of the finite self that is considered inalienable.

I would like to close with a remark of Wittgenstein's that fits in well with the quote from the *Phaedo*: we must give 'reasons' for our assertions, but what then 'reasons' are is itself a debatable matter upon which agreement must be reached. It is therefore important to bear in mind that the understanding of 'reason', or of that which is considered as a 'reason-for-x', is not something about which final certainty can be attained: 'Where there are no more reasons there is *persuasion*'.[22]

---

22. Ludwig Wittgenstein, *Über Gewißheit*, par. 612.

Panentheism

David A. Pailin

Panentheism is an attempt to identify and develop a concept of God that recognizes the proper ultimacy of the holy and takes seriously the self-conscious relationship of God to the world fundamental to the Judaeo-Christian-Islamic tradition of faith. While, therefore, the term 'panentheism' may be relatively new — it seems to have been coined by K.F.C. Krause (1781-1832) — what it connotes is arguably a way to understand the reality of God that satisfies both of the proper demands of adequacy for such theological understanding. One is adequacy to philosophical insights into that which is necessarily ultimate in being, value and rationality. The other is adequacy to actual religious belief in the living God of the faiths inspired by Abraham, Moses, Jesus and Muhammad. When properly understood, therefore, it is not a 'temptation' which lures believers away from their authentic faith. On the contrary, it provides a way by which the God in whom they believe may be apprehended in a rationally coherent manner.

According to Arnulf Zweig's article in *The Encyclopedia of Philosophy*, Krause's mystical and spiritualistic ideas were expressed in a style that is 'awesome' in its 'obscurity'. He employs 'an artificial and often unfathomable vocabulary' that includes 'monstrous neologisms' that are 'untranslatable into German, let alone into English'! Basically Krause maintains that God, as the primordial being who is without contraeity, contains and unifies the world while also transcending it.[1] In *The Ideal of Humanity and Universal Federation* Krause himself states that 'God is the one infinite ideal Being' from whose 'eternal power and wisdom and goodness' all that is 'arises' and in whom it 'subsists'. The creatures are finite, limited and independent. Both individually and collectively they are to be distinguished from God. 'No being *is* God except God alone.' While, however, God is 'over all His creatures', God never ceases 'to love His work, to maintain it, and to form it' into 'one universal

1. Zweig, Arnulf, 'Krause, Karl Christian Friedrich' in *The Encyclopedia of Philosophy*, edited by Paul Edwards, New York 1967, p. 363-5.

life.'[2] Using the analogy of the human body, Krause speaks of the universe as 'an organic whole, rich in free, self-dependent members'.[3] 'Every moment' God is aware of each of its members and reciprocally interacts with them, penetrating 'all its living parts' with 'new streams of life, love and beauty'.[4]

Another model for the God-world relationship used by Krause is that of a monarchy:'God is the monarch, and all beings are its citizens'.[5] The problem with this model — and with such other models for the relationship as that of the body — is to find a way of affirming the unity of all in God without denying the proper independence of the members. Some of Krause's comments illustrate the problem. On the one hand, he stresses that independence is the necessary condition of worth, life and love.[6] On the other hand, he sometimes casts doubt upon the reality of such independence. In one place, for example, he speaks of the world as being 'continually in the power of the Creator'.[7] In another, he expounds the monarchical model by stating that 'all things exist in predetermined harmony' but leaves it unclear whether this refers to the present or to a future resolution of 'the dissonances in the life of the world.'[8] Nevertheless, whatever the internal tensions in his expression of it, Krause's vision of the God-world relationship is basically one of love. In this love creatures 'realise themselves in the struggle of existence' and find their fulfilment in oneness with God:

Love is the living form of the inner organic unification of all life in God. Love is the eternal will of God to be lovingly present in all beings and to take back the life of all His members into Himself as into their whole life.[9]

While, however, Krause may have coined the word 'panentheism' to express his understanding of the relationship between God and the world and while the original provenance of the notion was what Dr. Meckenstock speaks of in his paper as 'the designs of philosophical systems in the succession of the

2. Krause, K.C.F., *The Ideal of Humanity and Universal Federation*, edited by W. Hastie, Edinburgh 1900, p. 5f.
3. Krause, *op.cit.*, p. 10.
4. Krause, *op.cit.*, p. 13.
5. Krause, *op.cit.*, p. 99.
6. Krause, *op.cit.*, p. 112.
7. Krause, *op.cit.*, p. 6.
8. Krause, *op.cit.*, p. 99.
9. Krause, *op.cit.*, p. 117.

critical philosophy of Kant', it is in the works of Charles Hartshorne (b. 1897) in the past half-century that this view of God and the world has received its classical and rigorous exposition. Hence, it is the understanding of the God-world relationship in what is called 'process theology', and Hartshorne's understanding of it in particular, that I wish to consider in this paper. Hartshorne's first major exposition of it is in *Man's Vision of God and the Logic of Theism* (1941). Later studies include *The Divine Relativity: A Social Concept of God* (1948), *The Logic of Perfection and Other Essays in Neoclassical Metaphysics* (1962), *Anselm's Discovery: A Re-examination of the Ontological Proof for God's Existence* (1965), *A Natural Theology for Our Time* (1967), and *Creative Synthesis and Philosophic Method* (1970) as well as numerous articles and a large work which he co-authored with William L. Reese, *Philosophers Speak of God* (1953).

Fundamental to Hartshorne's understanding of the divine reality is his recognition that an adequate analysis of the concept of God shows it to have a dipolar structure. Because of the way that Whitehead and Hartshorne are often linked together as the joint founders of a supposedly single system of understanding called process thought, it is important to appreciate that while there are various important similarities between the view of God put forward by Alfred North Whitehead (notably in *Process and Reality*, especially in its final part) and Hartshorne's analysis of the divine, the latter's notion of dipolarity is not the same as Whitehead's distinction between the primordial and consequent 'natures' of God. Therefore, although Hartshorne's dipolar structure provides a valuable model by which to develop what Whitehead suggests about the threefold character of God's reality and activity in terms of the primordial, consequent and (what is often overlooked) superjective 'natures' of the divine,[10] it is a fundamentally different conceptual structure. The result of failing to distinguish between these conceptual structures has been misunderstanding, confusion and, from some commentators, nonsense.

What, then, is Hartshorne's analysis of the dipolar structure of the divine and why is it important? This analysis shows, contrary to traditional under-standing, that it is not self-contradictory to predicate relative, contingent, temporal, changing and finite qualities of the divine in certain respects, as a well as absolute, necessary, eternal, unchanging and infinite qualities in other, systematically distinguishable, respects. While, furthermore, it may be a useful shorthand to speak of God as being in some respects

---

10. Whitehead, Alfred North, *Process and Reality: An Essay in Cosmology*, corrected edition edited by D.R. Griffin and D.W. Sherburne, New York 1978, p. 87f.

absolute, necessary, eternal ... and in other respects as relative, contingent, temporal ... these terms are more appropriately understood as formal, adverbial qualifiers which distinguish different aspects of the material attributes of the divine.[11]

Consider, for example, what is meant by speaking of God as having all knowledge (i.e., as having the attribute of omniscience). It is incoherent to deny this attribute to God. A being who was ignorant of anything would not satisfy the definition of God. Expressed negatively this means that there is nothing which is knowable that is outside the scope of God's knowledge. Expressed positively it means that in principle (and formally) God knows all that there is to be known absolutely, necessarily, eternally, unchangingly and infinitely. In other words, whatever may happen to be the case in any place at any time, God will know immediately every aspect of its internal and external relations without any distortion. Nothing whatsoever can be so without God knowing it to be so and, once it has happened, knowing it forever after as having so happened. In consequence there is an exact correlation between what has been and is, and the contents of God's knowledge of what has been and is: the contents of each can be defined in terms of the contents of the other. In practice (and materially), however, what God actually knows to be the case depends upon what actually happens to be the case. In the case of the events which constitute the empirical world these are contingent, relative, temporal and finite occasions in the changing processes of reality.

For instance, at whatever time and in whatever place and with whatever feeling a person might happen to read the previous sentence for the first time, God will know exactly when, where and how that person actually read it — and will know it without loss or distortion for evermore. Granted, however, that the successive states of human existence are not points on a predetermined world-line in the space-time of an everlastingly present block universe but are events in a reality whose temporal ordering is asymmetric (so that while the past of any state of coming to be is determinate, its future is indeterminate, even if minimally so), that place, time and feeling are basically contingent facts. While, therefore, no one (not even God) could have read that sentence before 7.15 p.m. GMT on 2 January 1992 (because it was

---

11. Cf. David A. Pailin, *God and the Processes of Reality: Foundations of a Credible Theism*, London 1989, p. 57ff, 96ff.

not written until then), a person could have read it in any place within the limits of accessibility and in any one of a large variety of moods at any time from then onwards. To the extent that when, where and how a person actually read it is thus a contingent matter, God's knowledge of it is likewise contingent. What is necessary is that God knows that event once it has come to be such.

Hence, contrary to what Dr. Meckenstock appears to suggest in his paper, according to this dipolar understanding of the divine the 'such-coming' of any contingent event is not necessary, nor is there a 'simultaneous determination and indetermination of events'. Indeed it is considered to be contradictory to hold that the occurrence of any particular genuinely contingent event is necessary from any perspective. This being so, it is a *contingent* event for God as for any other observer; what is *necessary* about it is not that it will happen but, in relation to God's knowledge, that once it has come about God will know it completely. Thus while divine omniscience embraces all that is knowable, future contingent events are not knowable for, as such, they are not 'there' (anywhere) to be known.[12] Although the resulting understanding of the divine does have 'existential consequences', as Dr Meckenstock says, it is not, I suggest, contrary to 'piety'. According to this understanding authentic theistic piety does not place its trust in the pre-established ordering of a block universe nor in a hidden puppeteer (cf. the song 'He's got the whole world in his hands') but in a God who is faithfully and graciously present with each individual in whatever happens to come about in the exciting openness of creative advance from the determinate past into the indeterminate future.

A similar dipolar analysis is to be applied to all the material attributes of the divine. God's love, for example, may be described as being absolute, necessary, eternal, unchanging and infinite in that in principle God's attitude to whatever there happens to be cannot be other than one of utterly pure, ceaseless, unwavering and limitless love. In practice, whether God's love for a particular person at a particular time and place is actualized in the form of interventionist activity or as a silent love that envisages and desires what is best for that person then, its actual form depends not only upon that person's existence but also on what is best for her or him in those circumstances. Since, furthermore, it is relative to those circumstances, it changes with them.

This analysis of divine love is not, as some seem to suspect, a magician's

12. Cf. Pailin 1989, p. 84-7 for more on the nature of divine omniscience.

trick whereby it appears that we can have both the penny and the bun as well. There is no logical sleight of hand to be detected. All that is happening is that a clear analysis is being made of what is meant when it is said that 'A loves B' and then that analysis is appropriately modified to take into account the unique status of the divine. When, for example, I say that 'Mary loves Sarah', I imply that in whatever situation Sarah may find herself, Mary will respond in a loving way. The appropriate expression of that love in practice will, however, vary according to Sarah's situation. When Sarah is suffering from influenza, Mary's love for her will involve sympathetic nursing; when Sarah is exuberant after winning a race, loving her means sharing her joy; when she is wanting to be alone, loving her means respecting her privacy; and so on. The essential difference between Mary's love and God's love is not that the actualization of the former changes while the latter, like the smile on the face of a statue of the Buddha, does not. The difference is that whereas Mary's love will be distorted by human failings (e.g., by not correctly appreciating what is the best for Sarah in the circumstances, by being tainted with jealousy, by being distracted by other concerns), the actual expression of God's love will always be the most appropriate expression of a love than which none greater is conceivable, which is inexhaustible and whose possible objects are limitless.

At the end of his paper, Dr. Meckenstock raises various questions about this way of understanding the divine attributes, especially those of the divine as loving, as eternal/temporal, as changing and as personal. Unfortunately there is not space in this paper to reply specifically to all these questions but these aspects of the divine reality are discussed further in *God and the Processes of Reality* and in the works cited there, and also will be further treated in my forthcoming *Probing the Foundations: A Study in Theistic Reconstruction*. When, however, Dr. Meckenstock suggests that 'believing God's love' is 'the confidence that all men, like [the] whole creation, have a full relationship to God', I am in hearty agreement: as I argue in *A Gentle Touch*,[13] it is this relationship that is the basis of the ultimate worth and salvation of all.

What Hartshorne means by 'panentheism' emerges when this formal dipolar structure is applied to the attributes used to describe God's

---

13. David A. Pailin, *A Gentle touch: From a theology of handicap to a theology of human being*, London 1992.

relationship to the world. In the 'Epilogue' to *Man's Vision of God*, he summarises the result as holding that

it distinguishes God from the 'all' and yet makes him include all. The apparent paradox dissolves when we see that the 'all' which is in God, yet not all of God, is the ordinary totality of actual, contingent existence, while the all which *is* God is that totality (stretching through infinite past time, and nearly all unknown to us) as involving, *besides ordinary causes*, the whole as an inclusive agent acting on its parts, further a supreme, abstract causal factor which contains no particular within itself.[14]

Panentheism is a distinct position that differs from 'classical pantheism' as much as from 'classical theism'. It is thus somewhat misleading to describe it, as Dr. Meckenstock does, as 'a synthetic position between theism and pantheism' since this may leave the impression that 'panentheism' is a kind of compromise between the other two positions, perhaps even as the result of an attempt to synthesise elements of theism and pantheism in an intellectually incoherent mishmash of ideas. Instead it is important to recognize, as Hartshorne puts it, that these three positions 'form a triad, any two members of which are about as far apart as any other two.' In one fundamental respect, however, panentheism differs in the same way from both of the other two. Whereas they deny 'contingency, and the possibility of a real increase in content, to deity', panentheism 'asserts of God both necessity and contingency, both immutability and openness to novelty'.[15] The significance of the panentheistic understanding of the reality of God and of the relationship of God to the world becomes clear when it is compared to the ways in which classical theism and pantheism understand these matters.

What Hartshorne means by classical theism (or, as he puts it in *Man's Vision of God*, 'pure transcendental deism'[16] is the position which holds that God is the super-cause taken as self-sufficient, a complete being, in

14. Charles Hartshorne, *Man's Vision of God and the Logic of Theism*, Hamden, Conn. 1964 (first published in 1941), p. 348.
15. Charles Hartshorne, *Beyond Humanism: Essays in the Philosophy of Nature*, Gloucester, Mass. 1975 (first published 1937), p. viii; but cf. Charles Hartshorne and William L. Reese, *Philosophers Speak of God*, Chicago 1953,: p. viii for a criticism of 'artificially limited options'.
16. *Man's Vision of God*, p. 347.

abstraction from any and all of his effects. God thus excludes the world; he is only its cause; in no sense is he effect, of himself or anything else. It is a concept of God that follows from holding that since God's nature must be thought of as being absolute, necessary, eternal, unchanging and infinite, the divine cannot be thought of in any way as having relative, contingent, temporal, changing and finite qualities. It is also a concept of God that considers that since, by definition, God as the proper object of worship is, as Anselm expresses it, 'that than which a greater cannot be conceived', it is incoherent for God to be conceived as lacking anything. Hence, on the grounds that to have potentiality is to lack the value of the actuality of that which is potential, the essential perfection of the divine is held to be a state of total completion, having all qualities (*ens realissimum*) and without any potentiality whatsoever (*actus purus*). Furthermore, because there is no potentiality in the divine, God cannot be in any way said to change.

The consequence of rigorously working out such a position is a concept of God who (or, perhaps better impersonally, *which*) is fundamentally at odds with the God of the living religious faith that considers God to be self-consciously active and so intentionally creative, aware of what is happening in the temporally ordered processes of reality and lovingly responsive to its constituents. It is a concept of God whose unchanging and essentially unchangeable perfection means, as Anselm argues, that God must be thought of as 'passionless' and so as unaffected by any sympathy for the wretched.[17]

Similarly, Thomas Aquinas maintains that God must be conceived as 'pure act, without the admixture of any potentiality'. Accordingly, it is 'impossible for God to be in any way changeable'.[18] While 'creatures are really related to God', it is a mistake to hold that God is really related to creatures.[19] Aquinas illustrates how he understands the divine relationship to the world by reference to the way in which a pillar remains unchanged while an animal changes in relationship to it — moving, for example, so that whereas the pillar was once on its left, it comes to be on its right. According to Aquinas' (pre-relativity theory) analysis of what happens, the pillar does not change but the animal changes in relation to the pillar. Furthermore,

17. Anselm, *Basic Writings*, translated by S.N. Deane, La Salle, Ill. 1962, p. 13f (*Proslogion*, ch. 8).
18. Thomas Aquinas, *Summa Theologica*, translated by the Fathers of the English Dominican Province, New York 1947, I,9,1.
19. *Ibid.* I,13,7.

while God is held to know 'all contingent things', it is 'not successively, as they are in their own being, as we do; but simultaneously' as they are all 'present to God from eternity'.[20]

So far as this understanding of God can be regarded as being compatible with affirmations of the reality of the temporal processes of contingent events and of the significant autonomy of human beings as persons (and it is far from evident that it is compatible), talk of such a God as 'loving' seems to be limited to referring to something which influences others rather like the way in which a statue affects those who see it. A statue may have all kinds of influence but it is totally unaware of those who see it, say, as smiling on them and of their responses to it. While, therefore, the divine as unmoved and unmoveable may unconsciously attract others towards itself by being a kind of final cause, it cannot coherently be thought of as being aware of the changing events constituting the contingent world in which we experience ourselves as existing, nor as responding intentionally to the changing states of the world since it cannot become aware of them. It is thus at least paradoxical that Anselm considered that there was point in praying fervently for aid from such a being[21] and that Aquinas has been dubbed 'the Angelic Doctor' whose 'arguments, doctrine and principles' are to be 'inviolately' held by those who teach philosophy and theology in the Roman Catholic church.[22] This 'God' may be the Good that, as a perfect ideal, attracts conscious beings towards itself. Its dominant inspiration is Aristotle's 'Unmoved Mover' who, as 'a primary being', is 'eternal and unmovable' and 'unalterable'.[23] It is not the living God of the Judaeo-Christian-Islamic traditions of faith who is held by the faithful to have internal relations with the world, looking with compassion on the needy and suffering with the wretched, nor is it a God to whom it makes sense to apply such verbs of intentional action as to create, to love, to save, and to preserve.

In understanding the relationship between God and the world, pantheism has generally been considered to be the only significant alternative to this form of theism. On examination, however, its classical form (with its criticism of the externality of the world to God) shows itself to be both a rationally justified, if radical and unexpected, exposition of the implications of the

20. *Ibid.* I,14,13.
21. Cf. Anselm, *op.cit.* 3ff (*Proslogion* ch. 1).
22. Cf. Canon 1366 § 2 quoted in the 1947 translation of the *Summa* (see n. 18), p. xvi.
23. Aristotle, *Metaphysics*, 1073a.

concept of God put forward in classical theism and a similarly unsatisfactory way of apprehending the object of religious faith in the Judaeo-Christian-Islamic tradition. This is because classical pantheism takes thoroughly seriously the notion that God's reality is infinite and, in every respect, the absolute and necessary ground of all that is. This being so, there can be nothing that is real (or, perhaps, 'truly real') that is not God, for there can be nothing that is beyond or outside or other than the infinite reality of God. Furthermore, everything that truly is must be necessary.

Baruch Spinoza, for example, argues in his *Ethics* that since God is an 'absolutely infinite' being which exists 'necessarily' it follows that there can be 'no substance' except God. Furthermore, the total absence of contingency in God means that as 'everything ... is in God', so everything must be 'made by the laws of the infinite nature of God, and necessarily follow from the necessity of his essence'.[24] God is thus 'the indwelling ... cause of all things' whose attributes are 'immutable' and whose products are eternal.[25] There is neither intellect nor will in God[26] and nothing can be other than it is: 'there is absolutely nothing in things by which we can call them contingent'. All that is follows necessarily from the 'most perfect nature' of God.[27]

This view of reality could be interpreted in accordance with some current notions in cosmology as affirming God as the space-time continuum in which we may trace the world-lines of individual entities so long as it is remembered that all such entities are themselves modifications or expressions of the reality of God. Such a concept of God (as being all that truly is — *Deus sive Natura*) casts puzzling doubts, however, on the reality of the empirical, contingent events which apparently constitute the world in which we experience ourselves as existing. They are doubts which invite a Moore-type common-sense response 'But they are real' (and cf. Galileo's — apocryphal — retort, 'e pur si muove', to those who compelled him to agree with those who demonstrated by sound reasoning that the earth does not move). Religiously the apparent incompatibility of this concept of God with assertions of the autonomy, however limited, of anything which is not God means that it seems incompatible with notions of reciprocal kinds of personal

---

24. Baruch de Spinoza, *Ethics and On the Correction of the Understanding*, translated by Andrew Boyle, London 1959, p. 11, 14f.
25. *Ibid.*, p. 18, 19.
26. *Ibid.*, p. 17.
27. *Ibid.*, p. 26f.

relationship between God and human beings. According to this pantheistic view, not only is all that is God; God is also wholly necessary and unchanging.

In view of these difficulties some have attempted to affirm both the infinite nature of God and the significance and autonomy of the constituents of the empirical, contingent world by a basically different interpretation of what is to be meant by pantheism. According to this interpretation of the notion, 'God' is to be understood as a cipher that stands for the totality of all that happens to be (or, if temporal ordering in that totality is stressed, of all that has been, is, and will be). While, however, this interpretation may safeguard the reality of the entities composing the world in which human beings consider themselves to exist, it does so by evacuating from the notion of God any sense of a personally-ordered (and so both unified and unifying) agency. Although the 'God' of this form of pantheism may be thought to have relations with what is, it is in the way that a totality has a relationship to its parts. It is not appropriate to speak of this 'God' as, for example, willing, purposing, knowing, responding and loving in relation to those parts, or even as consciously integrating them into a totality that is a 'whole'. Nor does it even follow that the totality of what is forms a coherent whole. This pantheistic view of 'God' as the 'all' may thus merely refer to an uncoordinated agglomeration of all agents and their products.

A less crude form of this interpretation of 'pantheism' does not merely call 'God' the sum of all that happens through the chance and necessity character of the processes of nature and of history. As well as affirming that whatever is is part of God, this 'pantheism' expresses some kind of value-judgement on what is with, in some cases, the important additional implication that all that is combines to constitute a single structure. In the latter case it is thus legitimate in some respects to think of 'the world' or 'the universe' or 'all that is' as referring to a coherent whole.

A sophisticated version of this kind of pantheism may be identified in the view of reality put forward in some American theological writings that attempt to preserve some significance for religion in what is described (but diversely understood) as the contemporary 'post-modern' culture. Although what is suggested is often referred to as 'naturalism', it is a position which may also be regarded as a form of pantheism. Since, however, its fundamental insights are empirically based, it is fundamentally distinct from the classical pantheism described by Spinoza. According to this way of understanding, the being of God as all is to be perceived through and identified with the temporal processes of contingent reality.

William Dean, taking up ideas of Henry Nelson Wieman, Bernard Meland and Bernard Loomer, has recently called for the development of what he calls a 'naturalistic historicism'. This is to augment and modify the radical historicism of recent theology with 'a naturalistic dimension' (or, a 'hermeneutics of nature') that takes account of what science tells us about reality while paying attention to the relativity of scientific views.[28] One example of the kind of faith and theological understanding that might result is described by Sallie McFague in the final paragraph of her contribution to the same volume of essays in which Dean's paper appeared:

To feel that we belong to the earth and to accept our proper place within it is the beginning of a natural piety, what Jonathan Edwards calls 'consent to being', consent to what is. It is the sense that we and all others belong together in a cosmos, related in an orderly fashion, one to the other. It is the sense that each and every being is valuable in and for itself, and that the whole forms a unity in which each being, including oneself, has a place. It ... is, finally, at a deep level, an aesthetic and religious sense, a response of wonder at and appreciation for the unbelievably vast, old, rich, diverse, and surprising cosmos, of which one's self is an infinitesimal but conscious part, the part able to sing its praises.[29]

This form of pantheism has many attractive features. To those for whom authentic existence in the 'post-modern' world requires the abandonment of notions of God as a personal, supernatural agency, it may offer the most satisfactory way of apprehending a credible faith which orientates the self by reference to a greater 'whole'. Nevertheless, although it affirms the significance of the contingent processes of reality implicitly denied in the classical forms of theism and pantheism, some of its expressions only do this by effectively denying the reality of God as a significant factor in shaping reality, and most of the others by substituting for God a vague sense of an immanent and value-caring superintendency.

While, then, both the classical form of theism which affirms God as essentially other and the classical form of pantheism which affirms the reality

28. Cf. William Dean, Humanistic Historicism and Naturalistic Historicism, in *Theology and the End of Modernity*, edited by Sheila Greeve Davaney, Philadelphia 1991, p. 57, 59.
29. Sallie McFague, Cosmology and Christianity: Implications of the Common Creation Story for Theology, in *Theology and the End of Modernity* (see n. 28), p. 40.

of God as essentially the all do so at the cost of undermining the significance (and even of denying the reality) of the world of contingent beings, what may be regarded as a naturalistic form of pantheism affirms the reality of the contingent world and the relative autonomy of its constituents at the cost of God's dissolution into the combination of a vague ordering of reality, a respect for values and individuals, and a warm sense of a whole to which all belong. It is an unhappy situation for philosophers and theologians who consider that these are the only available conceptual options but who wish to affirm both the reality of God as a transcendent, self-conscious, personal agent and the significance of the world as containing self-conscious personal agents whose reality is given ultimate worth by their relationship to God.

A further conceptual option is put forward by Samuel Alexander, for example in his paper on 'Theism and Pantheism'. Although he is aware of the danger of using philosophical conceptions in theological reflection,[30] Alexander identifies a fundamental problem for religiously adequate understanding of belief in the need to find a way of combining the notions of transcendence and of immanence in a coherent concept of God.[31] While these notions are not reconcilable when they are strictly understood (for 'If God is coextensive with the world, he does not transcend it. If he transcends it, he is not immanent to it.'[32]), 'neither pure transcendence nor pure immanence satisfies the mature religious sentiment.' What this 'sentiment' requires is a way to understand God as both 'coextensive with the whole' and yet not identical with it. This is because God, while having 'relations with every part of the universe', transcends it in some sense.[33] Classical pantheism is unsatisfactory because it denies the personal nature of the divine and the individuality of the believer; classical theism is unsatisfactory because its notion of a wholly transcendent God sabotages any affirmation of significant relations between God and the world.[34] It is, however, also the case that '[sc. classical] pantheism and [sc. classical] theism have each of them defects for the religious feeling which the other supplies, and merits which the other lacks'.[35]

30. Cf. Samuel Alexander, *Philosophical and Literary Pieces*, London 1939, p. 318.
31. *Ibid.*, 319f.
32. *Ibid.*, 323f.
33. *Ibid.*, 324.
34. *Ibid.*, 324-6.
35. *Ibid.*, 324.

Alexander refuses the solution essayed by some theologians, namely to try to evade the problem of conceptual reconciliation by holding that, while God 'in one respect is transcendent and in another respect immanent', the nature of the union of these qualities in the reality of God is 'a mystery'.[36] His own solution picks up some remarks by F.H. Bradley and implicitly uses ideas which he had earlier developed in *Space, Time, and Deity* (1920). This solution is based on the claims that 'time is a constituent of the very substance of reality' and that 'God is himself a creature of time'. On this basis Alexander suggests that in one respect 'God takes in within himself the whole world'. As thus 'immanent in it' (so that in this sense 'God' can be thought of as referring to the whole of the universe of space-time), God is 'nurtured' by all that comes to be. In another respect, however, 'deity' transcends the world since it is that quality that is always 'a stage in time beyond the human quality' and draws it creatively onward. It is a value that will never be actualized. In both respects the divine is infinite: immanently infinite in that God's 'body' incorporates 'the whole world', transcendently infinite in that 'deity' always lies beyond 'the inferior world' of what is actual.[37]

This is an interesting response to the problem of how to conceive God's relationship to the world. Unfortunately it seems that even if this way of understanding the object of faith is rationally coherent (and the nature and ontological status of that object may be considered to raise problems when God's 'body' is held to embody all that is actual while 'deity' is the regulative *nisus* of all processes), its religious adequacy is questionable. As Alexander makes clear (in remarks which are interesting to compare with some of Wolfhart Pannenberg's statements about 'the pure futurity of God'[38]), his position is that

God is not the already perfect being ... but is himself in the making... For the Universe as straining towards deity is a present reality. And the Universe so conceived is God. It is only the actual existence of deity which belongs to the future.[39]

36. Alexander, *op.cit.*, p. 328.
37. Alexander, *op.cit.*, p. 330-1.
38. Cf. Wolfhart Pannenberg, *Basic Questions in Theology*, translated by George H. Kehm, London 1971, vol. 2, p. 249; cf. pp. 232, 242, 244.
39. Alexander, *op.cit.*, 330-1.

If, however, a concept of God, in order to be religiously adequate, must satisfy the definition of God as 'that than which a greater cannot be conceived' or as 'the proper object of worship' or as 'the essentially perfect', it is arguable that Alexander's notion of God 'in the making' does not wholly provide what is required. It may come close to what is needed but his interpretation of the never-finally-to-be-achieved nature of God's 'deity' leaves it uncertain whether the object of faith and worship is a reality or an ideal *nisus* whose ontological status is unclear. The great achievement of Hartshorne's notion of panentheism, based upon his analyses of the dipolar nature of the concept of God and of the dual nature of divine perfection, is to have provided what can be reasonably held to satisfy the 'mature religious sentiment' that is appropriate to the Judaeo-Christian-Islamic tradition of faith in the reality of God. What this concept clearly affirms but Alexander's leaves puzzling is both the present actuality of the divine as perfect and the all-embracing and ceaselessly responsive reality of God as personally agential.

In *Philosophers Speak of God*, Hartshorne and Reese list five basic characteristics of the panentheistic concept of God.[40] God is to be thought of as (1) in some respects *eternal*, in that God is to be conceived as having no beginning and no end, as never having become God nor as being capable of ever ceasing to be God; (2) in some respects *temporal*, in that God is capable of creative activity and 'change, at least in the form of increase of some kind' — for example, by the increment of experiences of value through embracing all that successively comes to be in the world; (3) *self-conscious*, in that God is aware of God's own reality; (4) *knowing the world*, in that God is aware of every contingent actual event as it occurs in the universe; and (5) *world-inclusive*, in that, since God is internally as well as externally related to every actual event, all events are constituents of God's all-embracing reality. What this means is that

Panentheism holds that we are accidents in God, and thus it is equally opposed to the classical [theistic], 'there are no accidents in God but accidental realities outside him' and the [classical] pantheistic, 'Nothing is accidental but all is in God as essential to him'. Or, in other terms, panentheism conceives process, becoming, as real in God ... [41]

40. Cf. Hartshorne and Reese, *op.cit.*, p. 16.
41. *Ibid.*, p. 163.

One of the most common objections that is raised against this concept of God focuses on the notion of God as temporally ordered and internally related to the contingent processes of reality and so as able in a significant sense to change. It is argued that such a God cannot be considered to have the perfection of the proper object of worship which is a defining quality of the divine. J. N. Findlay even wonders if religion really wants 'an actual God'. In an appreciative response to Hartshorne's work, he suggests that 'a God which has even the exclusiveness involved in being one conscious person among others ... has not in my view the absoluteness necessary for a perfect, truly religious object'.[42]

This is an objection to which Hartshorne has responded in his analyses of the dipolar nature of the divine and of divine perfection as a state of 'dual transcendence'. By this means he seeks to show how God may be thought of both as perfect and as an actual, temporally ordered (but, as eternal, unending) individual.

As has been outlined earlier, it follows from the nature of the divine that the material attributes of God are to be understood according to a formal 'dipolar' structure. In principle God is to be held, for example, to be perfectly loving, perfectly knowing, and perfectly appreciative, in that God's response to whatever is the case expresses and cannot be other than an expression of love, knowledge and appreciation that is absolute, necessary, eternal, unchanging and infinite. These qualities, however, are not only abstract ideals: God's perfect being as loving, knowing and appreciating is also instantiated in actual relations with what is the case. This means that in practice what and how God actually loves, knows and appreciates is relative to and so depends in part on the accidents of what is there to be loved, known and appreciated. God's material qualities are thus perfect both abstractly in principle and concretely in practice.

God's perfection, furthermore, is to be conceived as a state of 'dual transcendence'. On the one hand, divine transcendence means that God is unsurpassable by any other. No-one can ever be more loving, more aware and more appreciative than God. This is true in principle as well as in practice. As Anselm perceived between writing the *Monologion* and the

42. J.N. Findlay, Some Reflections on Necessary Existence, in *Process and Divinity: Philosophical Essays presented to Charles Hartshorne*, edited by William L. Reese and Eugene Freeman, La Salle, Ill., 1964, p. 526.

Proslogion, God is not merely that than which none greater actually exists[43] but that 'than which nothing greater can be conceived'.[44] On the other hand, the nature of God's reality means that the actual contents of God's material qualities at any one time may be in certain respects surpassed by those contents at a later time. This temporal and incremental aspect of the divine reality does not imply that at any time God is less than wholly perfect. What it recognizes is that, for instance, God's knowledge at time t_1 will be all that has happened up to and is the case at t_1 while God's knowledge at a later time, t_2, will be of all that has happened up to and is the case at t_2. If, however, events have happened between t_1 and t_2, God's actual knowledge at t_2, in order to be an actual state of perfect knowledge, will contain more items than God's actual knowledge at t_1.

This interpretation of divine perfection may be regarded as open to two criticisms. One is that it considers that God's actuality as well as that of all other entities is temporally ordered. Those who consider that the divine reality is in every respect one of *totum simul* eternity will, therefore, doubtless reject this view of divine perfection. But then they have to find some other way of making sense of such matters as the attribution of personal activity and gracious relationships to God that does not imply a temporal aspect to the divine. It may not be possible — at least it does not yet seem to have been done satisfactorily. The other criticism is that this interpretation of divine perfection regards God as an actual individual. Those who hold that the proper object of religious worship is an ideal whose abstract qualities are never instantiated in a particular existing individual[45] will also presumably reject the notion of dual transcendence. In their judgment it introduces unwarranted notions of relationships with others and with Godself into the concept of the divine. But then this objection rests on a view of the reference of 'God' that is fundamentally at odds with the realist understanding of the object of faith typical of the Judaeo-Christian-Islamic traditions of belief in God.[46] What Hartshorne presents is a coherent way to understand divine perfection which accords with that realist position.

Another common objection to panentheism is that it presents a God who

43. Cf. Anselm, *op.cit.*, 41ff, 143f (*Monologion*, chs. 3f, 80).
44. *Ibid.*, p. 7 (*Proslogion*, ch. 2).
45. Cf. Findlay, *op.cit.*, p. 526.
46. Cf. David A. Pailin, *The Anthropological Character of Theology*, Cambridge 1990, pp. 9ff, 50ff.

is eminently passive and, as a result of this passivity, suffers. Such a view is clearly contrary to any notion of God as wholly impassible and unchanging, and, in relation to suggestions of divine suffering, contrary to notions of the divine state as one of total, untrammelled bliss. While, however, this objection is appropriate in the case of those whose notion of the divine is determined by Aristotle's idea of the perfection appropriate to the Unmoved Mover, it does not seem to be justifiable by reference to the view of God contained in faith moulded by the scriptures and beliefs of Judaism, Christianity and Islam. This is a God who takes heed of the sufferings of the people (cf. Exodus 3.7), who is typically addressed as 'the Merciful, the Compassionate' (cf. the openings of the chapters of the Qur'an) and whose nature is considered by Christians to be supremely manifested in the passion of Jesus. This being so, it appears to be a strength and not a weakness of panentheism that it presents a radical interpretation of the all-embracing nature of God according to which God shares to the full each experience of each subject, whatever its quality. Only so can God's knowledge be held to be a complete and genuine knowledge of all that occurs, God's love be what we understand by love, and God's appreciation of the value of each event involve internal relations in the divine reality. It was not merely an expression of his interest in bird-song that led Hartshorne to quote from William Blake's 'On Another's Sorrow' as a foreword to *Man's Vision of God*. That poem reminds us that to love those who suffer is to share their suffering as well as to seek to bring them joy.

The nature of divine awareness of each event raises some interesting questions when attempts are made to relate it to relativity theory and to current cosmological notions about the status of 'now'. This is not because of physical problems about the speed of communication and the location of the divine. God is co-present to all that is and the divine awareness of events does not depend upon the transmission of information over physical distances by physical processes. It would be ludicrous to suppose that God's awareness of Godself and of the world might be limited by communications that cannot reach God, wherever God is supposed to be, at speeds greater than that of light! What is puzzling is whether there can be said to be a cosmic 'now' which joins together a class of events as being absolutely simultaneous (taking God's awareness of those events as all being at the 'same' divine time as the absolute standard for simultaneity). The most likely answer seems to be that there is no such cosmic 'now' but that being 'now' is the state of an event at the moment of concrescence when it has determinate predecessors but no determinate successor to whose concrescence it contributes as a determinate object in that successor's past. 'Nowness' is thus not a property which is shared by a number of events as a common property which links them together as if they were points on a kind of privileged plane in the space-time continuum. It is a property that belongs to each individual event. From this it appears that there is no single temporal order in which God orders all events. There are as many temporal orders as there are events being temporally related. God's awareness includes an awareness of each of them. Furthermore, while God is immediately present to each spatially distinguished event, God is only present to those that are currently concrescent. God is not present to past events because they have perished into objects in the divine memory, nor to future possibilities for they have not yet come to be. What God knows as being actual 'now' is each event at that event's moment of actuality in the process of reality. Since it is immediate (i.e., simultaneous with the event's concresence — God does not have to wait for the information to arrive), it seems best understood as internal to each actual event. From this it follows that God is not to be thought of as having a single, absolute, privileged perspective on the processes of reality but as embracing the perspectives of all events. Whether, as a result, God's activity in relationship to the world is understood better as a series of divine responses concretely actualising in individual cases some general abstract principles than as the single co-ordinated response of an integrated, individual, personal agency is a question which cannot be taken up here. But it is an interesting one!

To hold that God is internally related to all so that in a real sense all is 'in' God — *pan-en-theism* — does not mean that God is not also conscious of Godself as in some respects other than the world and able to make decisions about the world. In this respect God's relationship to the world may be compared to the self's awareness of the body. What happens to my body is experienced by me as my experiences. When, for example, certain physiological events take place in my finger, I am aware of them because I feel pain. I am not, however, simply the sum product of such experiences; I can respond to my experiences of a part of my body by deciding to treat it, even to the point in some cases of having that part removed. In this sense I may be said to transcend my body. Similarly, panentheism considers that while God suffers all the pains and all the joys that are experienced in the world, with the result that the world may appropriately be described as God's 'body', God is also self-conscious of Godself as in some respects separate from the world and so as able to respond to its constituents.

It is, furthermore, a mistake to hold that since, according to panentheism, God is to be conceived as being eminently passive (so that no experience of any subject is not also God's experience), God cannot also be conceived as being eminently active (in that God influences every decision by which the actual form of every event is determined). The dipolar nature of the concept of God does not entail that a God who is actually passive cannot also be actually active. What it does entail is that both the activity and the passivity of the divine have to be interpreted in a dipolar manner — just as was illustrated earlier by reference to the notions of divine knowledge and divine love.

According to panentheism God both is affected by and affects all events. The activity of God, however, is not exercised through a monopolistic omnipotence (which is an incoherent notion since the relational nature of power means that no agent can coherently be thought of as having a monopoly of power) nor through a coercive supremacy that manipulates others by the exercise of irresistible forces. The panentheistic notion of divine agency struggles to make sense of it as a gracious, personal relationship which respects the integrity of the subjects whom it seeks to influence. I say 'struggles' because on reflection its preference for such notions as that of 'lure' to others of causal force not only seems, especially when applied to the natural order, to presuppose problematic panpsychic views of reality as a whole but also because, as advertisers know, a good 'lure' can sometimes be more compelling than brute force.

Although the model of the relationship between the mind and the body has many attractive features for exploring the panentheistic relationship of God and the world, it also points to many puzzles that need to be answered. On the positive side, for example, the mind-body relationship illustrates how God (as the 'mind') may be held to be aware of the parts of the world (as constituting the 'body'). On the negative side, however, psycho-somatic relationships by which the 'mind' belongs to and influences the 'body' are not well understood in terms of our own being and so provide only relatively unclear models for understanding divine activity in the divine-world relationship. In addition, while my finger's state may provoke me to do something about it, my finger is not a conscious agent in the implementation of that decision. This is not the case with God and persons. If it be correct to hold that God respects the integrity of the non-divine, then the activity of God must be understood as the activity of an agent on and with other agents. How this applies to the God-world case is far from clear.

It is a problem, for instance, which Grace Jantzen fails to solve in her interesting study of the world as God's 'body'. She rejects the idea that the human self can be 'split into mental and physical segments' (cf. mind and body) and adopts a holistic notion of human personhood as embodied selfhood. This she then uses as a model for perceiving the relationship between God and the world. According to this holistic understanding the world and God constitute one reality.[47] When, however, she considers the activity of God in relation to the world, problems arise. She speaks, for example, of the universe as 'God's self-formation' and as owing 'its being what it is directly to God's formative will'.[48] It is not made clear how such remarks are to be reconciled both with the apparent processes of cosmic evolution and with what she elsewhere says about God giving autonomy to the creatures.[49] Sometimes God's activity seems to be so all-embracing that is that is hard to see how on her understanding what happens in the world can be seen as anything other than God's self-activity. The question remains. How is the activity of God to be understood in a way that recognizes both the integrity and autonomy proper to the non-divine and the significance of the divine as a significant agent?

The nature of divine activity, however, is not a problem which is peculiar to panentheism. As is shown by the extensive literature about the issue that has appeared in the past couple of decades, it is a problem that confronts all attempts to make sense of realist understanding of God. Those who are impressed by the panentheistic concept of God should not be condemned out of hand for failing to solve a problem that those who adopt other concepts have equally failed to overcome! (Contrary to what Dr. Meckenstock suggests in his paper, this does not mean that panentheism — or any other understanding of the divine — leads in this respect to an 'unsolvable' problem, for if that were the case it would imply that such an understanding is untenable, but merely that in this respect understanding of the divine faces a problem that has not yet been satisfactorily solved. There is much work here for theologians who affirm a realistic understanding of the divine still to do.) One of the important contributions of panentheism to theological understand-

47. Grace M. Jantzen, *God's World, God's Body*, London 1984, pp. 8, 20, 124, 157f.
48. Jantzen, *op.cit.*, p. 134; cf. pp. 70, 90.
49. Cf. Jantzen, *op.cit.*, pp. 137, 152.

ing is that it has made this problem a serious one by showing that a realist concept of God is possible — a concept of God, that is, that understands God both as the proper object of worship and as an actual personal individual who is aware of all and responds to all.

When compared with classical interpretations of theism and pantheism and with some contemporary naturalist forms of pantheism, panentheism can at least claim to present a rationally coherent interpretation of the view of God that underlies the traditions of faith in God typical of Judaism, Christianity and Islam. Panentheism offers, therefore, not a temptation to err but an important source of insight. It also offers a way of understanding the nature of the divine and of the relationship of the divine to the world in general and to human beings in particular that, contrary to what Dr. Meckenstock suggests, not only is compatible with theological questions of christology and history but also (as various works in process theology indicate) provides valuable tools for identifying credible answers to those questions. In the end, however, all that the development of the notion of panentheism does is to make conceptually clear what believers in those traditions have considered to be the nature of God. It shows that it is possible to conceive of God as the proper object of worship and faith as being in significant respects both utterly absolute and totally related (and if, as Dr. Meckenstock indicates, questions remain about the possibility of reconciling the absoluteness and the objectivity of God, it must first be considered whether the problematic aspects of 'absoluteness' and 'objectivity' that he has in mind are appropriately to be attributed of the divine). What is strange and new and, apparently for some, frightening about 'panentheism' is the word and the conceptual clarity that comes with its analyses of the divine reality. But this is nothing new in theological understanding. Rigour and clarity and insight often seem frightening before the importance — and the usefulness — of what they disclose is appreciated.

Some Remarks on Pantheism and Panentheism

Günter Meckenstock

Introduction

Pantheism and panentheism are concepts which are concerned with doctrines in the European history of philosophy and theology. Both are contrary to the concept of philosophical and theological theism.

Christian faith, rooted in the bible, has theistic elements. In biblical statements God is thought to be a perfect, necessary, personal, intelligent, extramundane and manlike being; God is the creator of the world in the sense of creatio e nihilo; God established the beings of the world expediently; God may interfere with the events in the world; God preserves the world and deals with his creatures according to his plans like a potter with his pottery;[1] God informs mankind of his will to regulate the social, moral, political and religious affairs, by special revelations handed down to biblical writers; God has a special relationship to mankind through Christ.

Philosophical theism and pantheism are doctrines of the 17th and 18th centruries, which means they belong to the European enlightenment. Their background are the religious wars in Europe after the reformation and the maturification of the empirical sciences. In specific ways they try to manage the new intellectual situation of methodological atheism in natural empirical sciences and the cultural struggle of confessional wars. They formulate theology by reason and evidence, not by faith and confession. They understood themselves not as the framework of church-dogmatics, but as criticism of church-dogmatics and as better theory of rational theology. The liberation from church-dogmatics required a reformulation of metaphysical topics in such a way that the issues of confessional quarrel stood aside. Both doctrines are answers to the pressing mind-body problem.

Theism and pantheism are rational doctrines of the relationship between God and the world. They naturally presuppose that the concept of the world is only thinkable in relationship to the concept of God. Both concepts have a realistic view and a theoretical intention, which means they are interested

---

1. Cf. Romans 9.21.

in objective facts of the case. The relationship between the concepts of God and mankind is mediated by the relationship between the concepts of God and the world.

Pantheism and panentheism have different roots. The 'Sitz im Leben' of pantheism is the struggle between rationalism and supranaturalism, theism and atheism, church-doctrines and empirical sciences in the 17th and 18th centuries. Pantheism opposed a supranaturalistic theism. Moreover, at that time, pantheism was so closely related to the philosophy of Baruch de Spinoza (1632-1677), that saying 'pantheism' was nearly synonymous with saying 'Spinozism'. The theists accused the pantheists of being materialists or atheists. The 'Sitz im Leben' of panentheism is the design of philosophical systems in the succession of the critical philosophy of Kant. 'Panentheism' is one of the artifical terms which was created in the 19th century at the end of the German system philosophy to signify a system as a whole. Panentheism is interested both in giving final reasons for philosophical reflection and in establishing practical responsibility and divine causality. Atheism is not yet in the matter-of-fact context.

1. Some historical lines

The Irish philosopher John Toland (1670-1722) first used the term 'pantheist': 'The pantheists ... of which number I profess my self to be one'.[2] In 1709 Toland characterized pantheistic teaching by the formula: 'Nullum dari Numen a materia et compage mundi huius distinctum, ipsamque naturam, sive rerum Universitatem, unicum esse et supremum Deum'.[3] Toland, the first philosopher to be called a free-thinker, critizised in his anonymous first work *Christianity not mysterious* (1696) the Christian theology in the sense of deism. He accepted the divine biblical revelation only as far as there are rational sentences. He mentioned that the divine revelation is only aimed at renewing the law of nature (*lex naturae*), which is identical with the law of God's kingdom. The divine revelation takes the form of rational perceptions, not of mysteries. Toland rejected a super-rational or anti-rational understanding of the revelation and reminded his readers that the Christian faith became mysterious when it became licensed religion in the Roman Empire.

2. J. Toland, *Socianism truly stated*, London 1705, p. 7.
3. Toland, *Adeisidaemon. Annexae sunt eiusdem Origines Iudaicae*, the Hague 1709, p. 117.

The truth of Christian religion lies only in its identity with the rational universal morality and religion. Miracles are natural effects heightened to an enormous extent. The universal religion of the *lex naturae* is also an element of hylozoistic pantheism, formulated by Toland in his book *Pantheisticon sive formula celebrandae sodalitatis socraticae* (1720). The liturgy contained in it shows the religious character of pantheism. God is the soul of the world, the world is the body of God.

The term 'pantheism' was a concept of struggle. Concepts for situations of conflict are often of the kind that they show facts of the case from different points of view in very different respects. The pantheists refused the extra-mundane relationship of God to the world. Their motives were often of an ontological and theoretical basis. Opponents used the term 'pantheism' to charge the pantheists with atheism. This was not only an accusation of denying God's existence, but the polemical accusation of immorality and impiety. Pantheists were to be characterized as corrupt, totally bad men. The motives of their opponents were of a practical kind. Whereas the pantheists accepted that the theists were not up to the theoretical level of the time, their opponents denied the pure morality of them and predicted a breakdown of moral rules and systems.

Pantheism had an important function in the early history of the critique of religion in Europe. It supported a universally valid set of rules, not only in natural sciences, but in all perception and recognition, the predominance of mathematics and logic, and the autonomy of scientific methods. Pantheism shows a tendency toward determinism. But how is determinism consistent with morality? At this point, pantheism was judged to have immoral consequences. Pantheism could be misunderstood as justifying even the banal or evil and, therefore, blurring or blotting out the difference between good and evil. Because of the predominance of nature, pantheism has no interest in and no understanding of the openness of history.

Immanuel Kant (1724-1804) placed pantheism in the context of physico-theology. He discussed pantheism in his *Kritik der Urteilskraft* (1790), his doctrine of methods of teleological discernment in the philosophical explanation of the objective expedient forms of matter. Not in a highest intelligence, but in the totality of the world as a unique substance does pantheism have the last reason of the possibility of the forms of expediency of matter, whereas Spinozism comprehends the totality of the world as the quintessence of many determinations, which are inherent in a unique simple substance.[4] Kant makes a distinction between pantheism and Spinozism. Both view the relationship between God and the world as an inherent relationship. Pantheism focuses on the aspect of the inherent worldbeings, Spinozism on the aspect of the only substance.[5] Pantheism and Spinozism are answers to the question of absolute unity (demanded by reason) of the principle of the events and states of the world. Kant shows that pantheism and Spinozism do not answer the question of reason of natural expediency, but they do answer in the negative. They transform the causal relationship and the real expediency of natural things into a relationship of inherence with ideal final causes. The attempts of pantheism and Spinozism fail to explain the teleological expediency of nature from theoretical principles of reason.

Pantheism has been called irreligious and immoral. Therefore the book *Über die Lehre des Spinoza* (1785) of Friedrich Heinrich Jacobi (1743-1819), in which he reported that Gotthold Ephraim Lessing confessed the affirmation of Spinoza's formula ἓν καὶ πᾶν to him, launched a violent intellectual discussion in Germany. Jacobi's attack was aimed at Spinoza's philosophical system, which he judged to be a synthesis of rationalism, fatalism and atheism. According to common opinion, Jacobi considered Spinozism as a systematically elaborated pantheism.

As a result of that debate, pantheism and Spinozism enjoyed a higher standing in Germany, not in the sense of an elaborated philosophical doctrine, but in the sense of a true tendency in the rational understanding of the absolute and its relationship to the relative.[6] Friedrich Schleiermacher (1768-1834) described Spinoza as a prominent example of the articulation and representation of piety. In his speeches *Über die Religion* (1799), Schleiermacher declared that piety could be presented both under the categories of personality and freedom as well as under the categories of lawfulness and regulations. Schleiermacher showed Spinozism as an elaborate presentation of piety opposed to personalism. Piety, which is rooted in feeling, not in reason or action, is the intuition and feeling of the universe and has legitimate variants to articulate that intuition and feeling. It is an authentic sphere of human life quite different from metaphysics and morality.

4. Cf. I. Kant, *Kritik der Urteilskraft*, § 80.
5. Kant, *op.cit.*, § 85.
6. Cf., e.g., F.W.J. Schelling, *Sämmtliche Werke*, vol. 7, Stuttgart 1860, pp. 339-44.

Schleiermacher criticized that a lack of pantheism is the negation of trans-cendence in the idea of God.[7]

Georg Wilhelm Friedrich Hegel (1770-1832) defended pantheism against the accusation that it was 'Allesgötterei':[8] pantheism does not mean the deification of single concrete things,[9] but the unique substance which is imminent in all single concrete things.[10] Hegel criticized that pantheism views God only as 'Ansich' — as substance and absolute power, so that it does not view God as 'Fürsich' — as freedom and self-consciousness, not as 'Anundfürsich' — as mind.

The 'Atheismusstreit' (1798/99) about the philosophy of Johann Gottlieb Fichte (1762-1814) provided a latent argumentative contribution to the problem of pantheism. Fichte refuted the accusation that his philosophy of 'Ichheit', his philosophy of radical autonomy of the practical moral subject, was a special kind of atheism, with the remark that his system was no athe-ism, but acosmism. He criticized the realistic view of the world as entity of sufficient single finite things. He emphasized the nonentity of single finite things and the unique entity of God.

Panentheism is a philosophical doctrine which seeks to avoid some problems of pantheism and some problems of theism. Historically, it is a late concept in the struggle between pantheism and theism. Panentheism has a strategical intention to synthesize the moral autonomy of man and the ontological predominance of God. Karl Christian Friedrich Krause (1781-1832), who is the author of the term 'panentheism',[11] understood his phi-losophy as a continuation of the doctrine of Kant. Philosophy is the percep-tion of the absolute; it is 'Wesenschauung'. God is not or has not 'ein Wesen', is not 'das Wesen', but is 'Wesen'. To conceptualize reality, philosophy breaks into two branches.[12] In the analysis of self-consciousness ('Selbst-anschauung') the subjective-analytic branch deals with self-perception ('Selbstwahrnehmung'). The analysis of self-perception, of I-being, leads to 'Wesenschauung'. The objective-synthetic branch includes God-perception. From this basic point, Krause synthesizes the whole reality and develops the

7. Cf. F. Schleiermacher, *Sämmtliche Werke*, vol. III,4,1, Berlin 1839, p. 250.
8. G.W.F. Hegel, *Sämtliche Werke*, Jubiläumsausgabe, Stuttgart 1927-30, vol. 20, p. 118.
9. Cf. Hegel, *op.cit.*, vol. 16, p. 509-17.
10. Cf. Hegel, *op.cit.*, vol. 12, p. 486.
11. Cf. K.C.F. Krause, *Vorlesungen über die Grundwahrheiten der Wissenschaft*, Göttingen 1829, p. 484.
12. Cf. *Vorlesungen über das System der Philosophie*, Göttingen 1828.

different parts of concrete sciences. Krause comprehends the human subject ('Ich') as unity ('Vereinwesen') of natural body and rational mind. Both are contrary and interacting. Their unity is in God ('Urwesen'), absolute being, truly real, perfect and infinite. Krause combines mystic piety and systematic sophistication. Krause characterized panentheism as speculative theism.

The panentheism which is presented by David A. Pailin,[13] referring to Charles Hartshorne (born 1897), is much different from Krause's. Pailin defines panentheism in contrast to theism (*ens realissimum* and *actus purus*) and pantheism (Spinoza's concept of inherence). Panentheism regards world-beings as God's accidents, theism as accidents outside of God and pantheism as not accidental, but as essential. Pailin comprehends panentheism consequently in a third position between theism and pantheism. On the side of pantheism, how can one avoid deifying *all* finite world-beings, with demotivating consequences in morality? On the side of theism, how can one avoid increasing the difference between God and the world in such a way as to render a relationship between God and the world unthinkable? The theistic doctrine of God's attributes (perfect, absolute, necessary, eternal, unchangeable und endless) can be elaborated in a diastatic, dichotomous sense. The pantheistic doctrine of inherence of the world-things in God can be accentuated in the sense of essential identification. Panentheism tries to combine attributes of divine perfection and finite being, to produce a varied unity of God and the world. Therefore, Hartshorne stresses the structure of dipolarity and the idea of dual transcendence. The concept of God must include attributes of contingency, too. Panentheism intends to prove the compatibility of transcendence and contingency within the concept of God.

2. Some systematic aspects

The God-conception itself is the result and the articulation of the perennial efforts to consider the realm of ultimate values, the variety of religious feelings, the last causes of world-explanation, and the legitimation of social institutions.

The core of a doctrine is often cleared up by the issues stressed in a polemical debate with the counter-doctrines. The focus of theism is spirituality and personality, agency of a transcendent God. God is the creator of the world and the author of the moral designation of mortal-immortal mankind.

13. See above, pp. 95-116.

God's personal agency is conceived of as divine providence combining omniscience and omnipotence. Theism was opposed because of its alleged lack in the lawfulness of reality. The focus of pantheism is lawfulness, the rational understanding of world and nature. Pantheism was suspected of atheism, materialism and fatalism, was attacked by both a theoretical reproach as well as a moral reproach. In the theoretical respect, pantheism was thought of as the unification of God and nature, as the negation of transcendence. Strictly ordered nature itself is divine and self-sufficient. In the moral respect, pantheism was thought to deny human responsibility and liberty.

Pantheism is characterized by the kind of relationship between God and the world. From a realistic viewpoint, pantheism interprets the God-the world relationship as the inherence of accidents in a substance. The beings of the world as accidents are inherent in the divine unique substance. They are subsistent only by their inherence in God. Theism, however, interprets the God-world relationship as the causality of God to the world or as the dependence of the world on God. God is the cause, the world the effect. The struggle between realistic theism and realistic pantheism is the struggle about the adequate category of relationship.

Pantheism is rooted in rationalism. There are no reservations concerning the possibility of a rational perception of God. Reason is able to recognize God. Evidence and the logical coherence in the idea of God guarantee the truth. Pantheism recognizes God by reason, not by revelation. It refuses a doctrine of revelation and transcendence, which produces holes into the lawfulness of nature. Pantheism is abstinent against the religious experience of divine transcendence. It favours rational ethics with a determination of motives and behaviour. Spinoza's formula 'deus sive natura' shows his concentration on nature and his confidence in the methods of logical proofs in theological and ethical themes as well.

The assumption underlying pantheism is an explanation of world-beings and nature in their lawful reality by focussing on their relationship to the concept of God. In this way, pantheism underlines the universal validity of natural lawfulness and the capacity of reason. The unity of the principles of nature is not in a highest intelligence, but in the world's totality, which is understood as a unique substance in a theological way. The attributes of the world are synthesized with the traditional attributes of God. Pantheism refutes a concept of transcendence, which allows an arbitrary intervention of divine activity into the natural process of effective motion. Pantheism has no interest in the contingency of conditions and events of world-beings, but only in the stable existence, the rational change and the necessary shape of world-beings. Therefore, miracles are a central theme in the struggle against the dogmatic view of the world. God's miraculous arbitrary interventions into the natural process interrupt a lawful understanding of nature and a universal rationality. At this point there is a connection to deism. But whereas deism views the transcendent creator God as dismissed from the world after creation and as withdrawn from keeping and ruling the world, pantheism sees God active in preserving the world, especially in the validity of natural laws.

Pantheism has a physicotheological interest. Like Spinozism, pantheism is a special concept challenged by the dualism of body and mind. In the 17th century, the methodical elaboration of modern natural sciences and the conception of a transcendental philosophy integrating doubt as a way of intellectual advancement put body and mind in clear contrast. Therefore, the coordination of nature and reason became a central problem. As regards the ontological difference, is any acting of one sphere upon the other possible? Are both spheres of equal range? Is there any interaction? What is the function of God? Spinoza taught a parallelism of both spheres guaranteed by the concept of God, because he thought extension and thinking as God's attributes were in unseparable junction. Spinoza was convinced of the ontological insufficiency of finite things. They have subsistence only by their inherence in the unique substance, which is thought as *causa sui*. It is necessary for the understanding of the world to think God.

The physicotheological approach of pantheism is without answer to the epistemological question of how efficient reason is. In his transcendental critique of the idea of God, Kant argued that the categories which constitute the human rational perception of the world are unable to constitute metaphysics and its recognition of God. He reduced the idea of God to a regulative function in the objective world-perception, but gave him fundamental importance as a moral postulate. One shortcoming of pantheism is its concentration on the concept of substance and its neglect of moral freedom. Panentheism takes remedial measures against that by stressing the dependence of the world on God. Therefore, panentheism combines the category of causality with the category of inherence.

a. Religious context (reason and piety)
Pailin's way is to conceive God as an eternal and temporal, absolute and relative being. He combines divine attributes of necessity and contingency.

In the material doctrine of God's attributes, Pailin analyzes the notion of omniscience to demonstrate that the aspects of necessity and contingency are compatible in the concept of God.[14] Reading the sentences in his paper was not possible before a concrete time at a concrete place (before they were written at Manchester). That means God's recognition concerning space and time is contingent, but necessary when the event happens. That double aspect allows for the simultaneous determination and indetermination of events and actions. But the root of piety claiming God is omniscient is not adequately taken into consideration. There is a relationship between divine attributes and the type of human piety. The attribute of God's omniscience has existential consequences for man. It means that men are sheltered in all situations of life, but also responsible for all wanting and acting.[15]

The motive and direction of God-conception is not so much to describe a state of affairs, but to influence a movement of life. This claims special attention to the basic piety which Pailin does not give to it. For example Pailin's understanding of the statement 'God is love': God's love 'may be described as being absolute, necessary, eternal, unchanging and infinite';[16] in a concept of divine interventionist activity, God's love materialized for a particular person and ruled by the principle 'doing best for this person' is relative to the contingent circumstances of personal life. A lack of this understanding of love is that love may confirm the particularity of persons. This understanding cannot avoid conflicts evoked in managing the contingent best for many persons (for example contrary social desires of connected persons). The aim and principle of love can be better described as a perfect 'between', as a fulfilled relationship. Believing God's love is the confidence that all men, like whole creation, have a full relationship to God.

Pailin's message is that the coherent conception of panentheism is in keeping with the living ideas of Christian-Jewish-Islamic faith. Pailin gives an argumentation referring to 'the realist understanding of the object of faith typical of the Judeo-Christian-Islamic traditions of belief in God'.[17] He claims panentheism as 'a rationally coherent interpretation of the view of God that underlies the traditions of faith in God typical of Judaism,

14. Cf. Pailin above, p. 98f.
15. Cf. Psalm 139.
16. Pailin, above p. 99.
17. Pailin, above p. 111.

Christianity and Islam'.[18] Can all those traditions be identified by their realistic view of God? Schleiermacher summarized Judaism, Christianity and Islam according to the aspect of teleological piety,[19] but where is the evidence of unification, if the view is not on the type of piety, but instead on the object of worship? How can the multitude of beliefs be related to the concept of God and God's attribute of unity? Historical distinctions have influence in systematic analyses because systematic ideas are not indifferent to historical contexts. There should be a principal reflection on the religious function of logical coherence. How can the fact that faith and the articulation of faith are captives in the world's laws and, therefore, inadequate to the object of worship be taken into consideration? What is the mode of religious statements? Does the motivation to attempt a coherent reconstruction of religious concepts depend on special types of piety? Do the limits of rational reconstruction prove the predominance of spirited piety? It is also significant for religious experience that very different elements be managed in a fertile way. Coherence in theoretical and logical aspects is no religious need of prime order. Religious experience aims at perception and clarity, but the spiritual liveliness of the religious process has priority. This social and individual process shall be kept from an undesirable development and obstruction. Faith itself desires reason and reflection. Fides quaerens intellectum.

b. A realistic approach
Pailin claims that Hartshorne's panentheism with its dipolar structure of God's attributes gives a coherent understanding of divine perfection which is in accord with a realistic view. In respect to the objections to panentheism mentioned by Pailin,[20] some questions arise: How is God's eternity to be compared with temporality? Has eternity a temporal element, or is eternity without connection to space and time? Is it obvious to conceive God's eternity as causation of time? What is the ontological state of God's the world related attributes, by which he is thought changeable? What changes in God, the attributes, the modes of attributes, or the constellation of attributes? Is it necessary to think of God's activity in the sense of personal activity? Is there only the alternative between the concept of God as an ideal or as an actual individual? Is God's activity in accord with his unchangeability, or is an

18. Pailin, above p. 116.
19. Cf. Schleiermacher, *Der christliche Glaube*, 2nd ed., Berlin 1830-31, § 9.
20. Cf. Pailin, above p. 110ff.

active mode complementary to a suffering mode? But what about the world? Is the world such an evident brute fact as conceived? Is it almost clear what the world is? Or is one of the motives of the notion of God to clarify even what the world is?

In the summary at the end of Pailin's paper, there is an ambiguity in the assessment of the realistic point of view. On the one hand, Pailin claims to have given proof of the possibility of 'a realist concept of God'; here God is understood 'both as the proper object of worship and as an actual personal individual'.[21] On the other hand, he admits that all realistic concepts of God, not only panentheism, have a problem with the divine activity, and therefore, the activity-problem would be no argument against panentheism. If the problem is unsolvable in a realistic approach, we must draw conclusions to look upon efficiency and truthfulness of the realistic view. What about an approach which leads to unsolvable problems? Do the problems with God's omniscience and moral determination perhaps arise from realistic synthesis of God's attributes and the world's modes? The realistic approach is troublesome especially as pertaining to the relationship between God and evil: God cannot be omnipotent (almighty) and the supreme good without any evil in any way. If he is merely good and almighty and can prevent the evil, he must do it.

The intentional character of statements about God's attributes is not adequate or compatible with God's quality of absoluteness. The realistic approach promotes a statement-theology. But statements about God produce unsolvable contradictions between the presuppositions and structures of this mode of human knowledge and the unique quality of God. The realistic view of God has a tendency to make God a being like world-beings or like human persons. The thesis that God exists classifies God as a world-being, because existence is a modal category of the world reality.

c. The self-consideration of a doctrine

Like theism and pantheism, Pailin's panentheism is not conscious of the historical preconditions and real effects of its own theory. That the understanding of reality is an essentially historical one is no theme of its doctrine. I presume there are tendencies of self-justification and self-immunization in each doctrine.

The theorems of a doctrine ought to be consistent with the principle. Or

21. Pailin, above p. 116.

conversely: a philosopher is not allowed to neglect his propositions by his own theorems. He must think about what he is saying. For example, theism postulates that God is different from all other world-beings. But the attributes which are predicated to God are of the same genus like that of all world-beings. There is only a gradual difference. The notion of God as absolute, as being (not a being) makes sense only when it is formulated as absolute notion. The doctrine of God must be a non-statement-theory. But theism, pantheism and pantentheism are constructed as statement-theories. They make claims to know what God is in a direct way. That is the justification for giving God numerous attributes. And because some attribute are ambiguous in connection to God and the world, Pailin introduces the formal attribute of temporality and contingence into God with Hartshorne. But does God not get a double identity in that way? And is it enough to correct or to add some attributes, wherein the whole procedure producing them is wrong?

Each adequate doctrine of God must reflect its own insufficience to conceive God in an adequate way. Therefore, there can be no direct intentional speaking of God. But theism and pantheism consider in such a direct way. Theism speaks of the different attributes of God: omnipotence, omniscience. And it speaks of these attributes in such a way, so as to assert the notion of God by summarizing the attributes in the same way in which a tree or a window is described. Material statements in respect to God's attributes are established philosophically by three methods referring to human or mundane attributes. There is the way of negation (*via negationis*), the way of extension (*via eminentiae*), and the way of analogy (*via analogiae*). The three ways relate and connect the absolute to the relative things. Theism does not mention that the absolute must always be considered in its relationship to the relative. It postulates an apartheid, but cannot manage it. Theism does not view its own insufficience which it postulates as an attribute of God. Theism is still naive. The praying man speaks: there are no words to praise God. By speaking this, he praises God. The theist says, God is totally different. But in the doctrine, this falls into oblivion, the absoluteness becomes an attribute, and theism speaks directly by divine perfections what and how God is.

What makes the concept of God true? How is it conceivable to verify the God-conception despite of or because of its transcendence? It is not allowed to consider God as a thing like a stone or tree. To think about God means to formulate the way in which transcendence becomes thinkable in the way of a paradox. An adequate doctrine can only be the movement which shows the insufficience of human conception and gives way to the self-clarification of God in his self-disclosure in the absolute idea of himself by his own spirit.

After Theism

H.J. Adriaanse

> Gott ist ein lauter Nichts, ihn rührt kein Nun noch Hier;
> Je mehr du nach ihm greifst, je mehr entwird er dir.[1]
> Angelus Silesius

I. The incredibility of theism

Introduction

The conviction underlying the present paper is that theism in its traditional form has lost its credibility. Convictions, it is sometimes argued, are the sort of things you have or you have not. I think this is not quite right; reasons can be brought forward even for convictions, though these reasons cannot be considered as the premises from which the conviction necessarily follows as a conclusion. I shall mention three of the reasons for abandoning theism.

By theism in its traditional form I understand something not very different from what R. Swinburne understands by it in his book *The Coherence of Theism*.[2] He defines it as the belief in God as 'a person without a body (i.e. a spirit) who is eternal, free, able to do everything, knows everything, is perfectly good, is the proper object of human worship and obedience, the creator and sustainer of the universe.'[3] The phrasing differs slightly in various contexts in Swinburne's book, but that is of no great importance to me. Besides Swinburne suggests that theism does not involve that each of these properties is ascribed to God, nor that no other properties are ascribed to God.[4] This point does not matter either. Moreover, although Swinburne offers a very fundamental and detailed explanation of the properties under

---

1. 'God is a pure nought/ he knows no now or here/
   The more you reach for him/ the more he eludes you.'
2. R. Swinburne, *The Coherence of Theism*, Oxford 1977.
3. Swinburne, *op.cit.*, p. 1.
4. Although on pp. 222ff, Swinburne develops a sort of system of divine properties.

discussion, it is not impossible to have a different opinion about the precise meaning of this or that theistic predicate. Such differences about — as we say in Dutch — 'the decimal places' do not interest me either. What matters indeed is the mode of belief which is characteristic of classical theism. On this point I would like to lay further emphasis on Swinburne's statements or at least to connect them to a piece of argument which he develops in quite another place. I have in mind chapter 6 of his book in which he considers and dismisses the view that credal sentences — sentences which express the existence of a God with such and such properties — do not make claims but only express attitudes or commend ways of life. To him such sentences are or at least imply statements, that is 'claims about how things are'.[5] In this chapter he appeals — unusually, if I am not mistaken, for his way of arguing[6] — to 'the vast majority of normal users of religious language during the past two millenniums' and what they 'suppose to be implied by what they say'. I am inclined to agree with Swinburne on this point. Theism in its traditional form does not only ascribe a certain set of properties to God but in doing so claims also to contribute to human knowledge of 'how things are'. Doubtlessly theism has practical and affective aspects too but this 'cognitive' or 'descriptive' aspect is not absorbed by them. But, according to Swinburne (if I understand him correctly), it is precisely this cognitive aspect which renders theism philosophically relevant. Here too I agree with him. And I would almost say that by its cognitive aspect theism is rendered scientifically relevant. For science investigates how things are. The age-long conflicts in Christian culture between scientists and the faith of the Church indicate that theism has at least the tendency to compete with scientific or objective knowledge. But perhaps this last step goes too far. After all theism is not prepared to carry out empirical research. In this respect there has been an important difference, at least for the last couple of centuries. But as far as philosophy is concerned theism indeed presumes to be directly relevant. By philosophy we have to understand here a rational and criticisable discourse which consists mainly of assertions. The kind of belief which is constitutive of theism is a rational one: it is belief claiming to be true in a sense of 'true' which makes the difference between true and false decidable and intersub-

5. Swinburne, op.cit., p. 37.
6. Compare the remarks on pp. 87 and 93 on 'sociological and literary survey of what the utterers of theological sentences suppose to be implied by what they say'.

jectively stateable. In a theistic sense 'I believe in God, Creator of heaven and earth' is different not qualitatively but only in degree from 'I believe it is not going to rain this afternoon.' Both utterances express adherence to a phrastic component which is accepted to be true or false in the sense indicated above. In believing in God one is either right or wrong, just as in forecasting future weather conditions. Belief in God is concerned with what is the case, even if the tools of scientific research are insufficient to settle the truth or falsity of what this belief is alleging. For that reason philosophy is the proper tribunal and/or ally.

The philosophical discussion of the credibility of theism can be carried out on various levels. I distinguish three of them: the levels of coherence, probability and plausibility. My grounds for the conviction expressed at the outset will be spread over these three levels. Decisive in my eyes is the judgment according to the criterion of plausibility. That is not to say, however, that the credibility of theism provokes no objections on the other levels. The contrary is the case. I shall argue first that the coherence of theism entails at least one more difficulty than Swinburne admits in his monograph on this subject and next that the probability of it on inductive evidence is also more open to objections than Swinburne seems to think. I am well aware that if my argument on the first point were successful the issue would be settled for many a philosopher. If coherence cannot be stated, they might say, we have a case of incoherence and whatever is incoherent does not deserve further discussion. Swinburne — he again — can teach us that things are not as simple as that. But the middle course he opens up brings a considerable relativization of the importance of the coherence discussion. Questions as to the credibility of theism can hardly be settled on formal, logical grounds. We are relegated — that's my thesis — from that level to the long road of experience. But if we really take that road we cannot leave out the differences in view-point and historical situation of the various experiencing subjects. Here the distinction between probability and plausibility comes in. The first one operates with statistical grounds whereas the other leaves room for sociological and culture-historical considerations and even for common sense. But now to the point.

Coherence
As I announced already, in discussing the coherence problem I will concentrate on Swinburne's great and rich book. A coherent statement, he says, is one which it makes sense to suppose true. To meet this criterion, it

need not be true for that; 'the moon is made of green cheese' is an example of a false yet coherent statement. An incoherent statement is one with regard to which this supposition does not make sense because 'either it or some statement entailed by it is such that we cannot conceive of it being true'. One of the examples Swinburne adduces here is 'honesty weighs ten pounds'. This statement is incoherent because 'honesty is not the sort of thing which it makes sense to suppose weighs ten pounds'.[7] If one asks why this does not make sense, the answer obviously has to consist in an appeal to semantical and syntactical rules. These two kinds of rules are a matter of established and acknowledged use, but this use is not fixed once for all: it is open to modification.

Important for our purpose is the kind of modification made up by the analogical use of words. Whereas the normal use is rooted in a firm albeit sometimes vague relation of a word W to a set of (empirically specifiable) standard examples, analogical use means a loosening of the rules to the effect 'that to be "W" an object has only to resemble the standard objects more than objects which are standard cases of "not-W" objects, but need not resemble the former to the extent to which they resemble each other.' This is the semantical modification; the concomitant syntactical modification says that the rules governing the relations of W to other words and enabling inferences such as W → Y, W → Z etc., are loosened also, to the effect that 'some inferences are no longer valid'.[8] Thus analogical use of words presupposes their normal use. It should be distinguished carefully from univocal use, even if terms are concerned which are applied to God and man alike. Of course it cannot be denied that for instance wisdom as predicated of God amounts to something very different from wisdom as predicated of man, but that is merely a difference of degree. In both cases the same property is denoted; in the first case too the predicate 'wise' 'is being used in a perfectly ordinary sense'.[9] With this view, Swinburne turns against Thomas Aquinas for whom all God-talk is analogical, that is, neither univocal nor equivocal. According to Swinburne, analogical use is much rarer. Fortunately so, for analogy is used at the cost of informative content. 'If theology uses too many words in analogical senses it will convey virtually nothing by what it says'.[10]

7. Swinburne, *op.cit.*, p. 13.
8. Swinburne, *op.cit.*, p. 60.
9. Swinburne, *op.cit.*, p. 71.
10. Swinburne, *op.cit.*, p. 70.

Now Swinburne points out with a certain emphasis that his defence of the coherence of the theistic conception of God 'has in no way relied on supposing that words are used in analogical senses'.[11] Only once, in the final part of the book, where the coherence of the claim is concerned that the properties discussed previously belong necessarily to God, must he play 'the analogical card'.[12] Here my doubts begin. Firstly: the analogical use relates here to the term 'person' as a noun for a property of God. This term has been used all over the book. It seems very doubtful to me that on all preceding occasions it was completely devoid of analogicity. One could think here of a remark by A. Kenny about disembodied minds: 'The minds we know are embodied minds.'[13] Beginning with calling a being without a body (i.e. a spirit) a person is using from scratch the word 'person' in an analogical sense. Secondly: precisely the key-concept 'person'. This term is the core of an entire constellation of terms such as 'animate being', 'thinks', 'actions', 'brings about'. All these other terms are affected by this recourse to analogy. Swinburne himself says, but without attaching any consequence to it: 'Thereby we give all these words somewhat analogical senses'.[14] This consequence is that the corresponding concepts 'spirit', 'free agent', 'omniscient' and 'creator' are concerned too. Thirdly: it is doubtful whether this network of terms can be contained. Is not the concept of personhood so fundamental for theism that the analogical tincture pervades all discourse of God? If yes, then we would have to agree with Aquinas against Swinburne. Now the decisive point, however. Swinburne remarks: 'Once we give analogical senses to words, proofs of coherence or incoherence become very difficult'[15] and here again I wholeheartedly agree with him (perhaps against Aquinas). But if these three doubts are appropriate, then for the domain of theistic theology this remark is even an understatement. In reality the question as to the coherence of theism loses its hold very soon.

Probability
I arrive at the second point, the inductive evidence for the existence of a God conceived of in a theistic way. For the discussion of this point I stick to

11. Swinburne, *op.cit.*, p. 233.
12. Swinburne, *op.cit.*, p. 272.
13. A. Kenny, *The God of the Philosophers*, Oxford 1979, p. 123.
14. Swinburne, *op.cit.*, p. 274.
15. Swinburne, *op.cit.*, p. 61.

Swinburne, who rightly establishes a connection between the preceding point and the present one.[16] *Exempli gratia* I take the cosmological argument which he develops in his book *The Existence of God*[17] and I can declare that I agree for the most part with the criticism expressed by J.L. Mackie[18] against this argument. For the sake of brevity I limit myself to the exposition of two[19] of Mackie's objections which seem to me to be particularly important and to hit the mark. The cosmological argument argues from the existence of the world to God as the rational agent who has intentionally brought it about. God is, Swinburne specifies, the *explanans* of the existence of the world. It is a so-called 'personal explanation' which is at stake here, a kind of explanation which is to be distinguished sharply from the scientific or causal one and which owes its relevance to the fact that the world, even if it had an infinite history, still could have gone off otherwise or not at all. Now let *h* be the hypothesis that there is such a God whose intentional action has brought the world about, and *e* the evidence consisting of the existence of this world, this complex physical universe, and *k* the background knowledge which we take for granted before new evidence turns up. Then it may be true that the probability *P* of *e* in relation to *h* and *k* (in other words: the probability that if there is a God there will be a physical universe) is not very high. Yet according to Swinburne the probability of *e* in relation to *k* is still lower: a physical universe is very unlikely to come about but for God's agency. Consequently we have

$$P\ (e/h.k) > P\ (e/k)$$

and in accordance with generally accepted norms this counts as a good inductive argument for *h*. To be more precise: it is a C-inductive argument which is concerned here, that is an argument such that the premises add to the probability of the conclusion (i.e. make the conclusion more probable than it would otherwise be). Such arguments proceed under the condition

---

16. Compare Swinburne, *op.cit.*, pp. 5, 71, 279, 296 etc., where it is said that the question whether there are good grounds for supposing the truth of coherence claims lies 'outside the scope of this book'.

17. R. Swinburne, *The Existence of God*, Oxford 1979, esp. pp. 116-32.

18. J.L. Mackie, *The Miracle of Theism. Arguments for and against the Existence of God*, Oxford 1982, esp. pp. 95-101.

19. In distinguishing two main objections in Mackie's argument I follow W. Stegmüller's report of it in his book *Hauptströmungen der Gegenwartsphilosophie* IV, Stuttgart 1989, pp. 405ff.

that the initial probability P (h/k) is not 0. This condition gives rise to Mackie's first objection. He asks: 'How can we even think about the antecedent probability that there should be a god, given that there was no such universe?' This is hard to say indeed, for if e contains our knowledge of the existing physical universe then this knowledge has to be withdrawn from k. In that case k contains no more than logical and mathematical truths. What likelihood could the god-hypothesis have had in relation to these? If a physical universe like ours does not exist then there is no conceivable way to proceed in order to settle the initial probability of there being a God.

Swinburne, however, seems to have a different idea. In his view there are two rival hypotheses, one contending that there is no further cause or explanation of the complex physical universe, the other claiming that there is a an uncaused God who created it, but both taking for granted that this universe exists. The hypothesis of an uncaused God is more probable because it postulates a simpler explanation than its rival, i.e. one more likely in relation to our background knowledge — which can now include everything we know about ourselves and the world, though it must exclude any specifically religious beliefs. Here Mackie comes up with his second objection. The rival hypothesis is eliminated too easily. The fact that the universe would, by definition, have no further explanation does not justify Swinburne's claim that it is 'strange and puzzling' or 'very unlikely'. Moreover — and that is what particularly impresses me — the argument of relative unlikelihood can be turned very well against the preferred hypothesis of divine creation. The question, then, is not only whether it is likely that a God with the traditional attributes and powers would be able and willing to create such a universe as this, but also and preliminarily, whether it is likely that there is such a God at all. To answer this question one should ascertain the likelihood of what Swinburne's personal explanation attributes to God as his key power, namely the power to fulfill his intentions directly, without any physical or causal mediation, without materials or instruments. And then Mackie says: 'There is nothing in our background knowledge that makes it comprehensible, let alone likely that anything should have such a power. All our knowledge of intention-fulfilment is of embodied intentions being fulfilled indirectly by way of bodily changes and movements which are causally related to the intended result.' To my eyes Mackie is simply right here. I draw a quick general conclusion: If the explanatory force of theism as an inductive hypothesis about the origin of the universe is concerned, then at least on this point Swinburne's argument falls onto its own sword: an explanation is meant to diminish the extent of the non-understood but in fact this argument contributes 'nothing to support the claim that by adding a god to the world we *reduce* the unexplained element'.

Plausibility

As I said, I wish to draw a distinction between probability and plausibility. With the former, the phrastic component of credal sentences is all-important; the neustic component is thought to deserve hardly any attention: for why would anybody think or act against his own rational belief? Such a person would be irrational and making the supposition of irrationality means committing philosophical suicide. With the latter, at the risk of such suicide, the neustic component of credal sentences is given much more weight. It is no overstatement to say that on this view the entire distinction between phrastic and neustic components of such sentences is put into question; the idea is not accepted here that there are isolatable belief-contents which as propositions could be put before the mind whose judgment could thereupon decide freely between the affirmation and the negation of them. In this view beliefs are always embedded in the concrete biography of an individual which in its turn is a segment of the concrete 'biography' of a society. Consequently it hardly makes sense to deal with the credibility of credal sentences as long as the societal or historico-cultural context is not taken into account. Therefore one has to admit the relevance of such criteria as cognitive consonance, solidity of plausibility structures etc. In my opinion these new criteria are of the utmost importance for our question. Reckoning with them means a sort of self-relativization of philosophy but I think that philosophy indeed can no longer claim to be last court of appeal for truth. If beliefs are sociohistorical realities, philosophy cannot pass judgment on them without acknowledging that she herself is part of the sociohistorical process. This view implies the rehabilitation of empirical evidence and even of common sense as relevant for philosophical reflection.

As to the plausibility of theism, I think that the so-called secularization thesis should be taken very seriously. This thesis — I take here Peter Berger's book *The Social Reality of Religion*[20] as my point of reference — starts from 'empirically available processes'[21] which ensure that 'sectors of society and

20. Peter L. Berger, *The Social Reality of Religion*, Harmondsworth 1973 (first published as *The Sacred Canopy*, 1967).
21. Berger, *op.cit.*, p. 112.

culture are removed from the domination of religious institutions and symbols'.[22] This complex of processes 'affects the totality of cultural life and of ideation, and may be observed in the decline of religious contents in the arts, in philosophy, in literature and, most important of all, in the rise of science as an autonomous, thoroughly secular perspective of the world' (*ibid.*). To a certain extent the secularization process can be seen as 'a 'reflection' of concrete infrastructural processes in modern society'.[23] Its original 'locale' 'was in the economic area, specifically, in those sectors of the economy being formed by the capitalistic and industrial processes'.[24] In this milieu arose 'something like a 'liberated territory' with respect to religion' (*ibid.*). In modern industrial society the area of economy has conquered a central position to the effect that secularization 'has moved 'outwards' from this sector into other areas of society' (*ibid.*). This central position explains why any attempt to reconquer that liberated territory 'in the name of religio-political traditionalism endangers the continued functioning of this economy. A modern industrial society requires the presence of large cadres of scientific and technological personnel, whose training and ongoing social organization presupposes a high degree of rationalization, not only on the level of infra-structure but also on that of consciousness. Any attempts at traditionalistic *reconquista* thus threaten to dismantle the rational foundations of modern society. Furthermore, the secularizing potency of capitalistic-industrial rationalization is not only self-perpetuating but self-aggrandizing. As the capitalistic industrial complex expands, so do the social strata dominated by its rationales, and it becomes ever more difficult to establish traditional controls over them'.[25]

It is not difficult to see the consequences of this secularization process for theism. From the point of view we are now adopting theism is to be con-sidered as embedded or incarnated in a religious tradition. It cannot be detached from this tradition. Rather, it constitutes the heart or the organizing principle of it; it is its 'primary determinant of meaning'.[26] In a religious tradition a world is constructed and maintained.[27] The reality of this world

22. Berger, *op.cit.*, p. 113.
23. Berger, *op.cit.*, p. 131.
24. Berger, *op.cit.*, p. 133.
25. Berger, *op.cit.*, p. 136.
26. V. Brümmer, *Theology and Philosophical Inquiry*, London 1981, p. 134.
27. Berger, *op.cit.*, p. 13ff, 38ff.

'depends upon the presence of social structures within which this reality is taken for granted and within which successive generations of individuals are socialized in such a way that this world will be real to *them*'.[28] Religious traditions, in other words, owe their power to 'plausibility structures'. If these structures lose their integrity or continuity the world of that particular religion 'begins to totter' (*ibid.*) and comes in urgent need of legitimation. Now secularization precisely means the crumbling or even the collapse of the religious plausibility structure. The primary determinant of meaning is inevitably swept along in this fall. The problem is no more this or that detail of the theistic world-view which on the basis of an intact whole could be corrected or substituted; the problem is the whole itself, the idea that there should be something like a (theistically conceived) God.

In truth, there is much to object against the secularization thesis and *a fortiori* against the present exposition of it. Yet even if it were not 100% true, but only 50%, it would still be ponderable enough. And, once more, ponderable also in philosophy. It implies that there is a dialectical relationship between social structures and religious culture. 'The point is that the *same* human activity that produces society also produces religion'.[29] It is impossible, that is, that a secularization process should take place without impact on the religious, or in this case, theistic world-view. Concentrating on philosophy as a practice of knowledge one could even say: it is impossible that a liberated territory of science should arise without harming the plausibility of theism. In fact it seems that philosophy has to choose: she cannot both sustain theism and agree with the economy-based, autonomous, thoroughly secular world-perspective of science.

Corollary with regard to theistic religions
In my country it is sometimes argued that there is a generic difference between philosophical belief in (a theistically conceived) God and religious or at least Christian faith. The collapse of the former would hardly affect the latter. Even more, the collapse of the former would finally liberate the latter: from its age-long Babylonian captivity. At last the true, non-philosophical, non-metaphysical face of Christian belief in a personal God would come to light and it would be, so to speak, the grace bestowed to our epoch that we are in a position to see this. This is a kind of view which to a certain extent

28. Berger, *op.cit.*, p. 55.
29. Berger, *op.cit.*, p. 56.

I shall adopt myself too; in the last section of this paper I shall try to develop it a bit more. Still I think it is good first to state quite sharply that Christian faith largely coincides with theism and that the possibilities of separating Christianity from metaphysics are very restricted. This is a thesis which regards not only the historical essence of Christianity but also the nature of faith: one can hardly avoid thinking of faith as having an object, a really existing something or somebody to whom it is referring. Therefore the contrast that Pascal drew between the God of the philosophers and the God of Abraham, Isaac and Jacob is a very difficult one. It is, in my opinion, certainly untenable if it is posited on the level of conceptual content. Swinburne is right in saying that in the sense of his definition of theism Christians, as well as Jews and Muslims, are theists.[30] If Christian theology wanted to evade this consequence by retreating to a God-conception whose content differs not only specifically but even generically from that of theism, then it could hardly succeed. For in the first place Christian theology would then have to abandon very central, very fundamental elements of the traditional Christian God-conception, and in the second place — and even more important — it would *ceteris paribus* do nothing but exchange one metaphysical position for another. Even a 'wholly other' God-conception is a God-*conception* and entails as such certain metaphysical, that is existential claims. These claims can be made *pianissimo* or cloaked in flowery metaphors but as such this does not change anything. It merely produces the necessity of rational reconstruction,[31] i.e. of a transformation of theological phrasings into corresponding philosophical statements.

Needless to say, the trinitarian God-conception cannot figure as a God-conception which is generically different from theism. Perhaps it is not quite needless to emphasize that Jewish monotheism cannot either. It is sometimes argued that the Christian God-conception has lost the original purity of Jewish monotheism in that it has become amalgamated with Hellenism. In line with this view, a radical rejudaization of the Christian faith is often called for. Now it is without doubt that through its Hellenization the Gospel was brought into contact with metaphysical speculation. But it is an illusion to think that outside the sphere of speculation (which by the way has flourished in Jewish mysticism as well) metaphysical implications are non-

30. Swinburne, *op.cit.*, p. 1.
31. Compare H.G. Hubbeling, *Principles of the Philosophy of Religion*, Assen 1987, pp. 76ff.

existent. Jewish monotheism is theism just as much and it admits in principle of the rational reconstruction of a metaphysical equivalent which, then, is just as open to philosophical questioning as the traditional Christian God-conception is.

To sum up: if the argument in the sections preceding this corollary is valid then it is hard to contradict Wolfgang Stegmüller when at the end of his long review of Mackie's *Miracle of Theism* he observes that the author's philosophical position entails the rationally-founded statement that the monotheistic religions known to us are based on an existential assumption which is indispensable to them but which is presumably false.[32]

II. Theism as heritage

Heritage as charge and as benefit
Ideas can be tenacious and survive for centuries beyond the context of their appropriate use. To characterize this postexistence I choose the metaphor of heritage. This is no recognized philosophical concept; even the very voluminous *Historisches Wörterbuch der Philosophie* offers no entry for it, whereas the 31 volumes of the *Archiv für Begriffsgeschichte* do not contain any article or even abstract on it either.[33] Yet it is a juridical concept and for the fun of it I have looked a bit in a collection of proverbs and rules of Roman Law. I found there quite a lot of pithy sayings about heirs and legacies. I take the liberty to quote four of them:[34] (1) *Actiones heredi et in heredem competunt.*

---

32. W. Stegmüller, *op.cit.*, p. 518 '...aus Mackies philosophischer Position folgt die rational begründete Aussage, daß die uns bekannten monotheistischen Religionen auf einer für sie unverzichtbaren Existenzannahme beruhen, die vermutlich falsch ist.'
33. The *Dictionary of the History of Ideas* only mentions the biological sense of the metaphor which is irrelevant for my purpose. The only philosophical current I know of in which the idea of cultural heritage has been developed a little is Marxism. Thus we find it notably in Ernst Bloch, *Erbschaft dieser Zeit*, published in the ominous 1930s. An application of this view to the role of religion in culture can be found in his post-war books *Das Prinzip Hoffnung*, esp. pp. 1521ff and *Atheismus im Christentum*, esp. pp. 260ff. Jürgen Moltmann published an anthology of Bloch's texts on religion under the title *Religion im Erbe*, München/Hamburg 1967 in the preface of which the notion of heritage is made explicit.
34. Comp. D. Liebs, *Lateinische Rechtsregeln und Rechtssprichwörter*, Darmstadt 1982, p. 22 no. 20; p. 83 no. 8; p. 83 no. 13; p. 151 no. 11.

Claims can be made both by and against the heir. (2) *Hereditas pro parte adiri nequit*. Legacy cannot be accepted in part. (3) *Heres succedit in vitia realia defuncti*. The heir takes over the real [i.e. not the personal] shortcomings of the deceased. (4) *Partes renuntiantium accrescunt invitis*. An inheritance declined passes to the other inheritors, even though unwilling.

Sayings like these seem to me to signify that inheritance is a precarious affair in need of careful regulation. How easily quarrel can arise here, which then of course affects the most elementary and vital social unit, the family. Moreover, how dangerous and burdensome the position of the heir sometimes is. What is it that he receives? Will it not harm him or involve him in some misadventure? Sometimes it seems best entirely to renounce one's portion. Above all: if one accepts the heritage, what a burden one sometimes takes. The patrimony is to be carefully kept and administered. According to Roman law the head of the family would have the *heredium* in private property but it was in practice unavailable to him.[35] Especially this latter aspect provides a breeding ground for our metaphor.

It might be objected that this precarious and cumbersome character of heritage is but one side of the matter and that one cannot understand this institution adequately if one does not realize the benefits that are usually attached to it or expected from it. I concede this outright. Heirs enter into the possession of goods without labour. This prospect mostly brightens life to a considerable extent and one's comings and goings are not seldom strongly motivated by the hope of becoming a heir. I would like to instantiate this promising aspect of heritage also by some sayings. This time I prefer to draw them not from juridical but from evangelical wisdom. I take the liberty of quoting some significant verses from the New Testament.[36] (1) Hebr 9.15 'And for this cause he is the mediator of the new testament, that by means of death, for the redemption of the transgressions *that were* under the first testament, they which are called might receive the promise of eternal inheritance.' (2) Romans 8.17 'And if children, then heirs; heirs of God, and joint-heirs with Christ; if so be that we suffer with *him*, that we may be also glorified together.' (3) Galatians 4.7 'Wherefore thou art no more a servant, but a son; and if a son, then a heir of God through Christ.' (4) 1 Peter 1.4 'To

---

35. 'propriété privée du chef de famille, mais pratiquement indisponible', P. Ourliac & J. de Malafosse, *Droit romain et ancien droit*, Paris 1961, vol. II, p. 65.
36. Omitting the Greek text and using the King James Version.

an inheritance incorruptible, and undefiled, and that fadeth not away, reserved in heaven for you'.

If one compares the first set of sayings to the second, one could almost think of the opposition between law and gospel. This impression is of course due to my arrangement. Still I think it is true that the phenomenon of heritage is an ambivalent one and shows up two clearly different aspects. In dealing with the heritage of theism I want to depart from this ambivalence. We shall focus first on the encumbering side of it and then on the blessing that it might contain.

The heritage of theism as charge
'One has to be as naïve as a freethinker of the Saturday evening market to be happy in the illusion that one frees oneself from Christianity (...) by abjuring the Christian belief in God. For after the great heresy, after we have experienced that 'God is dead', we stand there with our Christian form as heirs of an age-long Christian discipline (...), Christians without Christianity, without faith, but nonetheless neither Brahmans nor barbarians.'[37]

These are words of the Dutch essayist Menno ter Braak (1902-1940), a fiery admirer of Nietzsche's individualism and therefore a firm adversary of modern collectivisms, whether communist or nazist. He was on the black list of the new rulers in Germany and was to be arrested immediately after the Dutch surrender in 1940. By killing himself, he was a few hours too quick for his executioners.

As subject of study, Ter Braak had almost chosen theology. But in his student years he had already taken leave of Christianity; the doubt with regard to 'the higher things' had gained the upper hand. He opted for 'the ordinary word'; his 1931 collection of essays *A Farewell to Clergymanland* (a book title which became famous in my country) does away with the sermonizing tone, the outward but also the inward sermonizing tone, by which truth is masked. It was also a struggle against himself he had achieved with this book: 'I had to combat the clergyman words of my vocabulary by other words', he wrote in the preface.[38]

The first quotation is drawn from a book he published 6 years later under the title *Of Christians Old and New*. The shadow of Nazism was falling over

37. Menno ter Braak, *Verzameld Werk* [Collected Works], 2nd ed., Amsterdam 1980, vol. III, p. 266.
38. Ter Braak, *op.cit.*, vol. II, pp. 167ff.

Europe; it was the supremacy of the Cyclops. What could honest people do to survive other than, just like Odysseus and his companions, making a stand together? The book is a plea for democracy. Of course it had to be a democracy without demagogy, without the usual phraseology and without the sacralization of equality, in short the democracy of Nobody. Still a democracy, a collectivity! The resentment of the herd towards the strong individual, from which this political form doubtlessly has its origin, should not only be unmasked but also be accepted. This resentment, then, was aroused and cultivated in Christianity; in consequence democracy is a result of Christianity and goes back to the Christian principle of the equality of all souls before God. And that is why, face to face with the Cyclops, people should become new Christians.[39]

What I have in mind concerning this example is two things particularly, one concerning the method and the other concerning the subject matter. As to the method: the heritage of theism asks for an approach different from that appropriate to theism itself. As inheritance theism has passed into other hands, other forms. It has been divided among many heirs; it is so to speak disseminated. Thus it is no longer a topic of philosophical theology *stricto sensu* but a ferment, an essence of certain religious traditions, or more precisely of the secularized postexistence of such traditions. Accordingly, the object of the philosophy of religion is not so much of a logical or epistemological kind; rather it is a factual entity or a plurality of such entities, namely the comprehensive cultural entities called religions. Therefore I think that it is not without reason that the name of our discipline contains the word 'religion'. To my knowledge this name arose at the end of the 18th century, and this simultaneously with a deep crisis — and on the Continent the almost complete extinction — of rational theology.[40] It is easy to establish a causal connection between these two events and to consider the philosophy of religion as the transformation, not to say the heir, of *theologia rationalis*. Philosophy of religion thus expresses by its very name a serious rupture of the metaphysical tradition. This name signals that it is impossible to know God by reason alone; we cannot have knowledge of God other than we have of the contingent entities called religions, in other words: the existence and

39. Ter Braak, *op.cit.*, vol. III, pp. 370ff.
40. Compare K. Feiereis, *Die Umprägung der natürlichen Theologie in Religionsphilosophie. Ein Beitrag zur Geistesgeschichte des 19. Jahrhunderts*, Leipzig 1965.

nature of God cannot be brought up[41] except in the forms of human worship. Dealing with the heritage of theism can take place only in the form of a philosophy of culture in which the task of philosophy does not so much consist in analysis or reconstruction but rather in reflexion and recollection. Its concern is to examine the transformations that religious belief in God has gone through and in which it has both gained and lost its identity. The reference to Menno ter Braak is meant to be an application of this different paradigm in philosophy of religion. A literary text was intentionally selected as point of departure, since it is not only the arguments of philosophers and theologians that are relevant here but also the texts of essayists and other belletrists whether pious or profane.

As to the relevance of our example for the subject matter under discussion, I would like to make two remarks. Firstly, the example shows the importance or the seriousness of the charge. It relates to no less a thing than the condition for decent survival. The foundation of society comes into play. In Ter Braak's view, theism is much more than the maintaining of credal sentences about a metaphysical being: it has shaped a political order and if it comes to pass away this order is seriously endangered. In this respect the book *Of Christians Old and New* seems to me to anticipate the turn to the problem of civil religion which in American discussions of the last two decades has become a hot issue. Meanwhile we should realize that in Ter Braak the argument is based not on religion in general but specifically on theistic religion. It is Christian faith that constitutes the charge. The heritage consists of the discipline Christianity brought about by its belief that in the last resort, in the sight of the Lord, there is no élite, no difference between the strong and the weak, the rich and the poor.

Secondly and more important: the selected example shows the tenacity, if not insuperability of the charge. As a motto for the second part of his book Ter Braak quotes Ernest Renan: 'I feel that my life is governed always by a faith that I have no more. Faith has this peculiarity that, when disappeared, it still works'.[42] The first-person voice of this quotation is, I think, appropriate. In lengthy explanations it is argued to what extent language in

41. Here my lack of mastery of the English language makes itself badly felt. I wished I had at my disposal here an English equivalent of the German word 'erörtern', which means simultaneously 'to bring something up', 'to discuss' and 'to put something in its place' (thus in Heidegger).
42. Ter Braak, *op.cit.*, p. 263.

Europe has absorbed Christian pretensions and has carried them along far beyond the limits of official, faithful Christianity. 'The Christian terminology becomes interesting to us particularly there where it is not the terminology of faith any more, where it is used unsuspectingly by freethinkers, Marxists, fascists and sceptics, for example *against* faithful Christianity. Language in its modern naivety is the most delightful masquerade (...): it outwits the ingenuous, it outwitted the Christians, but as dialectic it even outwitted Karl Marx, the enemy of Stirner!' But we should add — and that is my point — it has outwitted Ter Braak too. Even the values of this Stirnerian individualist are disguises of Christian spirit. There is at least one context in which he admits this quite overtly. Honesty (*honnêteté*) and human dignity are often pointed to by him as his highest values. In this context he says: 'By the notion 'human dignity' and its equivalents I express nothing but the 'equality of the souls before God'... without God. I cannot recognize an élite any more: no king, no dictator and no intellectual either; I only recognize that I am a Christian, a heir, in whom all has become instinct which in ancestry was built up out of compromises between pagan resistance and Christian discipline. (...) Human dignity is a concept which takes its comprehensive and absolute character from its Christian specificity. It is a concept that we cannot go beyond because it resumes our Christian heritage'.[43]

Our reaction might be: how very paradoxical all this is! Well, even that is conceded. 'Paradox' is indeed a key concept in Ter Braak's thoughts. On the final page he suggests that the very form of his book, its open end, 'is a symbol of Christian society that lets its symbols turn into paradoxes. The consistent non-conformist is the consistent proclaimer of non-metaphysical Christianity (...) because he has understood that Christian harmony comes to an end and that the epoch of Christian paradoxes is emerging'.[44] Yet, paradox is in Ter Braak not only a 'thematical' but also an 'operating' concept,[45] that is to say: it is not only in front of him, in his field of

---

43. Ter Braak, *op.cit.*, pp. 278ff.
44. Ter Braak, *op.cit.*, p. 377f.
45. E. Fink, 'Les concepts opératoires dans la phénoménologie de Husserl', *Cahiers de Royaumont n° III*, Paris 1959, pp. 214-41, esp. p. 217f.: 'La pensée, prise au sens philosophique du terme, (...) se tient dans l'élément du concept. La conceptualisation de la philosophie vise intentionnellement ces concepts dans lesquels la pensée fixe et conserve ce qu'elle a pensé. Ces concepts, nous les nommons <concepts thématiques>. (...) Mais, dans la formation des concepts thématiques, les penseurs créateurs utilisent d'autres concepts et d'autres modèles de pensée.

consciousness, but also at his back, like a *vis a tergo*. It runs off with him. And this might reveal what his new Christianity is really up to.

To us who stand at a distance of half a century it is all too evident that in receiving the inheritance of Christian theism this author is ridden by it. Does this mean that we ourselves are free from it? Has one merely to understand this disguise of the charge in order to be rid of it? I am not so sure. I am not fond of mystifications to the effect that whatever has become invisible counts as most real, even more real than it was before, but there is some truth — not only in psychoanalytical respects but also with regard to the history of culture — in the idea of the power of the Un-thought (*das Ungedachte*), the forgotten or the displaced. On this point I hesitantly agree with Heidegger and Derrida. So I think that it makes sense to address the question also to ourselves, I mean the question: under which disguises is theism still exerting its charge after its disappearance?

The heritage of theism as blessing

'De re' and 'de dicto'

In recent years the following story has been repeatedly quoted in my country:

When the Baal Shem had a difficult task before him, he would go to a certain place in the woods, light a fire and meditate in prayer — and what he had set out to perform was done. When a generation later the 'Maggid' of Meseritz was faced with the same task he would go to the same place in the woods and say: We can no longer light the fire, but we can still speak the prayers — and what he wanted done became reality. Again a generation later Rabbi Moshe Leib of Sassov had to perform this task. And he too went into the woods and said: We can no longer light a fire, nor do we know the secret meditations belonging to the prayer, but we do know the place in the woods to which it all belongs — and that must be sufficient; and sufficient it was. But when another generation had passed and Rabbi Israel of Rishin

Ils opèrent avec des schèmes intellectuels qu'ils ne conduisent pas à une fixation objective. (...) Leur compréhension conceptuelle se meut *dans* un champ conceptuel, (...) qu'ils ne peuvent eux-mêmes avoir sous les yeux. (...) Ce qui, d'une pensée philosophante, est ainsi utilisé couramment, pénétré, mais non réfléchi, c'est ce que nous nommons les concepts opératoires. Ils sont, pour parler en image, l'ombre d'une philosophie. La force éclairante d'une pensée se nourrit de ce qui reste dans l'ombre de la pensée.'

was called upon to perform the task, he sat down on his golden chair in his castle and said: we cannot light the fire, we cannot speak the prayers, we do not know the place, but we can tell the story of how it was done. And, the story-teller adds, the story which he told had the same effect as the actions of the other three.

The reason for the popularity of this story might be found in malaise. People would recognize in it their own situation, a situation at the end of a process of decay. In a series of generations the breakdown was accomplished, in steps that could almost exactly be marked: the breakdown first of the infallible authority of Scripture, then of the provident guidance of God in history and one's own life, then of the personal immortality or postmortem existence, then of the Church-going way of life. And just as in the story the process passed from thing to word; faith that initially was *de re* ended up as being *de dicto*. What more can happen? What else than that even the words will die down?

Of course malaise is an aspect of the situation and I do not exclude that in some cases the reference to this story is inspired by it. But the story itself — and perhaps the quotation of it too — has another tenor. We can become aware of this if we put the story into one of its best known contexts, the context of the conclusion of the book *Major Trends in Jewish Mysticism* by the great Kabbala expert Gershom Scholem. There we learn that the milieu which the story reflects is that of the mystical revival movement of hasidism in 18th-century Eastern Europe. But it is not only a story about hasidism but also, as Scholem makes plain, a story of the hasidim themselves. And the intention they had with it was (according to his interpretation) almost the contrary of what malaise is inclined to hear in it. The story about the words and deeds of famous Zaddikim is the greatest creation of hasidism. Not a few Zaddikim, above all Rabbi Israel of Rishin, the founder of the Eastern Galician Hasidic dynasty, have laid down the whole treasure of their ideas in such tales. Their Torah took the form of an inexhaustible fountain of story-telling. Nothing at all has remained theory, everything has become a story. In this sense I understand Scholem's puzzling comment on the story quoted above: 'You can say if you will that this profound little anecdote symbolizes the decay of a great movement. You can also say that it reflects the transformation of all its values, a transformation so profound that in the end all that remained of the mystery was the tale. That is the position in which we find ourselves today, or in which Jewish mysticism finds itself. The story is not ended, it has not yet become history, and the secret life it holds can break out tomorrow in you or in me.'[46] The comment is puzzling because of its lack of articulation. No 'but', no 'on the other hand', no 'nonetheless'. What is opposed to what in this text, what is to be stressed? As I said, I take it that this wonderful sequence of sentences means to embroider on the idea that everything has become a story. It then says that whenever the *dictum* comes to life the *res* itself is there.

The blessing of thick language

This idea is the point of departure of my thoughts about the heritage of theism as blessing. Briefly stated, the blessing consists in the availability of a very thick language. The adjective 'thick' refers to a context in G. Ryle.[47] 'What is *le Penseur* doing?', Ryle asks. The usual answer that the thinker is saying things to himself, fails badly. Perhaps he says nothing at all, and at any rate he is doing a number of other things which can best be described by saying that 'he is trying, by success/failure tests, to find out whether or not the things that he is saying would or would not be utilisable as leads or pointers.' Such a description is thick because it is using 'constitutionally adverbial verbs — active verbs that are not verbs for separately do-able, lowest-level doings'.[48] Examples of such verbs are 'to mimick', 'to do something experimentally' (which differs from just doing it), 'to do things as steps towards or stages in some ulterior undertaking' and — to my taste a particularly fine example — 'to undo'. Now the point that interests me is that in many cases these adverbial verbs are so to speak stackable. A good example is 'the adverbial verb "to think"'[49] itself. According to the description I just quoted, thinking is a sort of trying. The thinker is not so much guiding himself anywhere, but 'trying to find out whether this or that track of his own making would or would not qualify as a guiding (...) track'.[50] This kind of exploring is different from piloting others on a track that has already been cleared, and this in turn is different from following a pilot's lead. The difference lies in the levels of sophistication: of these three doings the first one according to Ryle lies on the highest sophistication-level and the last one

46. G. Scholem, *Major Trends in Jewish Mysticism*, New York 1946, pp. 349f.
47. Compare 'Thinking and Reflecting' and 'The thinking of thoughts. What is 'le Penseur' doing?', in G. Ryle, *Collected Papers*, II, London 1971, pp. 465-96.
48. Ryle, *op.cit.*, p. 486.
49. Ryle, *op.cit.*, p. 473.
50. Ryle, *op.cit.*, p. 494.

on the lowest.[51] Elsewhere he speaks in the same sense about 'accomplishment-levels' corresponding to the order in which the lessons of experience
must be learned. 'Some lessons are intrinsically traders on prior lessons. Such
tradings can pyramid indefinitely. There is no top step on the stairway of
accomplishment-levels'.[52] A thick description encompasses these different
levels.

In Ryle 'thick' is an adjective to 'description', whereas I want to use it as
an adjective to 'language'. That is quite a difference and I am afraid that Ryle
would have deemed this innovation a sign of confusion. With regard to those
adverbial verbs (and whatever classes of words) I merely think that it is not
a matter of course that qua bits of language they are on hand. Without the
availability of an appropriate language the pyramid of accomplishment-levels
could not be built up. The possibility of a thick description is dependent on
the existence of a thick language.

Three short remarks about what is to be understood by language here.
In the first place it is to be seen as an historical entity, susceptible to change.
It undergoes expansions as well as reductions. This explains the difference
between the phases of one and the same natural language and partly also the
difference between one natural language and another: one develops in a
tempo different from the other. Thus it may happen that in a given natural
language words fail: they are not yet there or they are not there any more.
In the second place: language is, although subject to change, yet relatively
stable. Usually the evolution proceeds rather slowly, so that people of
different generations can more or less understand each other. Moreover and
especially: What is not used actually is not at once gone. It is preserved like
a fund from which we can draw at the proper time. That is why speaking a
language always has the aspect of presentification of the past, or to borrow
a beautiful expression from Hegel, the aspect of *Erinnerung* (i.e. both
recollection and interiorization). In the third place: there is a connection
between language and experience. Language is the reflection of the contact
of a cultural community with reality. It is thus a reminder of the lessons
learned by this cultural community. Of course we have to understand this
distributively: the cultural community is a collection of communities which
partly fight each other. Language has this differentiation too; the experience
which it embodies is by no means homogeneous. Be that as it may, experi-

51. Ryle, *op.cit.*, p. 495.
52. Ryle, *op.cit.*, p. 483.

ence has the property of self-generation. Experience discloses new experience. That is to say that actual experience is prefigured in preceding experience. This feature is reflected in language. The language we speak in order to express our understanding of reality opens up by itself new possibilities of articulation.

A thick language, then, encompasses a wide range of accomplishment-levels — of experiences, memories, thoughts, fictions, feelings telescoped in basic doings. A very thick language encompasses virtually all accomplishment-levels. Theism has made language very thick — I mean the natural languages of the cultures in which it has lived or is still flourishing either as philosophical or as religious belief. The reason why this is so can easily be grasped. Both in its philosophical and in its religious form (and in the many, many hybrids) theism has been an exercise in sophistication of consciousness. The usual word for what I call here with Ryle 'sophistication' is 'transcendence'. Theism has been connected, at least since the beginning of modernity, with the demand to go beyond the world of everyday things. W. Trillhaas has brought his critical account of belief in God under the title 'intentional transcendence'. I recall some of the relevant contexts of his *Religionsphilosophie*. Transcendence cannot mean an object, a second world 'behind' ours; it denotes a movement accomplished by the religious subject. 'In its devotion the religious subject itself 'exceeds' the 'reality' which is confined by mere sense-data and which can be controlled experimentally and registered mechanically. It also 'exceeds' mere historical facticity.' With the terminology of Edm. Husserl one can speak here of an intentional surplus of meaning *(intentionale Mehrmeinung)*. It is as if something is added to normal perception, for instance a natural phenomenon is apperceived as 'creature', or a word addressed to me and touching my conscience is apperceived by me as 'Word of God'. 'In this surplus the horizon of the moment is widened so as to include past and future. In this surplus I leave my narrow shell; my fellow-human is not an object any more; I see myself in his mirror, I meet his expectation for me and experience my responsibility which, just as love and guilt, exceeds all momentary need. I come to myself, I become a person in that I gain distance from myself. All that, however, is but a beginning. Religion means a fundamental transcendence of experience, which impregnates the substance of mere everyday experience and fulfills it with 'meaning' in a density that perhaps never can be closed once and for all.' This ultimate opening is warranted by the religious idea of God. In accordance with the 'transcendence postulate' the word 'God' means the 'ultimate goal of intentional exceeding', that is "God' itself cannot be exceeded intentionally (...) *Deus semper maior.*' Trillhaas explicitly links up the transcending character of religious experience with language. This link is given by the fact that experience is a social event. It is the attempt to make sense of human existence in which I find myself involved together with other people. The meaning-structures resulting in this collective and personal attempt are not demonstrable but they find their 'intersubjective confirmation and interpretation in language. In language the transcendence of experience obtains its particular objectivity.'[53] So much for Trillhaas. My conclusion, once more, is that the theistic practice of surpassing everyday experience has helped to develop a virtually infinite stairway of accomplishment-levels or sophistication-levels, in other words, that it has substantially contributed to the birth and the maintenance of a very thick language.

Is this a blessing? We need not hesitate long about that. It can be a

---

53. W. Trillhaas, *Religionsphilosophie*, Berlin 1972, p. 67: '...das religiöse Subjekt selbst 'überschreitet' in seiner Zuwendung die durch bloße Sinnesdaten begrenzte, experimentell kontrollierbare und mit Apparaten registrierbare 'Wirklichkeit' wie die der bloßen historischen Tatsächlichkeit.' p. 69: 'Auch die religiöse Zuwendung (...) vollzieht sich in der Weise einer solchen intentionalen Überschreitung, in einer Mehrmeinung. Es ist zunächst so, als ob der Wahrnehmung noch etwas hinzu-gefügt würde. Wenn Naturerscheinungen als 'Kreatur', wenn ein an mich gerich-tetes Wort, das mich im Gewissen trifft, als Wort Gottes wahrgenommen wird...' p. 213: 'Erst im intentionalen Überschreiten leuchtet 'Sinn' auf. Dieser Sinn ist immer ein Mehr als das, was vor der Hand und vor Augen liegt. In diesem Mehr erweitert sich der Horizont des Augenblicks und begreift Vergangenheit und Zukunft ein. In diesem Mehr verlasse ich mein enges eigenes Gehäuse, der andere Mensch ist nicht mehr Objekt, sondern ich sehe mich in seinem Spiegel, begegne seiner auf mich gerichteten Erwartung und erfahre meine Verantwortung, die ebenso wie Liebe und Schuld alles momentane Bedürfnis überschreitet. Ich komme zu mir selbst, werde Person, indem ich von mir Abstand gewinne. Aber das ist nur ein Anfang. Religion meint eine grundsätzliche Erfahrungs-transzendenz, welche die Materie der bloßen Alltagserfahrung durchwirkt und in einer vielleicht niemals ganz abschließbaren Dichte mit "Sinn" erfüllt.' p. 82f: '"Gott", bzw. das "Göttliche" meint in der Religion immer ein letztes Ziel intentionaler Überschreitung. Vom Menschen aus gesehen ist "Gott" selbst nicht mehr intentional überschreitbar.' p. 213: 'Diese Erfahrung von Bindung und Trans-zendenz (...) ist (...) ein sozialer Vorgang. Es ist Sinngebung des menschlichen Daseins, in dem ich mich selbst ebenso wie den anderen Menschen begriffen finde. Es ist keine objektive Sinnstruktur, sie ist nicht demonstrierbar, aber sie findet ihre intersubjektive Bestätigung und Deutung in der Sprache. In der Sprache gewinnt die Erfahrungstranszendenz ihre eigentümliche Objektivität.'

blessing, without doubt. It is a magnificent language to play in. Acting, pretending, simulating, ironizing, imagining, joking, singing, praying all go very well in it. And of course story-telling also. What for instance would a novel like *The Name of the Rose* be without the very thick language of theism? Eco manages to show up the traces of this language virtually everywhere. Due to these traces the movement of intentional transcendence can be triggered at any moment. Thus I think that the heritage of theism guards us from the enthroning of thinness, i.e. from a culture which ignores system- atically and on a large scale that which Ryle makes clear with his example of *le Penseur*, namely that what *le Penseur* is 'thinly' doing, e.g. producing *sotto voce* words, phrases and sentences, '*must* have a "thicker" descrip- tion.'[54] About this thinness could be said much more. If I am not mistaken, philosophical analyses of modern culture converge in the diagnosis of a thinning down, a loss of substance with its unfathomable depth. I leave all that aside here but there is one more remark to be made. One could also characterize this tendency of our culture (if it is one), in a far echo of E. Cassirer's terminology,[55] as functionalization. Then it is to be stressed that the counterweight that the language of theism provides for this tendency cannot itself be functionalized. Theism or at least its language is not the kind of thing that could be appreciated because of its functionality. The point is that this language is a real blessing, that is a good which is not a means, a good which in a sublime sense of the word is useless.[56]

Enjoying the blessing
But how can the blessing of the heritage of theism be enjoyed without making the metaphysical claims implied in theism? *Hereditas pro parte adiri nequit*. This is the problem I want to face in conclusion of this paper. I should like to say two things about it. I do not conceal the fact that there is a huge tension between these two things.

The first of them concerns the *ceteris paribus* proviso I made above on p. 138. As long as metaphysical, i.e. existential claims are implied, theist

54. Ryle, *op.cit.*, p. 478 (italics mine). Ryle continues interestingly: 'What he is "thinly" doing must be in one or more ways and at one or more removes an intention- parasite.' And again: 'Intention-parasites may pyramid.'
55. E. Cassirer, *Substanzbegriff und Funktionsbegriff. Untersuchungen über die Grundfrage der Erkentniskritik*, Berlin 1910.
56. Compare Klaus-M.Kodalle, *Die Eroberung des Nutzlosen. Kritik des Wunschdenkens und der Zweckrationalität im Anschluß an Kierkegaard*, Paderborn 1988.

religions remain on a par with theism as rational belief and share the destiny of the latter, it was said there. But by now the moment might have come to remove this proviso and to focus on the difference which is relevant here.

It is the difference between making a metaphysical claim and echoing it. Making a claim can be done in many different ways: you may whisper it, or wrap it up in curlicues and flourishes, or merely signal it without words. In such cases it may be necessary to make inquiries. But then the matter will be settled: if the claim is indeed made, it will be affirmed upon inquiry. In this sense the theist, as I defined him, is indeed making metaphysical claims. Willingly and knowingly he assumes the pretension that his belief in a person without a body etc. is rational — i.e. on a par with objective (philosophical or even scientific) knowledge — and that it is even true.

Let us take on the other hand the example of Menno ter Braak. In vindicating the discipline of Christianity, he received the remnants of the language Christianity had developed in order to achieve this discipline, and therewith he consciously took in the metaphysical claims implied in this language. Is this to say that he also made these claims? Clearly not. He plainly rejected them. He opted for a secular way of life and thought, even in his capacity of 'new Christian'.

Now the point is — under this first heading — that this is possible and that consequently the distinction under discussion is valid. Ter Braak and kindred spirits cannot simply be said to be victims of delusion. Here I would wish to express my reservation with regard to a certain use of the idea of an ubiquitous metaphysics. It might be argued that the echoing of a metaphysical claim is not really different from the making of it because the distinction between knowing and willing and not-knowing and not-willing is not tenable. Reference might for instance be made to Derrida's magnificent text 'Préjugés. Devant la loi'[57] in which the freedom of judgment which is necessarily implied in such a distinction is shown to be founded on prejudice. Judgment under all its forms — attitude, operation, statement — is conditioned by a pre-judice which is absolutely heterogeneous to its rules, to the rules, that is, of any possible judgment. The law by virtue of which judgment is performed is not there, is not at our disposal: rather we are 'before' it, just as in Kafka's tale. In this way the idea of an original and inescapable 'guilt' towards metaphysics can be made very tempting indeed.

57. J. Derrida, 'Préjugés. Devant la loi', in J. Derrida et al., *La faculté de juger*, Paris 1985, pp. 87-139.

But this does not take the edge off the distinction. There is quite a large gap between our debt to this (quasi)-transcendental kind of prejudice and our would-be debt to the pretty solid and positive existential claim of theism. Derrida's negative theology[58] does nothing to bridge this gap, quite the contrary.

If, then, the distinction under discussion should not be abandoned too soon it might be applied to the field of religious belief also. Whatever holds for the form of life of the completely secularized 'new Christian' Ter Braak, why should it not hold too for a worshipping form of Christianity? As a matter of fact, Christian faith (as well as theist faiths in general) is used to claim the objective truth of the knowledge it embodies. But why should it be incapable of desisting from that claim? Why should it not be in a position to say the prayers, sing the hymns and tell the tales it has always cherished, just for the joy and the pleasure and the relief and the edification of performing them? It might well be that in faithfulness to the *dictum* the *res* itself is given. And I do not see why in this non-metaphysical vein it would not be possible even to develop some sort of theology. Why should reflective faith, instead of constantly accounting for the rationality of incredible existential claims, not be able to swerve round them? Why could it not step to a higher sophistication-level and start playing with that echo, modulating, counterfeiting, quoting, displacing, interpreting, hiding and seeking it?

The second thing I want to say as to the enjoyment of the blessing is this. At least as far as the apex of the heritage of theism is concerned there is no escape from metaphysics. This apex consists in the word 'God'. I simply do not see how we could use this word or even how it could cross our minds[59] without getting entangled in metaphysics, i.e. in that general idea of what there is which has been settled in the 25 centuries of Western philosophy. Here we can learn a lesson from Heidegger. As is well known Heidegger announced in his earlier writings the programme of an *Überwindung* [surmounting] of metaphysics. But later on he found that this term is too straightforward and he replaced it by *Verwindung* which means not only 'surmounting' but also 'coiling'. Metaphysics cannot be undone; the *Schritt zurück* [step back] cannot mean that we go back on it. Metaphysics rather is

---

58. Compare especially J. Derrida, 'Comment ne pas parler', in *Psyché. Inventions de l'autre*, Paris 1987, pp. 535-95.
59. Compare E. Levinas, *De Dieu qui vient à l'idée*, Paris 1982.

the background or even the 'partner'[60] in the face of which philosophical thought has to go its way. It is hard not to attach this sense also to the new term 'postmetaphysical', even though this interpretation goes against the *mens auctoris*.[61] What comes after metaphysics is indeed metaphysics again.

But perhaps there are examples of honourable entanglement in metaphysics. I would think then especially of Th. Adorno and M. Theunissen.[62] For the sake of brevity I limit myself to pointing to one idea of the former. In the last chapter of his *Negative Dialektik*, entitled 'Meditations on Metaphysics', Adorno states that, in order to be truthful, thinking should, at least nowadays — i.e. after Auschwitz — think also against itself and match itself with the extreme which retreats from conceptualization. It should, that is, confront itself with the 'other-than-concept', with the non-identical. In doing so it takes over the task of metaphysics, the knowledge of the Absolute, which in the last couple of centuries has fallen in a process of marginalization. It was expelled from its institutional housing; it was fatally thrust into the realm of the apocryphal; it had to flee also from (positive) religion into profanity; at present it is leading a homeless and unsightly existence. It has been overthrown, but that thinking which confronts itself with the non-identical, Adorno says in the last line of his book, keeps solidarity with it in the moment of its downfall.

I take this word 'solidarity' in its strong original sense, as joint and several liability. The thinking of the non-identical takes the place of the dethroned. The question then arises in what sense the heritage of theism which at least in its apex is entangled in metaphysics can be said to be an enjoyable blessing. Is it not the gravity and mourning of deposition instead of joy that sets the tone here? One part of the answer to this question might be found in the *Historisches Wörterbuch der Philosophie*, in the article 'Genuß'. There I learned that this word has meanings other than that of cheerful consumerism which is dominant today. In J.G. Herder for example, at the end of the 18th century, *Genuß* is seen to underlie the whole way in which the subject appropriates his world; it means the original opening up of reality. Thus existence itself is *Genuß*. Quite so: the blessing of the heritage of theism is not the kind of thing we can have in an external manner,

60. Compare H.-G. Gadamer, *Das Erbe Hegels*, Frankfurt 1979, p. 84.
61. Compare Jürgen Habermas, *Nachmetaphysisches Denken*, Frankfurt 1988.
62. M. Theunissen, *Negative Theologie der Zeit*, Frankfurt 1991.

keeping ourselves out of it.[63] That this involvement must needs make us feel jolly is not at all implied. The other part of the answer I find in Adorno. The gravity of despair knows its own strange bliss and this momentary bliss is *pars pro toto*. I cannot resist quoting the context:

The disturbed and damaged course of the world is, as in Kafka, incommensurable [with concept] also in the sense of its pure meaninglessness and blindness. It cannot be stringently constructed according to these principles. It contradicts the attempt of the despairing consciousness to posit despair as something absolute. The course of the world is not absolutely closed (...) All traces of the other in it are fragile; all happiness is distorted due to its revocability. Nonetheless in the faults which belie identity the beings are pervaded with the constantly broken promises of that other. Each happiness is a fragment of the entire happiness (...).[64]

III. By way of conclusion

God does not reign over the spirit of all people. Many of them, and among them the most learned, the best, the wisest, reject and deny him, as a useless hypothesis, as a sort of crutch that mankind, finally recovered, would not longer need. Yet I have some doubt that this idea of God can ever be torn loose, up to the root, up to the heart, from the restlessness of man. Science, morals, history can do very well without God. It is humans that cannot. Not so much to understand but to dream. To suffer and to rejoice. To commemorate and to hope.

It is under the look of a dream that I write these pages. And when they will be

---

63. *Historisches Wörterbuch der Philosophie* (ed. J. Ritter), vol. III, p. 319.
64. Th. Adorno, *Negative Dialektik*, Frankfurt 1966, p. 356: '...Denken müsse, um wahr zu sein, heute jedenfalls, auch gegen sich selbst denken. Mißt es sich nicht an dem Äußersten, das dem Begriff entflieht...'; p. 395: '....Metaphysik, als Wissen vom Absoluten...'; p. 390: 'Alle metaphysischen [Spekulationen] jedoch werden fatal ins Apokryphe gestoßen.'; p. 392: '...ob Metaphysik allein im Geringsten und Schäbigsten überlebt, im Stand vollendeter Unscheinbarkeit...'; p. 398: 'Solches Denken ist solidarisch mit Metaphysik im Augenblick ihres Sturzes.'; p. 393-4: 'Der verstörte und beschädigte Weltlauf ist, wie bei Kafka, inkommensurabel auch in dem Sinn seiner reinen Sinnlosigkeit und Blindheit, nicht stringent zu konstruieren nach deren Prinzip. Er widerstreitet dem Versuch verzweifelten Bewußtseins, Verzweiflung als Absolutes zu setzen. Nicht absolut geschlossen ist der Weltlauf (...) So hinfällig in ihm alle Spuren des Anderen sind; so sehr alles Glück durch seine Widerruflichkeit entstellt ist, das Seiende wird doch in den Brüchen, welche die Identität Lügen strafen, durchsetzt von den stets wieder gebrochenen Versprechungen jenes Anderen. Jegliches Glück ist Fragment des ganzen Glücks...'

ready this dream will have taken a shape. In the beginning was God. And then, step by step, his own creation will have repressed God. It will have found him oppressive, ridiculous, absurd, entirely useless and superfluous, truly pernicious. It will have reduced him to the humiliating status of one of those child's dreams that we shake off in the awakening (...) in order to pass on to the serious things: money, power, revolution, science. I have resumed on my own account this feeble child's dream. I have not said: 'This is God. He has such and such figure, and a beard. It is him. Listen to him. Tremble. Obey.' I say: 'The dreams are ideas. And the ideas are real.' At the end of this book God will be an idea, a memory, a hope. In my modest way I shall have recreated God. That is merely just conpensation. Because God has created me.

(...) I believe it, I feel it, I know it, I am sure: I have been borne by some-thing. By what? Who will tell me? By time, by history, by the whole of man-kind, by the laws of nature. It is all this that I call God. Vocabulary is free and I have a generous mind: I have been created by God.

And I bless him for having created me. For having let me be. For having permitted me to deny him. For permitting me to sing for him and to be, after so many others (...) the herald of his glory and his omnipotence.

(...) I wrote somewhere that I was a sceptic. That is true: I do not believe much, in fact almost nothing. Or perhaps even nothing at all. I do not believe in myself nor in others. I believe that the moral values, the societies, the forms of art, the political and intellectual systems, all these human constructions will do nothing but go by and are not worth a jot. I believe only in time, in history and in God. Because God is time. He is all the rest too, by the way, because he is all at once. But, at any rate, time. He is the absence of time, and at the same time, time.

We — I mean mankind — fall short of earnestness to a bewildering extent. We are dealing with everything except the whole, I mean God. I do not believe anything. Take all away: I believe in what remains. Due to a marvellous paradox which is the key of this book, if you take all away, what remains is all. The first whole, that is the details, the anecdotes, the futility of knowledge, the frivolity of power. The second whole is all. It is God. And it is this book about which I am prepared to say anything except that it can be modest. Lord! Bless it! And that thy holy name be blessed.

So here I write, this book, under the look of God who is nothing else than my dreams. And my dreams are from God. And all that I am is from God. And all that you are is from God. And when you read these lines while I am already elsewhere you will wonder perhaps where this book has been before it was written. Well, it was in God. (...) And when there is nobody any more to read it, it still will be in God's bosom. And because it is not finished yet, it still is in the bosom of God.

There is, I admit, something fairly comic in seeing that God through me glorifies his holy name. What do you want? That is the way it is. I cannot change it. I shall not speak about myself. I shall only say that God bloweth where he listeth. He blows upon Karl Marx, upon the clochard around the corner, upon Caesar, upon Galileo (...) He blew upon Lucifer. He blew upon Judas. He may also blow upon me.[65]

---

65. Jean d'Ormesson, *Dieu, sa vie, son oeuvre*, Paris 1980, pp. 113-16.

After 'Post–Theism'

Christoph Schwöbel

Our outlooks on whatever there is are, at least before the *visio beatifica*, irreducibly particular and perspectival. Even when we share important elements in our background, our occupations, our beliefs, our convictions, our intellectual and cultural heritage, our respective standpoints, our ways of perceiving, interpreting and organizing matters on hand and our notions of what these matters are, are in important respects person-relative, shot through with our particular personal characteristics of interacting with one another and with the world. Yet, in order to communicate, to cooperate and to coexist as relational and social beings we have to discover and establish some common ground in our use of signs in order to interpret and to organize our interaction with reality, however different our perspectives on and conceptions of 'reality' may be. The diversity and personal particularity of our specific perspectives of action and interaction are what makes life interesting and rich, enabling conversation, dispute and agreement, conflict and joint action. Only if it were to be interpreted in terms of a rigid linguistic, epistemological or even ontological perspectivism for which the only non-perspectival universal truth is the incommensurability of relative standpoints, means of interpretation and ultimately of reality itself, would the variety of our perspectives on whatever there is become, at least, boring and, at most, life-threatening.

Philosophical discussions are no exception. They are only interesting if the partners in dialogue present different perspectives on the topic under discussion, but they can only be productive if there exists enough common ground for disagreement and perhaps even agreement. Ideally, one might wish for the logical complementarity of perspectives in philosophical discussion, so that thesis and antithesis, criticism and anti-criticism, position and opposition can be presented in tidy symmetry. Hegelians might even hope that a creative synthesis, sublating the original opposition might emerge as the result of such a dispute. In ideal circumstances, Professor Adriaanse's stimulating and provocative critique of 'traditional theism' would be answered by a defence of traditional theism by one of its exponents, and his programmatic prospect of philosophy of religion 'after theism' would be answered by an equally programmatic statement on 'The Future of Theism'. My contribution is only a poor substitute for the ideal scenario. Unfortunately, my perspective on theism is, albeit different from Professor Adriaanse's, not its logical complement, since my understanding of 'theism' differs from his, and my view of the future of philosophy of religion after theism is also different from his suggestions. The question is whether we share enough common ground to make the difference of perspectives interesting. However, hopes for a synthesis would appear to be premature.

I. The Critique of Theism Revisited

Professor Adriaanse's paper starts by expressing the conviction 'that theism in its traditional form has lost its credibility'.[1] In consequence, the first part of the paper reads, if I may be allowed the flippancy, in part like a declaration of bankruptcy on behalf of a third party and in part like an obituary. In philosophy and in the history of ideas both are somewhat risky pronouncements. Declarations of bankruptcy might always be answered by the third party concerned demonstrating that their business is far from insolvent. Obituaries might find their response in the statement 'Reports of my death are highly exaggerated', issued on behalf of theism by one of its representatives, indicating that theism is alive and well and residing at Oxford.

The comparison with those rather different genres brings out an ambivalence in the reasons Professor Adriaanse offers for his conviction that 'theism in its traditional form has lost its credibility'. On Adriaanse's analysis, 'credibility', it seems, is established through the three criteria of coherence, probability and plausibility. The first two groups of reasons, summarized under the headings of coherence and probability, refer to logical and epistemological criteria, to the question whether claims expressing belief in God as 'a person without a body (i.e. a spirit) who is eternal, free, able to do everything, knows everything, is perfectly good, is the proper object of human worship and obedience, the creator und sustainer of the universe'[2] are internally coherent (i.e. not self-contradictory) and whether claims about the existence of such a God can be shown to be true. The application of these criteria, in the sense in which Professor Adriaanse employs them, does not depend on a specific socio-historical context. The application of the first

1. Above, p. 130.
2. R. Swinburne, *The Coherence of Theism*, Oxford 1977, p. 1.

criterion indicates whether in stating a specific claim certain syntactic and semantic rules have been observed, i.e. whether the statement is logically and semantically well formed and thus succeeds in stating a claim. The logical and semantic rules which define coherence in this sense are not dependent on such criteria as 'cognitive consonance, solidity of plausibility structures etc.' which are themselves dependent on a particular socio-historical context. The second criterion, probability, is introduced to assess 'the inductive evidence of a God conceived of in a theistic way'[3] and is applied to a specific form of arguing that the hypothesis that there is a God whose intentional action has brought the actual universe about is more probable than a rival hypothesis that there is no further explanation of the complex universe, given the evidence consisting of the existence of this universe and our background knowledge concerning the states of affairs in such a universe. The way in which Adriaanse criticizes this form of Richard Swinburne's recasting of the cosmological argument by rehearsing J.L. Mackie's criticism of it concerns the logical form of this particular C-inductive argument and its application to claims about the existence of a creator God. This criticism does not refer to changed states of affairs which would constitute new evidence or to a different description of our background knowledge. There is nothing to suggest that a changed state of affairs and, consequently, different knowledge of this state of affairs has rendered the argument invalid. The application of both criteria suggests that Professor Adriaanse's claim is, in fact, stronger than the tensed form in which he expresses his conviction that theism in its traditional form 'has lost its credibility'. On the basis of the first two criteria Adriaanse introduces, theism never possessed credibility, if credibility is seen as defined by coherence and probability, and, consequently, could not lose it. The criticism is, in fact, as strong as W. Stegmüller's summary of Mackie's position, which Adriaanse quotes, and which suggests, that on the basis of Mackie's reasoning 'the monotheistic religions known to us are based on an existential presupposition which is indispensable to them but which is presumably false'.[4] This strong conclusion has, however, problematical implications for the overall strategy of Professor Adriaanse's paper: if theism is and always has been incoherent and with regard to the probability of its existential claims false, then there is

3. Above, p. 134.
4. Above, p. 11.

nothing to inherit, neither as a 'charge' nor as a 'blessing', apart from a self-contradiction and a falsehood.

The third criterion, plausibility, is, as Professor Adriaanse emphasizes, of a different kind. It refers to the socio-historical process, to the changes which occur in the plausibility structure of societies. It presupposes the view, programmatically developed in the sociology of knowledge, that beliefs are socio-historical realities which have a history of acceptance, rejection or indifference in particular cultural scenarios that are open to empirical investigation. There are good reasons for not ignoring such empirical findings in the philosophy of religion, although this has the consequence that the validity or, at least, the relevance of certain philosophical theories becomes dependent on particular findings of, for instance, sociological research. Professor Adriaanse refers for the validation of his claim that theism has lost its credibility to the so-called secularization thesis developed by some sociologists of religion in the 1950s and 1960s. This thesis, which I will discuss in a little more detail below, describes according to Adriaanse 'the crumbling or even the collapse of the religious plausibility structure' so that '(t)he primary determinant of meaning [(a theistically conceived) God] is inevitably swept along in its fall'.[5] If this is correct and theism in its traditional form is indeed dead, then the tasks of philosophers are somewhat restricted. They may as historians of philosophy record the demise of theism, discuss its possible causes and engage in reflections about how to dispose of the legacy, but to argue against it would not only appear as a flagrant violation of the rule *de mortuis nil nisi bene*, but would also seem slightly futile — unless theism belongs to the group of philosophical theories which one might dub the 'living dead' (like Platonism, realism and idealism) which seem to haunt philosophers especially assiduously after they have been pronounced dead and obituaries have been published. This third criterion is the only one of the three criteria which meets the requirements of Professor Adriaanse's tensed statement that theism in its traditional form 'has lost its credibility'; but if this is correct, then why offer arguments that it should be so?

So far I have only looked at the three different groups of arguments Professor Adriaanse offers and have indicated some of the implications that follow if they are successful. But are they? Let us therefore look at the three arguments in a little more detail.

5. Adriaanse, above, p. 139.

I.1 Coherence and Analogy

Professor Adriaanse's first argument for what he calls the 'incredibility of theism', the test of the coherence of theistic statements, concentrates on the problem of analogy. His argument is introduced in the form of three 'doubts' which he employs to voice the general suspicion of the incoherence of theism. He exemplifies them all from Richard Swinburne's *The Coherence of Theism*. The first is the observation that the term 'person' is applied to God analogically, something that Swinburne freely admits and considers necessary. Adriaanse illustrates his doubt with a remark by Anthony Kenny that 'The minds we know are embodied minds.'[6] The second is the observation that this concept is at the centre of a whole cluster of concepts of intentional agency, a fact, which Adriaanse interprets in such a sense that '(a)ll these other terms are affected by this recourse to analogy'.[7] The third point is the suspicion that because of the central status of the concept of person in theism analogical use of language cannot be contained so that 'the analogical tincture pervades all discourse of God'.[8] The 'decisive point' is again expressed by a quotation from Swinburne: 'Once we give analogical senses to words, proofs of coherence or incoherence become very difficult.'[9] This remark Adriaanse regards as 'an understatement' and states that '(i)n reality the question as to the coherence of theism loses its hold very soon.'[10]

The problem of the analogical use of language in statements about God is one of the most extensively discussed issues in philosophical theology. One of the most illuminating recent accounts of analogy is the one by J.F. Ross in his *Portraying Analogy*[11] which Richard Swinburne employs in his recent *Revelation. From Metaphor to Analogy*.[12] Ross works with the notion of a 'predicate scheme' which refers to the meaning-relevant possible substitutions of a word W in a given sentence which leaves the sentence itself well formed. Meaning-relevant are such substitutions which have connections of meaning with the original word like synonyms, antonyms, contraries, determinates of the same determinable etc. We can now, with Swinburne, define univocal, analogical and equivocal uses of words through the notion of a predicate

6. Adriaanse, above, p. 134.
7. *Loc.cit.*
8. Above, p. 134.
9. Swinburne, *op.cit.*, p.61.
10. Adriaanse, above, p. 134.
11. J.F. Ross, *Portraying Analogy*, Cambridge 1981.
12. Richard Swinburne, *Revelation. From Metaphor to Analogy*, Oxford 1992, pp. 40ff.

scheme: 'Words have the same meaning, are being used univocally, if they have the same predicate scheme (...); similar meaning, are being used analogically with respect to each other, if they have overlapping predicate schemes; and are equivocal with respect to each other if their predicate schemes do not overlap.'[13] From this notion of a predicate scheme it is not difficult to point to syntactic rules in the form of a general statement of the conditions that govern the use of a given word W and to formulate semantic rules pointing to correct and incorrect cases of the application of W to particular objects or kinds of objects. It is also quite clear that the use of the predicate scheme for successfully analysing analogical uses of words only functions successfully in a given realm of discourse if this analogical use can be compared to univocal and equivocal uses, uses of synonymity or near-synonymity, and uses of clear equivocity where we have no overlap of the respective predicate schemes of two words. By comparison to the limiting cases of univocity and equivocity we can establish the degree of analogy that obtains in a given case. This is important since the analogical use of words changes — as Adriaanse rightly points out — the inferences that can be drawn from a statement containing analogically employed words to the extent that some inferences that can be drawn from the identically construed statements in which the same words are used univocally are no longer true. The predicate scheme gives a good indication where to expect changes concerning the possible correct inferences from a statement containing analogically employed words.

There is no good reason based on semantic or syntactic observations to suppose that all theistic language has to be used analogically. First of all, the discourse of theism comprises far more forms of language than only uni-vocal, equivocal and analogical uses (and this is, strictly speaking a problem of predication), but also metaphorical, allegorical, parabolical uses and so on. Secondly, where the suggestion has been made that all theistic language is to be interpreted analogically as (perhaps) in Thomas Aquinas' case or in J.F. Ross' thesis that analogy is the 'rule of meaning for religious language'[14]

---

13. Swinburne, *op.cit.*, p. 40.
14. Cf. J.F. Ross, 'Analogy as a Rule of Meaning of Religious Language', *International Philosophical Quarterly* vol. 1, 1961, pp. 468-502. Swinburne (*op.cit.*, p. 153, n. 9) points out that Ross allows that words are used in religious discourse which are either univocal or equivocal in the senses defined by the application of the predicate scheme.

this proposal has usually been justified by general metaphysical considerations and covers, as in Aquinas' case, uses which would not be seen as analogical according to the criteria mentioned above. For Aquinas, for instance, univocal predication is only possible with regard to entities belonging to the same genus, the ascription of meaning is ultimately based on our experience of sensible objects, and some forms he classifies as analogical uses like the *analogia attributionis* would on the above rule have to be counted as clearly equivocal. I do not suppose that Professor Adriaanse's agreement with Aquinas expressed in the statement that 'the analogical tincture pervades all discourse of God'[15] implies that he subscribes to the same metaphysical and epistemological views which form the background of Aquinas' thesis of the comprehensive range of analogical uses in God-talk. Thirdly, one can argue that some of the 'oddities' of God-talk arise not because the meaning of predicates are stretched analogically, but because they are predicated of God. Duns Scotus' view that terms denoting divine attributes are predicated of God univocally does not commit us to the view that the predications in questions are therefore not different at all. As Swinburne, who shares Scotus' view on this point, shows, there are real differences. Most theists would claim that 'God is wise' entails 'God is essentially wise', whereas 'Socrates is wise' does not entail 'Socrates is essentially wise'. Swinburne explains that 'the difference does not arise because "wise" has different meanings when applied to God and when applied to Socrates. Rather, the entailment arises because of the meaning of the word "God". "God" is a word used to denote a kind of being who cannot but be wise... the contributions of "wise" to the meaning of "God is wise" are just the same.'[16] The predicate scheme of 'wise' does, in this case, not require analogical expansion. One could develop that argument by showing that the differences are not only introduced through the semantics of the word 'God', but also have to be considered in their pragmatic dimension, i.e. by reflection on what people do when they predicate attributes of God in a specific context.

Professor Adriaanse's thesis that ultimately all God-talk in theism is infected by the virus of analogy is not offered as a thesis concerning the language, but in order to suggest that the analogical use of language

15. Adriaanse, above, p. 134.
16. Swinburne, *op.cit.*, p. 152.

somehow undermines the coherence of theism. He agrees with Swinburne who writes: 'Once we give analogical senses to words, proofs of coherence or incoherence become very difficult.'[17] However, this sentence does not seem to offer support for Adriaanse's view that the analogical use of language threatens the coherence of God-talk in theism. What it does state is that *proofs* of coherence *or incoherence* become difficult, because the truth conditions of statements containing analogically used words may change and it may therefore be difficult to point to circumstances which would demonstrate the correctness or incorrectness of their claims. It is claimed not that theistic language becomes incoherent, but that *proofs* of coherence become difficult. However, a given statement does not become incoherent because we cannot offer any direct proof of its coherence. There may be other strategies to provide an indirect proof of coherence by pointing to parallel cases. The point, however, is that proofs of *incoherence* are just as difficult as proofs of coherence. They would require unveiling a self-contradiction contained in the theistic statement, and whatever analogy is, it is not a self-contradiction. The same circumstances which make proofs of coherence difficult make proofs of incoherence just as difficult.

Furthermore, if Professor Adriaanse's thesis that the analogical use of language threatens the coherence of theism is correct, this must apply to all areas of discourse where analogy is used. If the thesis is asserted in this general form, this would mean that large areas of science, especially the most sophisticated forms of modern science, would also have to be incoherent. As Mary Hesse has shown in her *Models and Analogies in Science*,[18] modern science is in its theory formation dependent on the development of models which are based on the detailed comparison of 'positive analogy', 'negative analogy' and 'neutral analogy' as the presupposition for the coherent interpretation of experimental data. The case of science is especially relevant for Professor Adriaanse's argument since he claims that 'science investigates how things are'.[19] If it is true that the use of analogy threatens the coherence of any discourse, the fundamental choice he postulates for philosophy where philosophy 'cannot both sustain theism and agree with the economy-based, autonomous, thoroughly secular world-perspective

17. *The Coherence of Theism*, p. 61.
18. Mary Hesse, *Models and Analogies in Science*, London 1963.
19. Adriaanse, above, p. 131.

of science'[20] is merely a choice between two forms of incoherence.

Professor Adriaanse is right in focussing attention on the use of the concept of the person in theistic discourse because this is indeed one of the points where theism, in some of its varieties, takes a different route from orthodox Christianity where God is interpreted not as a person but as three persons in one substance. Proponents of unipersonal theism and of Christian trinitarian thought would, however, agree that it is necessary to assert personal relations of God and to talk about God in terms of personal agency, and that it is necessary to qualify personal concepts in their application to God. The use of the term 'person' is indeed one of the cases where Swinburne would concede that there are good reasons for an analogical use of the word. The reasons for this are, however, different from Adriaanse's, who seems to restrict the literal use of 'person' to embodied agents. The reason for Swinburne is that personal identity has to be defined independently of the gain or loss of certain abilities. In the case of the God of theism, God possesses attributes like omniscience and omnipotence as essential attributes which cannot be lost or gained, so that it is this difference which requires the analogical use of 'person'.[21] A further step that is recommended by Swinburne and others is to develop the analogical use of the concept of person into a systematic model and to qualify this model by the introduction of a second model which brings out those aspects which are not covered by the person model. (Swinburne suggests the use of the model of a law of nature or a supreme form that could never lose its powers and is thus able to develop the view of God's perfections as essential perfections[22]). One can argue that the rules for the use of these models and the criteria of their compatibility are not logically different from the two model situation in the sciences, which has been exhaustively discussed with regard to the wave/particle models of light and can be developed to a very high standard of coherence. The employment of a similar strategy does not automatically make the discourse of theism incoherent.[23] A refutation of this claim would require to show that the use of analogies and models in science inevitably

20. Above, p. 139.
21. Cf. Swinburne, *The Coherence of Theism*, ch. 14.
22. *Revelation*, p. 156f.
23. I have argued for the complementarity of the model of personal agency and of that of a transcendental relation in *God: Action and Revelation*, Kampen 1992, pp. 23-45, esp. 36ff.

generates incoherence and has therefore to be purged from science altogether, which would leave us with a very primitive form of science indeed. We can conclude that there do not seem to be good reasons for supposing that the analogical use of words in the discourse of theism leads to the kind of incoherence which would render theism 'incredible'.

I.2. Probability and Ultimate Explanations

We can deal with Professor Adriaanse's second point, the application of the criterion of probability, much quicker since it concerns a far more specific problem and does not have such wide-ranging implications as the claims about the connection between analogy and incoherence that we have just discussed. The target of Professor Adriaanse's criticism is one particular form of arguing for the existence of a creator God. It is characterized by a set of presuppositions which have not only been criticized by anti-theists such as Mackie, but also by many theists. Among these presuppositions is the suggestion to analyze 'God exists' as a contingent proposition, so that God's existence is a brute fact which is inexplicable. God's existence is thus interpreted as the 'ultimate brute fact' which explains everything, but cannot itself be explained. The contingent thus has primacy over the necessary in God, although God's essence can nevertheless be interpreted as an eternal essence. This corresponds to Swinburne's understanding of an 'ultimate explanation' which posits a set of initial conditions and laws of behaviour which entails all states of affairs in the actual universe (and so functions as their explanation), but which cannot itself be explained.[24] Other proponents of theism have objected to this view and have restated the traditional view that God should be understood as necessarily existent and as the source of all possible and actual beings, and that the contingent attributes of God must necessarily be based on the necessary properties, so that God as the wholly self-explanatory being is the ultimate explanation of everything other than God.[25] The notion of ultimate explanation which can be employed in such a conception can incorporate modal elements of sufficient causal explanations, and would have to qualify the notion 'personal explanation' heavily because of the 'kind' of being God is on such an understanding. These other forms of theism are not touched by the type of criticism Professor Adriaanse offers and can even agree with the criticism that Swinburne's postulate of a

24. Cf. R. Swinburne, *The Existence of God*, Oxford 1979, 92ff.
25. Keith Ward, *Rational Theology and the Creativity of God*, Oxford 1982.

simple ultimate brute fact is counter-intuitive and has less probability than the hypothesis of a complex set of brute facts, such as a complex universe. The point is, that even if the theist were to concede Mackie's criticism of Swinburne's argument, it would only render one particular strategy of defending the claim of the existence of God problematical, but would not provide good reasons to conclude 'that the monotheistic religions known to us are based on an existential assumption which is indispensable to them but which is presumably false'.[26] In order to substantiate this claim, a decisive disproof of the existence of God would have to be offered. For postulating the 'incredibility of theism' by questioning one particular form of arguing for the existence of God is not enough.

I.3 Plausibility and Secularization

The third point is arguably the one to which Professor Adriaanse attaches the most weight. He draws attention to the point that beliefs are always embedded in the concrete biography of an individual and the changes in the socio-historical context. This applies also to theism: '(T)heism is to be considered as embedded or incarnated in a religious tradition. It cannot be detached from this tradition.'[27] Adriaanse even claims that it constitutes the organizing principle of a religious tradition, its 'primary determinant of meaning'. The thesis is that the secularization process in which 'sectors of society and culture are removed from the domination of religious institutions and symbols'[28] leads to 'the collapse of the religious plausibility structure' where the primary determinant of meaning, now described as 'a (theistically conceived) God' is 'swept along in this fall'. Sociological theories like the secularization thesis are empirical hypotheses which are open to empirical confirmation and disconfirmation. Here I would claim that the general form of the secularization thesis to which Adriaanse refers and which enjoyed considerable popularity in the 1960s has not stood the test of empirical confirmation. The situation is more ambiguous than the thesis allows. In Berger's form the secularization thesis referred in any case primarily to the fact that the Christian religious tradition could no longer serve as the integrative framework, 'the sacred canopy', for the different sectors of society

26. W. Stegmüller as quoted by Adriaanse, above, p. 141.
27. Adriaanse, above, p. 138.
28. P.L. Berger, as quoted by Adriaanse, above, p. 138.

and culture in North American and Western European societies. This aspect of the thesis may be correct. However, Western societies, and of course not only Western societies, have since seen the rise of religious influence on societies to an extent which had seemed highly improbable in the 1960s.[29] This phenomenon comprises such divergent aspects as the rise of different forms of religious fundamentalism, the growing influence of non-Christian religious traditions in the life of Western societies, the astonishing growth of new religious movements and the increasing political influence of religiously motivated groups.[30] What has been decisively falsified is the corollary of Berger's thesis that 'the secularizing potency of capitalistic-industrial rationalization is not only self-perpetuating but self-aggrandizing'[31], and Berger himself who is among the foremost sociologists of religion who have charted these processes, has in the process modified his original hypothesis.[32] The changes are indeed astonishing and challenge us to change our perceptions of the presence of the religious dimension in industrialized capitalist societies. Church attendance in the United States, sociologists tell us, is at present higher than ever before in the country's history, and the highest increases are recorded in the big cities, seen by sociologists thirty years ago as the centres of secularizing tendencies. The growth of Protestant (in most cases Pentecostal) churches in South America makes the European Reformation appear a minor incident by comparison. This is not to deny that there are significant secularizing tendencies in North American and Western European societies. But it challenges the view that the secularization thesis is sufficiently supported by empirical evidence to claim that secularization is a uniform trend which leads to the collapse of religious traditions and to

29. Cf. Daniel Bell, Return of the Sacred? The Argument on the Future of Religion, *British Journal of Sociology* vol. 38, 1977, pp. 419-49; Charles Glock and Robert Bellah (eds.), *The New Religious Consciousness*, Berkeley 1976; Andrew Greely, *Unsecular Man*, New York 1975 and Richard John Neuhaus (ed.), *Unsecular America*, Grand Rapids 1986.
30. Cf. Erling Jorstadt, *Evangelicals in the White House: The Cultural Maturation of Born Again Christianity 1960-1981*, New York 1981; cf. also Richard John Neuhaus and Michael Cormartie (eds.), *Piety and Politics: Evangelicals and Fundamentalists Confront the World*, Washington 1989.
31. Berger as quoted by Adriaanse, above, p. 138.
32. Cf. Peter L.Berger, *The Heretical Imperative*, New York 1979; on Berger's development see: James Davison Hunter and Stephen C. Ainsley (eds.), *Making Sense of Modern Times: Peter L. Berger and the Vision of Interpretive Sociology*, London 1986.

the dominance of 'the economy-based, autonomous, thoroughly secular world-perspective of science'. As a candidate for empirically disproving the credibility of theism the secularization thesis has to be discounted. Its significance can only be assessed within a wider framework of assessing the different and sometimes contradictory tendencies that characterise the religious situation of modern industrial societies.

I have discussed the reasons adduced in support of Professor Adriaanse's conviction that theism has lost its credibility in order to show that they offer only questionable support for the claim that philosophical discussion has inevitably and irrevocably moved beyond the discussion of theism. A declaration of bankruptcy seems to be open to the challenge that theism is, with regard to its capacity of refuting its critics, far from insolvent. An obituary seems to be equally premature, since it would seem that we cannot presuppose the demise of theism in our reflections on the future of philosophical engagement with religious traditions. Theism remains (whether we like it or not) a live option and philosophers of religion cannot be excused from engaging in debate with its representatives.

II. Theism Redefined

We have so far presupposed the term 'theism' in the sense in which Adriaanse employs the concept on the basis of Swinburne's definition. Adriaanse even extends this use by claiming that 'theism' is the common denominator or even the genus of Christian, Jewish and Islamic faith, so that his criticism directly affects Christian, Jewish and Muslim theologies unless they are programmatically post-theistic like Adriaanse's own conception. Along with this extension of the range of application of the term goes a subtle shift of the meaning of theism, insofar as Adriaanse now applies the term to all forms of faith which state a relationship to an 'object', a 'really existing something or somebody to whom it is referring'[33] and which therefore imply ontological claims. All forms of faith making, implying or presupposing ontological claims which require metaphysical elucidation are thereby classified as forms of 'theism'. This strategy has the effect that all religious forms of faith and their theological and philosophical expressions are presented with the alternative of defining their identity either as theistic or as post-theistic. In my view, this renders the notion of 'theism' so

33. Adriaanse, above, p. 139f.

indeterminate as to be virtually uniformative. Furthermore, it restricts the choices that can be made in the philosophy of religion to the choice between the theistic and the post-theistic option, so that we are presented with the alternative of two rather totalitarian conceptions. It seems therefore necessary to give a sharper focus to the understanding of 'theism' to provide a basis for investigating its relationship to religious traditions and their theologies. Let us try to find a sharper focus for 'theism' by, first of all, considering the historical location of the use of the term and, secondly by listing a number of its systematic characteristics.

II.1. Some Historical Aspects of the Rise of 'Theism'

Historically, we find that the term 'theism' is introduced and comes to prominence in the aftermath of the confessional wars in Europe. The period of its programmatic use in European thought almost exactly coincides with what one could call the 'century of theodicy' which Ann Loades has dated from the publication of Sebastian Schmid's commentary on the book of Job in 1680 to Kant's *On the Failure of All Attempted Theodicies* in 1792. Theism can be interpreted as an attempt to provide a response to a number of inter-connected challenges.

The confessional wars, although, at least in part, fuelled by nationalistic, economic and other political motives, were accompanied by the theological polemic of the opposing confessional parties concerning issues in the doctrine of the sacraments, the understanding and status of ecclesial authority and the underlying christological and pneumatological questions. The confessional wars contributed to the impression that a state of peace within nations with a population of mixed confessional allegiance which would guarantee the functioning of social institutions and a state of peaceful coexistence between nations of different confessions providing the basis for trade relations and political cooperation could not be based on the doctrines of the Christian church. They seemed to have been shown to be unsuitable for this purpose because of their inherently contentious character. The church appeared to be irrevocably divided into different confessional parties. Theism originated in this situation — this is my thesis — as an attempt to formulate a framework of rational consensus of fundamental beliefs as the basis for communication and cooperation between the parties that existed in a state of continuing conflict because of their different theological interpretations of specific Christian beliefs and practices. In order to achieve this aim a conceptuality had to be provided which, on the one hand, offered a common ground of possible agreement for the parties in conflict and, on the other hand, excluded all those issues which had proved to be the source of disagreement and conflict. The requirements for this framework were by no means simple if it were to offer a unifying basis for the internal cohesion of societies of different confessional status and for the external contact of societies of different confessional identity. Since the conflict concerned religious beliefs, beliefs about the fundamental orientation of human life and therefore about the fundamental constitution, order and destiny of reality, the new framework could not be located on a lower conceptual level, but had to comprehend fundamental religious beliefs about the metaphysical structure of reality within itself. Those beliefs, however, which appeared as the source of conflict and strife, had to be relegated to a lower conceptual level, so that disagreement about these convictions would no longer threaten the very foundations of society. This double aspect can also be identified with regard to the strategies of justifying claims for the basic consensus. The way in which the fundamental beliefs, formulating the envisaged consensus, were justified had to be based on grounds transcending the confessional conflict, while the significance of the traditional authorities for the justification of religious beliefs and practices had to be played down because they had been implicated in the conflict of the confessional parties.

As a response to the challenge of confessional conflict, theism introduced, in effect, a radical disjunction into the doctrinal scheme of Christian beliefs which corresponded to a certain extent to the traditional distinction between natural theology and supernatural theology. The beliefs which became candidates for inclusion into the unifying framework were those about the existence of God, the divine attributes and the relationship between God and the world that were expressed in the doctrines of creation and providence. The set of fundamental doctrines also contained a number of beliefs about human nature, such as the rationality of humans, the immortality of the soul and human freedom, not however, doctrines about sin and salvation. The latter were located together with the doctrine about the church, the sacraments, the last things and their christological and pneumatological presuppositions on the lower level which did not define the basis of consensus, but were issues in which one could agree to differ once the consensus was secured. While the beliefs defining consensus had to be seen as being based on publicly accessible evidence and universally accepted criteria, the group of doctrines which were excluded from the consensus had to be interpreted as matters of private conscience, based on historical and communal sources of authority which could not be strictly universal. The dissolution or, at least, the displacement of the doctrine of Trinity in theism is a symptom of the disjunction it introduced into the doctrinal scheme of Christianity, and not, as, for instance, Theodore Jennings argued,[34] its source. That theism and the doctrine of the Trinity are alternative ways of structuring the system of beliefs and cannot be simply added together appears plausible not least from the attempts to reintroduce the doctrine of the Trinity as a speculative device for reordering the system of beliefs in the 19th century.

Because of this disjunction theism had to present beliefs and arguments about God in such a form that they were no longer dependent on their original setting in the communal practice of faith. The doctrines of God and human nature which were isolated as providing a viable road to consensus could therefore no longer be presented in their original religious, and that means particular confessional, context, but had to be abstracted from it. Theism therefore took the form of a philosophical theory which programmatically transcends the given particular contexts of religious practice. This had the consequence that the beliefs and arguments constitutive for theism were taken out of their conceptual location in the doctrinal scheme of Christian faith and out of their context in the practice of Christian faith. This is especially interesting with regard to the theistic proofs which in medieval times had been firmly embedded both within the doctrinal scheme of Christian theology and within the practice of worship and which now, in order to establish their potential universal validity, had to be abstracted from their original religious context. In the process their use and function in providing reasons for the existence of God changed.[35]

The second challenge which formed an important part of the context of the rise of 'theism' as a programmatic concept and to a large extent defined its agenda was the renewal of an atheistic critique of Christian faith after the Reformation. Although it had roots in the Renaissance and its retrieval of the ancient critique of religion in some strands of hellenistic philosophy and rhetoric, it only seems to have developed into an explicit denial of the existence of God at the end of the 16th century. Since then we find a sudden increase of apologetic and polemic literature, beginning perhaps with Henry

---

34. Th.W. Jennings, *Beyond Theism. A Grammar of God-Language*, New York 1985, pp. 14-20.
35. Cf. John Clayton, art. 'Gottesbeweise', in *TRE* XIII, pp. 760-76.

Smith's *God's Arrow against Atheists* (1593), directed at first against a rather diffuse set of beliefs deviating from Christian beliefs. The charge of atheism could become an issue of public debate, focussed on people like the second Earl of Rochester (1647-80). The discussion overlapped in most European countries with the confessional polemics during and after the confessional wars. Catholic writers made the Reformers responsible for the rise of atheism,[36] Protestant writers, in turn, blamed the emergence of atheism on 'popery'.[37] The anti-ecclesiastical polemics represented in France by the *libertinage érudit*[38] led to the debates, which are documented in Jean Bodin's *Colloquium heptaplomeres de rerum sublimium arcanis abditis* (c. 1592), about whether religious belief contributed to the benefit of society or was an impediment to public order. The concept and programme of theism were part of a philosophical attempt at suppressing the growing atheist influence by refuting its claims.

However, there is one aspect where the theistic refutation of atheism introduced an element that is not to be found in its response to the confessional polemics. It is the attempt to respond to the possible atheistic implications of the newly autonomous natural sciences which followed Roger Bacon's programme of a *scientia experimentalis*. Here the challenge consisted in the thesis that the assumption of a God who is the creator of the universe and its regular structures and governs its course through divine providence does not contribute anything to the explanation of natural phenomena in the investigation of the sciences. This thesis, which had already fuelled the controversies over Galileo and Giordano Bruno, found its fullest theoretical expression after various prefigurations in the early 17th century, first in the pantheism of Spinoza's *Tractatus theologico-politicus* (1670) and then at the end of the 18th century, now as a scathing response to the theism of Samuel Clarke and Newton, in d'Holbach's *Système de la Nature* (1770). The effect of this view was that it provided the background for the development of theism as an explanatory hypothesis of the origin and the order of the universe. The concept of God therefore had to be employed in such a way as to form the central term of such a universal explanation. Its coherence in this way

36. Antonio Possevino, *De sectariorum nostri temporis Atheismis liber*, Cologne 1586.
37. Jakob Friedrich Reimann, *Historia universalis Atheismi et Atheorum*, Hildesheim 1725.
38. Cf. René Pintard, *Le Libertinage érudit dans la premiere moité du XVVe siècle*, 2 vols., Paris 1944.

becomes the lynch-pin of the coherence of philosophical interpretation and scientific investigation of the world. This required not only to show that the categories of theism are compatible with the theory and practice of the sciences, but also to offer an ultimate explanation superior to other attempted ultimate explanations. Theism was thus confronted with the requirement to develop its statements about God as explanatory hypotheses of a universal range and of 'ultimate' logical status, so that they themselves could not be explained by any other explanatory hypotheses. On such a view, deism appears as a reduced form of theism in that it restricts the explanatory power of the God-hypothesis to the originating relation between God and the world, and so also reduces its logical status in that it is not required as the ultimate explanation of all other explanatory hypotheses. By contrast, it is the universal character of theism's claims to offer explanations of all states of affairs that obtain in the world, be they the result of natural regularities or their apparent exceptions, that logically requires a movement from the assumption of a cause of the world to the view of a living author of the world.[39] In turn, deism had to appear to theists merely as a form of atheism. It is this claim of theism to offer a universal ultimate explanation of everything there is and everything happens that made the question of theodicy its central theme. This also explains why for theism theodicy becomes a *theoretical problem* that is capable of a *theoretical solution*. In its attempts to respond to that problem theism was, however, severely restricted, in that it could not refer to those christological and eschatological doctrines which had formed the background for reflection on the existence of evil and suffering and for a view of the love of God in traditional Christian doctrine.

Historically, the fate of the concept of 'theism' gives important pointers to the fate of theism as a philosophical theory. In continental Europe, the programmatic use of the term is not continued after the Enlightenment, and 'theism' is already established in the 19th century as a historical term denoting particular strands in the philosophy of the 17th and 18th century. The philosophical question of 'ultimate explanations' found its context mainly in the context of transcendental philosophy and the discussion of the transcendental character of human subjectivity, or in philosophical materialism. In the Anglophone world, and, more precisely, in England, the concept of theism and the philosophical programme it denotes survived the Enlightenment. One of the reasons for this seems to be that after the early radical

---

39. Kant, *Critique of Pure Reason*, B660f.

phase of the Enlightenment in England, Enlightenment ideas found a success-ful response and refutation in philosophical theories which rejected the conclusions of the early English, French or German Enlightenment, but adapted its philosophical methods for the defense of theism. The classic example for this form of theism is, of course, William Paley's *Natural Theology*, which served as the paradigm of theistic reasoning throughout the 19th century and to a certain extent defines the agenda for philosophical theism until the present day. If one talks in a reasonably precise sense of traditional theism, one can only refer to the tradition for which Paley's work stands as the paradigmatic example. The term 'classical' theism seems by comparison like a recent invention designed by the proponents of 'neo-classical' theism such as Charles Hartshorne to contrast their own philosophical programme to that of Thomas Aquinas. However, reference to Aquinas in this context is only partially correct, since for Aquinas the themes which in theism are abstracted from their place in the conceptual scheme of Christian doctrine are, as the 'praeambula fidei', firmly embedded in the integrated framework of Christian doctrine structured by the organizing principles of nature and grace. Historically, it would then appear, 'theism' is concerned with the creation of a philosophical framework for defending a conception of God (which is in some respects similar to that of Aquinas) which was to take the place of the different confessional doctrinal frameworks since they could no longer provide common ground between different confessional parties. However, the survival of 'theism' as a programmatic concept for a particular form of philosophy of religion in the Anglophone world, and especially in England, which makes it a live option for contemporary philosophers, cannot disguise the fact that it did not achieve what we have interpreted as its original aim, i.e., of providing a common ground of consensus for rapidly diversifying plural modern societies. In England, it has, however, provided a common ground for dispute for much longer than in most other European societies, and to a certain extent still does so today.

II.2 Some Systematic Aspects of Theism

Systematically, the sketch of its historical setting provides sufficient material for a reasonable precise description of theism. In its core element theism appears as the reversal of Christian Wolff's definition of an atheist: '"*Atheus*"

dicitur, qui negat dari Deum, hoc est, ens a se, mundi auctorem.'[40] Theism
appears thus as a philosophical theory which offers arguments for the
existence of God who is described as a self-existent being and a personal
agent, and who is the source of all being, meaning and truth, the ground of
the existence and intelligibility of the world, and, as the highest good, the
source of all value. Theism has the logical status of an explanatory theory
which is intended to offer the ultimate explanation of everything that is and
everything that happens, of all possible and actual events, states of affairs,
processes and values in the world. For this purpose theism requires a
demonstration of the coherence of its concept of God which elucidates the
attributes of God who is, as a personal agent, the source of all being,
meaning and truth, and shows that these attributes can without self-
contradiction be ascribed to one being. Because of the universal range of
theism as an explanatory theory the question of theodicy becomes the test
case of the coherence of theistic claims, since it raises the question whether
the existence of certain states of affairs in the world is consistent with the
existence of a God as described in the theory of divine attributes.

As a philosophical theory theism is dependent on the doctrines and
practices of Christian faith for its *content*, and on their atheist criticism for the
form of its arguments. It represents, in effect, a *de-contextualisation* of the
Christian concept of God which is abstracted from its conceptual setting in
the doctrinal scheme of Christian theology and from its context in the
practices of Christian faith. This de-contextualisation may account for some
of the striking differences between orthodox Christian doctrine and the
philosophical understanding of God in theism which is most prominent in
the contrast between God as 'a person' and the doctrine of God as three
persons — one substance in credal formulae, and in the notion of God as 'a
being' and not 'Being' as in traditional doctrine. As a philosophical theory
the theistic understanding of God does not function and does not have to
function in concrete contexts of application in personal piety or communal
worship. This de-contextualisation is, however, not accidental. It is a
necessary component of the attempt at transcending particular and therefore,
at least potentially, controversial forms of belief and their particular
communal contexts. This requires that the arguments theism presents must
be shown to rest on universal foundations for the validation of knowledge,
and its strategies of giving reasons must meet universal criteria for what

40. *Theologia naturalis*, 2 §411.

constitutes a correctly formed and successful argument. Theism is, in contemporary philosophical jargon, inherently 'foundationalist'. All its arguments must be accessible to natural reason, the kind of reason, which, as a constitutive element of human nature, is universal to humanity. However one may assess this implication of theism's strategy of de-contextualization, it necessarily implies that its theses and arguments are firmly placed in the realm of public discourse. Because of the character of its claims and arguments theism has to make its stand in the realm of public contestability. It functions in this way as an antidote to the tendency towards the privatization of religious beliefs in the modern and also in the post-modern era. This is, albeit indirectly, witnessed by Professor Adriaanse's criticism.

This consideration of theism in its historical context must suffice to point out that theism is a phenomenon that is both more restricted and more specific than the rather general definition Professor Adriaanse employs. Reflections on the tasks and prospects of philosophy of religion 'After Theism' can therefore not be presented as the fundamental transition from one epoch to another. The fundamental difficulty such an approach presents is not only that it employs a notion of theism which is problematical because of its indeterminate character comprising Christian philosophical theology from the second to the twentieth century, yet ultimately going back to Plato and Aristotle, while also taking in metaphysical reflection on God in Judaism and Islam. The difficulty is also that a possible alternative to theism is presented in the same form as a general theory resulting from a paradigma shift in the philosophy of religion and in the plausibility structures of society. This seems to be a somewhat ambitious strategy, which can neither account for the continuing presence of theism as a live option in the philosophy of religion nor would it seem to be able to do justice to the variety of possible other routes for contemporary philosophies of religion whose plausibility or implausibility cannot be decided beforehand on the basis of a particular interpretation of the course of philosophy of religion from a theistic to a post-theistic era. My thesis is therefore that the theory of a necessary transition from a theistic to post-theistic era is not supported by sufficient reasons either with regard to the interpretation of theism or with regard to the claim of the advent of a post-theistic era, and that it unnecessarily restricts the possibilities available for philosophies of religion in the contemporary situation. In my view, the context in which we do philosophy of religion today is decisively shaped by the pluralism which characterizes modern

Western (and to an increasing extent Eastern) societies and which forms the background of discussion of both the place of religious beliefs in such a context and of the possible tasks of philosophical engagement with religious beliefs.

III. Religious Beliefs and the Challenges of Pluralism

III.1. Pluralism, Views of Life and Religious Beliefs
The word 'pluralism' is one that has suffered from inflationary use in recent years. Let me therefore outline briefly how I suggest to use the term in this paper.[41] Following a proposal by Eilert Herms, I use the concept 'pluralism' to describe the state of a society, where there is a diversity of systems of fundamental beliefs and values held and subscribed to by members of a society.[42] We can call these systems of fundamental beliefs and values views of life. In a pluralistic society these diverse views of life exist in a competitive relationship that is not (or no longer) contained by a set of shared convictions about the meaning and destiny of individual and social life in the world. Views of life constitute a dimension of individual and social life which is relatively independent of the other fundamental dimensions of society though not unconnected to them.

Even a minimalist description of a society[43] must include reference to

41. For the argument in this section I have made extensive use of Eilert Herms' paper 'Pluralismus aus Prinzip', in: *'Vor Ort.' Praktische Theologie in der Erprobung.* Festschrift für Peter C. Bloth, Nürnberg 1991, pp. 77-95. It is Herms' particular achievement to have shown that the 'pluralism on principle' he advocates is fully compatible with the Reformers' notion of revelation. This implies that Christian faith is capable of appropriating pluralism on its own terms and does not have to be transcended in order to accomodate the requirements of a pluralistic society. John Clayton's Stanton Lectures for 1992, *Religions, Reasons and Gods* have provided many important insights into the relationship between the private dimension of religious beliefs and their 'public contestability'.
42. This notion of 'pluralism' is very different from the theory of 'religious pluralism' as represented by the authors of *The Myth of Christian Uniqueness*, John Hick and Paul F. Knitter (eds.); for my criticism of this theory see 'Particularity, Universality, and the Religions. Toward a Christian Theology of Religions', in: Gavin D'Costa (ed.), *Christian Uniqueness Reconsidered. The Myth of a Pluralistic Theology of Religions*, New York 1990, pp. 30-46.
43. This description follows the standard analysis of four spheres of social interaction which Schleiermacher first developed from an analysis of the structural elements

the provision of means of survival of the members of a society (the *economic* dimension), reference to the fundamental rights, duties and rules of ordered interaction which regulate the participation of members of a society in the processes of decision making about the internal order of a society and its external relations to other societies (the *political* dimension), and reference to the acquisition, development and application of knowledge which is required for securing an adequate basis for the survival and development of a society (such as knowledge about the functioning of the economy, the provision of an adequate infrastructure of a society, of health care etc.) and for the functioning and development of the forms of social interrelationship of the members of a society (the *'knowledge'* dimension). This knowledge dimension covers areas of research, investigation and inquiry such as the sciences, medicine, law, the humanities, the social sciences etc. All these dimensions of the life of a society exist as ordered forms of interaction where the requirements of order increase with the size and complexity of the social group under consideration. These forms of interaction can be organized in different degrees according to the existing requirements through the creation of institutions and codified systems of rules. Since human beings are by

of personal being, cf. F.D.E. Schleiermacher, 'Entwürfe zu einem System der Sittenlehre', in O. Braun, J. Bauer (eds.), F.D.E. Schleiermacher, *Werke. Auswahl in vier Bänden*, vol. II, Leipzig 1913. My brief description only differs in that it allows for the expansion of the four fields by pointing to the development of an independent 'cultural' dimension. Historically this is a development which, to a significant extent, postdates Schleiermacher's theory. Schleiermacher's analysis of four fundamental cultural spheres which can be systematically derived from the constitution of finite personhood has in recent years been constructively developed by Eilert Herms and applied to a variety of problems in social ethics and ecclesiology. Cf. E. Herms, 'Religion und Organisation', in: *Erfahrbare Kirche. Beiträge zur Ekklesiologie*, Tübingen 1990, pp. 49-79. The advantage this analysis has, is, that it identifies the four cultural functions which are constitutive for every society (and in this respect it is superior to Hegelian forms of analysis which distinguish between society as the system of rules governing the possession, acquisition and distribution of goods and the state as the system of rules regulating political rule and which are therefore in danger of overlooking the interrelationship of these two dimensions and their relationships to the other two [or three] dimensions). Alternative proposals, as, for instance, Talcott Parsons' suggestion to view society as the interaction of the personal, the cultural and the social system, point to the internal differentiation which we find in each of the dimensions and in their interrelationships. Cf. T. Parsons, *The Social System*, New York 1951.

nature cultural beings human interaction in all these spheres transcends the realm of the purely functional. When basic needs are satisfied, forms and means of interactions can be elaborated which, when the process of internal differentiation of a society progresses, can become independent as a *cultural* dimension of the life of a society resulting in independent forms of social interaction (documented by cultural institutions such as museums, theatres. concerts, art galleries etc.). All these areas of interaction which are constitutive for the life of a society form complex interrelationships in which the economic, the political and the 'knowledge' dimension interact in various ways.

Human action in these various dimensions of interaction is informed and shaped by a fourth dimension, the *religious-ethical* dimension of views of life or fundamental religious beliefs and moral convictions. Views of life incorporate fundamental beliefs and convictions about the aims and goals which are to be realized in the economic, the political, the 'knowledge' dimension and the cultural dimension. They therefore contain fundamental beliefs about the constitution, the structure and the ultimate destiny of human being in the world. These beliefs have an orientational function for individual human agents and for groups and societies, since they prescribe the norms and values of action in the different fields of interaction in a society by asserting a distinctive view of the possibilities of human action in the world. Views of life therefore always have a metaphysical dimension in that they, at least implicitly, contain an ontological dimension which bases our ethical responses in claims about their objects and their intrinsic qualities.[44] That views of life represent an independent dimension of social interaction is itself a contentious thesis. The history of modernity since the breakdown of the medieval synthesis which characterized the *Corpus Christianum* gives evidence of various attempts to ascribe this orientational function not to an independent dimension of views of life, but to one of the other dimensions which constitute society. It has been claimed, for instance, that the economic dimension, in the interaction of labour and capital or in the free play of market forces produces the fundamental orientation for individuals and for societies, or that the historical dialectics of the class struggle provide the ultimate aims and goals of individual and social action, or that the

---

44. For a detailed analysis of ontological accounts as articulations of our moral 'gut' reactions, e.g. respect, cf. Charles Taylor, *Sources of the Self. The Making of Modern Identity*, Cambridge 1989, chapter 1, 'Inescapable Frameworks', pp. 3—24.

progress of science will function as the reliable guide for the goals society should achieve. It can, I think, be shown that the ascription of the fundamental orientational function to one of the dimensions of society, and the denial of a dimension of fundamental reflection which is concerned with views of life, leads to an ideological distortion of economics, politics or science which is ultimately counter-productive to the functioning of economic or political interaction and scientific research. There seem to be good reasons to claim that the economic, the political and the 'knowledge' dimension of social interaction are in need of orientation and cannot themselves function as the source of orientation for the whole of society in all its dimensions.

In the modern era one can distinguish a variety of different views of life, although they can roughly be grouped into two categories: religious and what I will call 'meta-religious' views of life. Meta-religious views of life are in many respects structurally similar to religious views of life, although there are a number of decisive differences. Meta-religious views are not only programmatically *post*-religious in that they claim that the history of humankind has moved beyond its religious stage (classically in Auguste Comte's law of the three stages of the development of the human race), they are also *meta*-religious in that they offer an explanation of religion which is intended to unveil its true character (as a primitive form of science, or as a projection of human ideals). Meta-religious views of life incorporate a critique of religion. In this way the religions are reinterpreted as unenlightened or misguided or even fraudulent forms of human activity, as the product of the mythopoetic imagination of the human mind, or as means of social domination. In contrast, religious views of life claim that religious beliefs are not the product of human activity in inquiry and investigation, but are ultimately grounded in experiences of disclosure (in the religions of revelation) or discovery (in mystical traditions) which are given as the foundation of human activity. In meta-religious views of life the human agent rules supreme, in religious views of life human agency is seen as relative to the agency of a divine agent, or an ultimate reality which transcends human activity as its ground and source.

Religious views of life are distinguished from meta-religious views of life in that they claim to be based on experiences of disclosure or discovery which are not the result of human epistemic activity, although they are, of course, interpreted and appropriated in human epistemic activity. A paradigmatic disclosure or discovery experience therefore provides in religious views of life the reference-point of religious traditions. Religious beliefs are distinguished from other forms of knowledge in that they contain fundamental beliefs about the constitution, structure and ultimate destiny of created being. They are characterized by their *comprehensiveness,* so that they refer to the totality of reality, its beginning and end, and are claimed to apply to everything there is. It is, furthermore, claimed for religious beliefs that they refer to an *ultimate dimension* of reality which is fundamental for every attempt at describing and comprehending reality. In religious beliefs ontological claims are therefore asserted, presupposed or implied which refer to the ontological make-up of what there is. However, in spite of the 'objective' ontological character of religious beliefs, the believer does not remain external to the content of belief. Religious beliefs are *self-involving* so that the situation of the believer is an implication of the content of belief. Religious beliefs are therefore not only characterized by their propositional content, they also possess a commissive and prescriptive force, so that subscribing to specific beliefs commits believers to specific attitudes and dispositions which are the prescriptive basis for formulating norms of action and values of life. Because of their fundamental content and prescriptive force religious beliefs are always *personal* in so far as they are constitutive for shaping the relational being of persons in their relationships to other persons, to themselves and to the world of nature. All these relationships are shaped by the relationship to the content of the disclosure or discovery experience (be it God or a state of enlightenment) which is the fundamental content of religious beliefs. Since they are rooted in historical traditions and apply to the social existence of human beings, religious beliefs have a *communal* character which finds its expression in communal worship, ritual and social action. Although they are personal in shaping the fundamental orientation of individual believers, religious beliefs do not remain private, but have *public* consequences in virtue of their function in shaping believers' policies of action.

The different aspects which characterize religious beliefs as orientational beliefs are constituted and mediated by language, by linguistic communicative interaction. Religious discourse which constitutes and mediates religious beliefs provides a fundamental framework for interpreting the totality of reality as rooted in the unconditional ground of everything there is, and in this way determines the possibilities of action, the norms and values of action for believers. It specifies their position as agents in the world and the forms of action that are in accordance with their fundamental beliefs about the constitution, structure and ultimate destiny of life. Religious discourse is, on the one hand, a relatively autonomous realm of discourse which has its specific identity in its relation to the paradigmatic experience of disclosure or discovery that forms the foundation of a religious view of life. This specific character of religious discourse is cultivated in religious traditions which hand on specific ways of referring back to this foundational and paradigmatic experience. On the other hand, religious discourse is also relatively interdependent with other realms of discourse in that it forms and expresses the fundamental orientation of action for believers and therefore necessarily enters the public realm of social interaction. The public contestability of religious beliefs expressed in religious discourse is a necessary condition for the accountability of the religious believer as an agent in a social context of action. Religious discourse must therefore be capable of interpretation not only to members of a specific religious community, but also to those belonging to other religious communities or to society at large. This capacity for interpretation of religious discourse is a requirement of the function of religious beliefs to provide a comprehensive and fundamental orientation for the believer's policy of action.

I have throughout stressed the pragmatic significance of views of life, whether they are meta-religious or religious views of life. It seems that one can indeed defend the thesis that views of life are constitutive for our capacity for intentional action. Once our choices move from the trivial level of whether to have corn flakes or rice crispies for breakfast they very soon involve beliefs about our role as agents in the world, about our possibilities of action and the norms and values we try to actualize in our actions. Our capacity to act in larger contexts or in situations where the outcome of our actions is crucial for our well-being and that of others depends on our capacity to give coherence to our policy of action. The attempt to give coherence to our policy of action, especially in cases where we have to relate different fields of action, such as the economic, the political and the 'knowledge' dimension of society, depends on our having beliefs and convictions about the constitution, structure and ultimate destiny of life and on our ability to draw inferences from these beliefs which shape our policy of action. Only such beliefs can provide the background for the responsible selection of aims and means of action and can provide reasons for accepting choices the consequences of which reach beyond our immediate context. If views of life become opaque, the agent's capacity for intentional action is restricted and becomes arbitrary. This situation is experienced as a loss of freedom.

If this view of the constitutive role of views of life for our capacity for intentional action can be validated, then it also applies to the field of social interaction in societies. The thesis would then be that only such societies possess the capacity for determining their development in which decisions can be taken which are based on fundamental beliefs about the aims and values of society as a whole and about the worth, rights and duties of its individual members. More precisely, one can say that views of life are constitutive for society's capacity to come to decisions in complex situations which require the correlation of different dimensions of the life of society, of the economic, the political and the 'knowledge' dimensions. If views of life become opaque, society's capacity for social interaction becomes restricted and society comes in a state of crisis, either with regard to the actual processes of decision-making or with regard to the plausibility and acceptability the decisions that are taken have for significant parts of society. At this point conflicts between individual freedom and communal justice appear and a loss of the transparency of processes of decision-making is experienced.

At this point we can again point to the difference between meta-religious views of life and religious views of life. In meta-religious views of life the status of the human agent is either individually or collectively absolute, and individual freedom or collective freedom is seen as absolute and self-constituted, i.e. not constitutively related to a reality or agency other than that of the agent. In religious views of life the status of the human agent is always relative to the ground and source of reality (be it a divine agent or an ultimate reality). This implies that the agents are not only accountable to themselves but also to a reality outside themselves. Reasons for actions must therefore go beyond a consensus between the agents, so that every consensus that can be reached about what ought to be must be based on beliefs about what really is the case, on beliefs about the fundamental constitution, structure and destiny of life.

This interpretation of views of life emphasizes their pragmatic aspects insofar it focusses on the capacity for intentional action and social interaction. It is, however, not pragmatist insofar as it acknowledges that there are criteria for assessing and performing actions which go beyond their pragmatic viability and are based on ontological beliefs. On this view, one would have to say that religious beliefs have the pragmatic action-orientating function I have attempted to describe in virtue of the fact that their precepts about what we *should* do are based on beliefs about what there *is*. The action-directing capacity of views of life depends on the ontological beliefs they incorporate. Furthermore, I would like to emphasize that this account of religious beliefs, although it stresses the way in which religious beliefs function as an ultimate framework for interpretation and action, is not functionalist. Religious beliefs *function as they do* because of *what they are*, beliefs about the ultimate constitution, structure and destiny of life which is beyond the control and manipulative grasp of human agents. Only meta-religious views of life can on the basis of this description be open to the charge of pragmatism or functionalism.

III.2. Civil Religion and its Dissolution

We have so far presented an interpretation of views of life which could be characterized as the description of an 'ideal type' in that we have con-centrated on certain structural aspects which constitute views of life. This strategy is not necessarily one that leads into empty abstractions as long as it can be shown that the elements identified in the 'ideal type' can be reidentified in concrete contexts of application which, of course, always form the background to descriptions of ideal types. I have referred to the situation which characterizes most Western European societies and North American society as one of pluralism in which different views of life exist in a competitive relationship which is not (or no longer) contained by a shared set of beliefs and convictions that provide the basis for moral consensus in a society. The bracketed proviso 'no longer' refers to the fact that, according to an important school of thought of the sociology of religion, pluralism appears in Western European and North American society succeeding a stage which has been described by Robert Bellah and others as the dominance of a *civil religion*. The term refers to a state of society where there exists 'a common set of moral understandings about good and bad, right and wrong, in the realm of individual and social action', and it is postulated that 'these common moral understandings must also in turn rest upon a common set of religious understandings that provide a picture of the universe in terms of which the moral understandings make sense'.[45] Civil religion is based on the presupposition that all members of a society subscribe to this common set of moral understandings and religious understandings and that society is willing to preserve this state against tendencies to question its validity.

45. Robert N. Bellah, *The Broken Covenant: American Civil Religion in Time of Trial*, New York 1975, ix.

Because of its consolidating function for the stability of a society, civil religion tends to assume the status of a state religion and can develop marked totalitarian tendencies because any attempt to require justifications of its central tenets appears as an attack on the social cohesion of society. The Greek *polis* and the Roman Empire, with its succession of civil religions until it accepted Christianity as the religion most likely to preserve *salus publica*, offer evidence of both tendencies, with Socrates documenting the example of one who had to pay the price of questioning and requiring justifications for the tacit consensus of society.[46]

For our purpose it is significant that the role of theism as we have interpreted it in its historical setting in the 17th and 18th century is not unlike that of a civil religion, and one could even argue that in English society theism is until the present day its operative civil religion. This could be supported by observations that the public presence of religion is mainly reduced to those aspects of religious beliefs and practices which are compatible with theism.[47] In Continental Europe the development is more complicated in that the civil religion of theism has from the end of the 18th century been counter-balanced and modified by the convictions of the French Revolution which exercised a much stronger and historically increasing pressure towards the religious and ideological neutrality of the state.

The links between theism and civil religion which we can establish may vary in different contexts and would require a far more detailed investigation. What is, however, structurally similar is that civil religion operates with a similar disjunction of beliefs that we have also observed as constitutive for theism. It introduces a distinction between the common set of moral and religious understandings which must be subscribed to by all members of society because it is fundamental for the social cohesion of a society, and moral and religious beliefs which do not have this foundational function in defining the moral consensus of society. Religious beliefs which do not belong to the common set become optional extras, they are thoroughly privatized. They are tolerated as private choices as long as they do not

---

46. Cf. E. Herms, *op.cit.*, pp. 82ff.
47. The Boy Scout Movement is an interesting example of this since it incorporates Christians, Jews, Muslims and Sikhs and even brings members of the different religions together once a year for an act of communal worship at their renewal of promise. ('I promise that I will do my best to do my duty to God and to the Queen and to keep the Cub Scout Law.') A classic example of theism as a civil religion!

impinge on the foundations of society defined by the common set. Civil religion can therefore incorporate an *apparent pluralism* of private religious beliefs which is compatible with the shared common understandings of the public realm. The tendency towards the privatization of religious beliefs and their relegation to the strictly personal level goes together with a secularization of the public realm. What sociologists observe in societies the cohesion of which was once defined in terms of a civil religion is that this twofold tendency of the privatization of religious beliefs and the seculari- zation of public moral values contains in itself the seeds for social crisis through the dissolution of the foundations of civil religion. The common set of moral values cannot be stable as a strictly secular set of moral under- standings if it is no longer based on a 'common set of religious understand- ings that provide a picture of the universe in terms of which the moral understandings make sense'. Robert Bellah and his co-authors have charted this development in their classic *Habits of the Heart*,[48] where the common understandings of morality are overtaken by the culture of the primacy of self-fulfilment.

What Professor Adriaanse advocates in the second part of his paper under the heading 'theism as heritage' as a programme of philosophy of reli- gion is, in my view, an accurate description of the functioning of theism (or in the case of the example of Menno ter Braak, Christian theism) as a civil religion and its dissolution. The example of Ter Braak's 'new Christian', who still supports the moral values of Christian faith but denies their 'theistic' or 'metaphysical' foundation in claims about God and God's relationship to the world, highlights the paradoxical character of the 'secularized postexistence' of religious traditions. The moral precepts and values that are implied by religious beliefs, such as the equal dignity of all human beings 'in the sight of the Lord',[49] are affirmed, while their foundation in beliefs about the constitution, structure and destiny of life is denied. The action-directing inferences of religious beliefs, their commissive and prescriptive force, are affirmed while the propositional content of the beliefs is denied. Here the paradoxical seems to merge into the contradictory. As I have tried to show above, religious beliefs have an orientational function in determining our possibilities of action, the norms and values we try to realize in our actions,

48. Robert Bellah, Richard Madsen, William M. Sullivan, Ann Swidler and Steven M. Tipton, *Habits of the Heart: Middle America Observed*, London 1988.
49. Cf. Adriaanse, above, p. 145.

because of their ontological commitments, because of the ontological claims about the constitution and nature of reality they assert, presuppose or imply. Where these ontological claims are denied, the norms and values one wants to affirm must be based on other grounds. The 'charge' still exercised by theistic claims cannot fill that place. As a 'condition for decent survival'[50] the memory of ontological claims one can no longer accept seems insufficient. One could point to the empirical evidence provided by such studies as *Habits of the Heart* to show that the moral stance that is recommended by Ter Braak is, as a matter of social development, indeed in danger of being replaced by an 'ethic' that is reduced to the demands of self-fulfilment and procedural fairness.

Professor Adriaanse's second main point in his reflections on the 'heritage of theism as blessing' which he supports with an intricate analogy (sic!) of Gilbert Ryle's theory of 'thick descriptions' can, I think, be interpreted in a similar way as an accurate description of significant tendencies in the process of the dissolution of civil religion. Where religious beliefs are consistently privatized and thereby declared irrelevant for the public realm, where they lose their capacity of functioning as orientational beliefs, religious faith is indeed in a position where there is not much more left than 'to say the prayers, sing the hymns and tell the tales it has always cherished, just for the joy and the pleasure and the relief and the edification of performing them'.[51] Theology would than have no other option then 'to step to a higher sophistication-level and start playing with that echo, modulating, counterfeiting, quoting, displacing, interpreting, hiding and seeking it' (*ibid.*). The *dictum* has replaced the *res*, and words, mere words, are all we are left to play with. If the thesis that I have presented above is correct and views of life using *dicta* to make ontological claims about *res* are constitutive for an agent's capacity to act in complex situations and for the accountability of agents for their actions, this view presents us with a categorical refusal to act and, consequently, with an escape into unaccountability. But not only that. Once the *dicta* no longer refer to *res*, they lose the capacity of providing reasons for actions by explicating the beliefs that form the background of choices. Ethical discourse is deprived of reference to values that are valued not only because I choose to do so, and can no longer attempt to find justification for what I *ought* to do in what there *is*. Without the *res* of ethical values and moral

50. Adriaanse, *loc.cit.*
51. Adriaanse, above, p. 155.

norms, the *dicta* of moral discourse are entirely open to the manipulation of what Iris Murdoch has called 'the fat relentless ego'.[52] If we cut the chord that binds *dictum* and *res* together, the language of religious and moral discourse atrophies to the expression of choices and desires, what Charles Taylor has called 'the ethics of inarticulacy',[53] and the post-theist may not even be left with many words to play with. The parallels to the culture of self-fulfilment seem quite pronounced. Again, I do not deny that Professor Adriaanse's thesis correctly describes a significant trend in modern societies, but I do not see how this description can offer a promising programme for philosophy of religion 'after theism'. It may be that in the end philosophy leaves everything as it is, but that does not imply that philosophers have to become accomplices in the erosion of the social interaction of society which philosophy presupposes as its context. If this is the price theologians have to pay for stepping on to that 'higher sophistication-level'[54] they should decline the invitation.

III.3. *Genuine Pluralism and Philosophy of Religion*

I have indicated earlier that I accept that some of the trends Professor Adriaanse describes are to be found in modern societies, but that I find it difficult to accept the general thesis of the inevitable process of secularization with all its implications and its corollary of the transition from theism to post-theism. A more promising picture of the cultural context of contemporary philosophy of religion seems to me that after the dissolution of theism and its apparent pluralism of privatized views of life we also find evidence for the rise of a situation of *genuine pluralism* in which different views of life, religious and meta-religious, co-exist in a competitive relationship. Tendencies like secularization and privatization are aspects of that wider picture so that we find examples of a continuing secularization together with examples of a revival or new birth of religious traditions, including fundamentalism of various traditions, new religious movements and a variety of meta-religious views of life. In such a scenario, which I believe to be the situation in which we already live or towards which we are on the way, the

---

52. Cf. her essay 'On "God" and "Good"', in Stanley Hauerwas and Alasdair MacIntyre (eds.), *Revisions: Changing Perspectives in Moral Philosophy*, Notre Dame 1983, pp. 69—91, p. 72.
53. *Sources of the Self*, pp. 53ff.
54. Adriaanse, above, p. 155.

plurality of views of life is no longer contained by a set of common understandings of a moral or religious character, but exists in a relationship of competition. For all the perils of such a situation, one has to acknowledge that it presents us with a genuine reassertion of religious beliefs, since they can only be in a competitive relationship, or a situation of possible conflict, if religious beliefs are indeed held as orientational beliefs which present public truth claims and have public consequences for the formation of believers' policies of action. Genuine pluralism indicates the end of the privatization of religion.

This situation of pluralism contains opportunities as well as dangers. The opportunity it presents consists in the fact that, with the eclipse of the privatization of religious beliefs, religious beliefs again become part of public discourse. This means that in public discourse in a pluralistic society orientational beliefs, fundamental religious beliefs and moral convictions become again themes of social interaction. The structure of society requires that members of different communities of believers act together, and the nature of their religious beliefs requires that the rationale for their actions is based on their fundamental views of life. What is required in such a situation is a *culture of dialogue* in which members of different religious communities and representatives of different meta-religious views of life can engage in discourse about the aims they can accomplish together in the different dimensions of social interaction, in the economic, the political and the 'knowledge' dimensions of society. Such a culture of dialogue can only function under two fundamental conditions: that the autonomy of the different views of life is respected by all participants in this dialogue, and that they can recognize the necessity for interaction as a presupposition of joint action in society. In a pluralistic society which is, in Martin Marty's phrase 'a community of communities',[55] there exists no longer a common ground of shared beliefs or values which is to be presupposed in the processes of social interaction in society. The only 'common ground' that exists is the recognition of the situation of pluralism and the acknowledgment of rules for a successful dialogue. Every other common ground cannot be presupposed, but will have to be established in the process of dialogue. This has a number of far-reaching implications for the communication structures in society. Among them is the end of the alleged autonomy of the economic, political and 'knowledge' dimensions. In a situation of genuine pluralism economic,

55. Cf. Martin Marty, *The Public Church*, New York 1981.

political and scientific decisions will have to come back into the arena of public discourse. Decisions in these realms can no longer be left to technocratic expertise that requires no justification with reference to orientational beliefs. This has a surprising consequence: genuine pluralism requires the acknowledgment of the autonomy of different views of life, but it questions the autonomy of the dimensions of social interaction in the economy, in politics and in scientific investigation in the widest sense. In this way, pluralism expands the realm of public contestability rather than restricting it.

Recent writers on pluralism have emphasized that pluralistic societies can only be safeguarded from chaos and open conflict if their members learn to communicate in two languages: a public language of common citizenship and a second language which expresses the relationship of members of society to their particular groups and traditions.[56] If our observations about the orientational character of views of life are correct, then the order must be reversed. The first language would be the language in which we express the foundational beliefs that we share with a community of believers, the language that constitutes our capacitiy for intentional action. The second language would be the language of interaction between the different communities, the language of dialogue that is required in order to cooperate in pluralistic societies, and it is the language of dialogue which will be the language of common citizenship.

If this sketch of a genuinely pluralistic society points in the right direction, then there is indeed a 'paradigm shift' required for philosophy of religion. Professor Adriaanse has already indicated the first decisive paradigm shift, the one from natural theology to philosophy of religion. This paradigm shift implied that philosophical reflection no longer concentrated on the questions of the *praeambula fidei* as they are accessible to observation and reason, but concentrated on religion as a universal human phenomenon, expressed in the dependence of humanity on 'transcendence'.[57] This introduced a concept of religion into philosophical reflection where 'religion' was interpreted as a universal relationship between the finite and the Infinite, and particular religions could be assessed with regard to the degree in which they

56. Cf. Jonathan Sacks, *The Persistence of Faith. Religion, Morality and Society in a Secular Age*, London 1991, esp. 66ff.
57. Professor Adriaanse's interpretation of W. Trillhaas' notion of 'intentional transcendence' (pp. 19ff.) is a non-realist version of philosophy of religion in this paradigm.

instantiated the concept of religion. The religions could be viewed from a
neutral philosophical perspective which programmatically abstracted from
the particularities of specific religious traditions. The advent of pluralism
means that there is no longer a universal concept of religion which can be
seen to lie at the root of all religions. Religion only exists in the plurality of
religions. This implies that there is no longer a neutral perspective, a
standpoint above the different religious traditions and views of life. There are
only internal perspectives, perspectives located within particular views of life,
and external perspectives, the perspectives from which other religious
traditions are viewed from a perspective located within one specific tradition.[58] Philosophy of religion becomes the philosophy of religious views
of life as they are incorporated in particular religious traditions. Philosophical
questions will therefore have two locations. On the one hand, they will be
concerned with inquiring into the internal rationality of beliefs and their
justifications within a particular tradition. In the Christian traditions this can
in many ways be seen as a renaissance of philosophical theology as Norman
Kretzmann describes it:

Philosophical theology shares the methods of natural theology broadly conceived
— i.e. analysis and argumentation of all sorts accepted in philosophy and the
sciences — but it lifts natural theology's restriction on premises. In particular,
philosophical theology accepts as premises doctrinal propositions that are not also
initially accessible to observation and reason. From a philosophical point of view,
it takes up such premises as assumptions. Argumentation based on such premises
may be (and historically has been) as rigorous as any, but the status of its premises
of course precludes its satisfying the peculiarly stringent criteria of Aristotelian
demonstration. A philosophical theologian engaged in such reasoning tests the
coherence of doctrinal propositions, develops their implications, attempts explanations of them, discovers their connection with other doctrinal propositions, and so
on, with no pretence at offering proofs of the sort putatively available in natural
theology.[59]

In contrast to the de-contextualization of theism this represents, in effect, the
re-contextualisation of philosophical reflection in religious traditions. On the

58. Cf. Ingolf U. Dalferth, *Kombinatorische Theologie. Probleme theologischer Rationalität*,
    Freiburg 1991, esp. pp. 59-98.
59. N. Kretzmann, 'Reason in Mystery', in G. Vesey (ed.), *The Philosophy in
    Christianity*, Cambridge 1989, pp. 15-39, pp. 15ff.

other hand, philosophical reflection will be located on the interface between the internal and the external perspective where religious beliefs enter the arena of public contestability when members of different traditions engage in dialogue. There seems to be no reason to suppose that the paradigm shift from a philosophy of religion to a philosophy of religious views of life will make philosophers redundant.

IV. And Theism?

I have argued that theism remains a live option in a pluralistic context. There are no good reasons to suppose that theism is relegated by historical necessity to the history of philosophy. Philosophical theism will, of course, continue to be an option for those who disagree with the scenario of a pluralistic context for philosophical reflection I have tried to sketch. But, also within a pluralistic context and for those who accept this scenario, theism will have an important role to play. In my view, this role will, however, be different from the programme of theism in its original historical setting. It is no longer concerned with *demonstrating* the coherence of a concept of God, with providing reasons for the existence of God and with offering a theoretical solution to the problem of theodicy on the basis of universally acceptable evidence in reason and observation. Instead of a *foundational* role, theism's concern for coherence, the validation of existential claims and its engagement with the question of theodicy can be transformed into a *grammatical* or *criteriological* role for the ways in which believers attempt to explicate the internal plausibility of their beliefs and their capacity towards aims and goals which can be shared in social interaction by members of different religious traditions and representatives of different views of life. Even in a pluralistic context theism remains the advocate of public contestability. That theism can be successful in playing this role in provoking argumentative exchanges — 'after theism' as well as 'after post-theism' — may have been documented by the present conversation.

A Reply to Christoph Schwöbel

H.J. Adriaanse

First of all I would like to thank my opponent and friend, my *Duzfreund* Dr. Christoph Schwöbel for his extensive and penetrating criticism of my paper. He has offered a rather complete alternative to my position; I admire his conception for its consistency and thoroughness as well as for its subtlety and originality. Yet my role at this moment is not to extol my critic but to clarify and to defend my own stand. The best way to do this might be to follow roughly the line of Christoph Schwöbel's paper. There are 6 points on which I would like to make a briefer or longer remark.

1. About the ambivalence of the reasons for my judging theism incredible. I do not deny this ambivalence but I do not feel bothered by it; the way in which one has to argue in this matter is by accumulation of reasons. I refer here to the remarks on method made by Basil Mitchell in his book *The Justification of Religious Belief*. The first phrase of my paper is tensed since in my opinion a truth is concerned which may be timeless in itself but the discovery and general acceptance of which is by no means timeless. Now Christoph says that if theism is and always has been incoherent etc, then there is nothing to inherit, neither as a charge nor as a blessing, apart from a self-contradiction and a falsehood. This conclusion is too straightforward in my view. There are magnificent errors. Let us take the example of early Christian eschatology. I take it that the belief in the second coming of Christ in its elementary, literal form has turned out to be wrong. Still I admit and wish to emphasize that this belief while sublimating and transforming its original form has developed a huge civilizing power. Christian Europe has learned to understand life in the tension between 'now already' and 'not yet'. The charge and the benefit of this view of life are to a large extent independent from the original belief and the truth or falsity thereof.

2. About the problem of analogy in the section on the coherence of theism. My argument is construed as an internal criticism of Swinburne's argument. So my own view about this problem is not developed. If I were to develop it, one of the first things I would stress is: that in this issue the question has to be dealt with whether on principle the analogy has the

carrying capacity needed for the onus of proof. I could refer here to the remark of Philo to Cleanthes in the final section of the second part of Hume's *Dialogues concerning Natural Religion*. One cannot with impunity extend the range of analogy beyond experience. So the first thing I think should be done is to distinguish between cases in which the use of analogy is appropriate and helpful and the cases in which it increases confusion. This distinction is not always immediately evident; reasonings can go astray imperceptibly. But if we go beyond all possible experience things are clear; the carrying capacity is zero in this case. So of course I do not reject any use of analogy but to extend it from natural science, however speculative and theoretical, to theology is in my eyes a leap in the dark and in fact on principle question-begging. I agree wholeheartedly with Swinburne, therefore, when he applies his idea that one has to use analogy sparingly and carefully to the realm of theology also. My point is that he seems to be not sparing and careful enough. The fact that his statement refers to the *proofs* of coherence or incoherence, and not to coherence or incoherence themselves, does not alter very much. I think that strict proofs in this field are altogether impossible, so that our judgment has to rely on other grounds. This is in short the purpose of my argument in the section on coherence. On the level of the coherence/incoherence discussion the theistic claim cannot be substantiated and I take it to be no good thing for the credibility of theism that this is so.

3. Now for the probability of ultimate explanations. I do not understand how my opponent can feel so much at ease *vis-à-vis* Mackie's criticism of Swinburne. Of course it is only one particular strategy of defending the claim of the existence of God which is rendered problematical here, but is his, *i.e.* Christoph's own account of ultimate explanation not highly dependent on Swinburne's? I think it is. In order to show this, two clarifications should be made preliminarily.

Firstly: we should distinguish here more sharply between the logical and the ontological order. The contingent proposition Swinburne is said to offer is opposed to 'the necessary in God'. This opposition is crooked. A proposition about what is necessarily existent can itself quite well be contingent — for example 'Zeus exists necessarily', since this proposition is false (as most of us will believe) — whereas a proposition about a contingent being can quite well be a necessary one (in the sense that it is necessarily true). Secondly: Stating that God is necessarily existent and the source of all possible and actual beings, is not enough in the context of the problem under discussion. For a theistic conception of God it is indispensable to claim that

God is not only being but also *a* being. And the question, then, is of course how the predicates *esse* and *ens* can be combined. An important difference between them is at any rate that whereas *esse* perhaps — perhaps! — can be said to exist necessarily, *ens* can not. To quote Hume once more: 'There is no being whose non-existence implies a contradiction. Consequently there is no being whose existence is demonstrable. The words, therefore, *necessary existence* have no meaning.' I would qualify: with the possible exception of being itself. But this qualification does not secure divine being if taken in a theistic sense. Now my point: any argument claiming necessary existence must needs claim plain or factual existence. Necessary existence is a modality of factual existence; one cannot affirm the former while not affirming the latter. *A necesse ad esse valet consequentia.* The weaknesses discovered in Swinburne's personal explanation in terms of an ultimate brute fact do not fail to affect any ultimate explanation in terms of necessary being. Finally: I leave aside Christoph's distinction between an ultimate explanation which cannot itself be explained and ultimate explanation in terms of 'the wholly self-explanatory being'. I simply do not see what the explanatory power of this latter term could be.

4. As for the argument on secularization which is the main point in the first part of my paper. My argument is meant in a more specific way than Christoph seems to think. I am still concerned with theism, not with religion in general. Religious revivals (which of course I acknowledge) do not falsify my idea that theism suffered a heavy loss of plausibility from secularization. To my opinion these revivals do not even per se falsify the secularization thesis. Religion can come to new flourishing *after* having lost, and *because of* having lost its role of ascertaining the foundations of society and culture. Our postmodern situation seems to me to provide an example of that development. Postmodernity opens up new horizons for religion, yet not in the centre of culture, but *in margine*, in the play area. Now theism, as I defined it, implies the claim to be at the centre, the heart, the basis of society and culture. For it claims to know what is ultimately real and good and as such binding, worthy of obedience for all individuals and for society as a whole. If theism has no place any more in the centre of culture its plausibility is seriously threatened. The secularization thesis, as I exemplified it with the help of Peter Berger, says that the complex of economy, science and technology is at the basis of our society. What is the role of God (seen theistically) in present-day economic life, in scientific theories, in technological processes? To raise the question is to answer it.

5. About the definition of theism, Christoph takes my notion of theism to be so indeterminate as to be virtually uninformative and he proposes and elaborates another understanding which is both more restricted and more specific. Here we have a very interesting part of his paper which is of utmost importance for our conference. Once again, I would like to express my admiration of the impressive consistency of his view. But it is not my view! That is my first point here. Of course everybody is free to stipulate the meaning of a concept but he is in danger then of missing the problem under discussion. I can only declare that my way of stating the problem seems to me to be an adequate one, even an obvious and imposing one. Theism is a very comprehensive notion indeed. It comprises both a variety of religious traditions and a variety of levels of reflexion, from spontaneous experience up to metaphysical conceptualization. However, I deny that it is uninformative for that reason since it allows for clear contrasts: for instance the contrast with God as impersonal being, or the contrast with polytheism, or with no God at all. This sense of theism has become accepted in philosophical language at least since Schopenhauer.

Next to this point I would like to make a second point under the same heading of this fifth remark. It is about Christoph's alternative view of theism and I must confess that, in spite of the qualities just pointed to, his argument has not convinced me, neither in its historization of this concept nor in its philosophization (if I may say so) of it. The historization cannot account for one of the most significant features of Christoph's notion of theism, namely that it is connected with the dissolution or displacement of the doctrine of the trinity. Theism and the doctrine of the trinity are alternative ways of structuring the system of beliefs, he says. If theism originated in the situation of confessional conflict as an attempt to formulate a framework of rational consensus, why, then, the doctrine of the trinity would be thus affected? The confessional conflict was not at all about the Trinity. To the contrary, one of the few topics the warring parties entirely agreed on — at the cost of the unitarians — was trinity. As to the philosophization of the concept of theism, this move seems to me to be an exaggeration. Philosophy was a constant companion of theology from the first century on. All key doctrines of Christian faith have been formulated with the help of philosophy, including for instance the doctrine of the trinity. So why is theism a philosophical theory, whereas trinity is not? Is it because theism, as Christoph says, transcends *programmatically* the given particular contexts of religious practice, whereas trinity does not? If we look to Swinburne's (and my) definition of theism, there is no sign of such a programme. Furthermore: I feel somewhat at a loss with regard to the relationship Christoph establishes between theism and pluralism. On the one hand he seems to think that theism frustrates genuine pluralism, on the other hand the public contestability, which is indispensable even in genuine pluralism, is presented as a virtue of theism. My reaction to this ambiguity amounts roughly to: you can't have it both ways. But perhaps I miss the point here. Finally: why the grammatical or criteriological theism, introduced on the last page, still deserves the name of theism (according to Christoph's own restricted understanding of this term), is a thing that I fail to grasp.

6. Christoph's criticisms of the second part of my paper are quite severe. He suspects a categorical refuse to act and an escape into unaccountability, moreover, pronounced parallels to the culture of self-fulfilment and, finally, complicity in the erosion of the social interaction. It might not be as serious as that. I do not see why post-theism cannot give a loyal contribution to the genuine pluralism advocated by Christoph. It is one of the orientational beliefs competing in this pluralist situation. And it is not essentially privatisationalist, as Christoph suggests: its very name bears witness to a religious and theological belief. So if it were to operate in the public realm as one of the orientational beliefs, how could it prevent from bringing up religious and theological questions? But there are three things that to my opinion we should keep in mind here. First: if we allow orientational beliefs to play a constitutive role in the public realm, then we must be ready for the eventuality that the problem of the stability of 'the common set of moral values' is still unsolved. Pluralism and stability of foundation do not go together as a matter of course; to the contrary they tend to mutual exclusion. Any modern society is in a situation of unstable equilibrium. No pluralism, however genuine, will be able to change that. Quite the reverse — and that is my second point — it is very likely that an open and unrestricted competition of views of life will either paralyse or restrict the public realm. Pluralism is inevitable but that does not mean that it is a good. It is something very dangerous indeed, particularly with regard to the foundations of society and I think I would definitely prefer the apparent pluralism of civil religion to the genuine pluralism of unimpededly competing views of life. This preference does not entail in my case a preference for theism, however. Thirdly, the most important thing. Orientational beliefs are ontologically rooted, Christoph says. And I agree with him! I wonder how he can expect me to 'cut the chord that binds

dictum and res together'. Didn't I emphasize both the charge and the benefit of theist dicta? What character the heritage of theism has in fact if not an ontological character? I called this 'metaphysical' instead of 'ontological'. Is that the point? Christoph writes 'The dictum has replaced the res and words, mere words, are all we are left to play with.' That is the only phrase in his beautiful paper I protest against. It does not apply to somebody who tries, without the banality of overstatement, to point at the miracle implying 'that whenever the dictum comes to life the res itself is there'.[1] Apart from any personal involvement, I think we as philosophers of religion would do our job in a better way if we took it for granted that words are *never* 'mere words'.

I stop here. These remarks will be enough to verify at least one of Christoph's assertions, the one expressed in his final sentence, that theism is still successful in provoking argumentative exchanges.

1. Adriaanse, above, p. 149.

Philosophy of Religion in Sweden and Finland: a Survey

Anders Jeffner

In the Nordic countries, the small paths in the landscape are often the most intriguing and interesting. The same may perhaps be said for the intellectual terrain, and there is a considerable risk that these significant paths will be overlooked in a brief survey where in many cases it is not even possible to describe all the main roads. This paper is an invitation to investigate some of these side paths together with the main road and share some of my personal reflections.

Many of the books and articles discussed here are available only in Swedish, but it is not totally impossible for scholars familiar with Germanic languages such as English, German or Dutch to understand philosophical works written in Swedish. Finnish on the other hand, belonging as it does to the Finno-Ugric language branch, poses a linguistic problem. I myself do not have a command of Finnish and this survey therefore does not include works available only in Finnish.

I intend to point to tendencies in the Swedish and Finnish philosophical debate which existed during the mid-1900s and are still significant for present-day discussions. Influential scholars who were active at the beginning of this century, such as Axel Hägerström and Nathan Söderblom of Sweden and Edvard Westermarck of Finland, are consequently not included here. I must also refrain from discussing philosophers who, though they have achieved important results relevant for philosophy of religion, have not dealt directly with our subject. This is why I have not taken up such famous and well known Finnish philosophers as G.H. von Wright and J. Hintikka.

My starting point is the Swedish philosopher of religion, Anders Nygren. The presence of philosophy of religion as a distinct subject at Swedish theological faculties owes much to Nygren's writings, and he has also had considerable influence on the Finnish counterparts. Nygren's first philosophical work appeared in print as early as 1921. After serving many years as a bishop, he returned to the philosophy of religion, attempting to relate his earlier theories to a new philosophical and theological situation. The result of this effort was published in English: *Meaning and Method. Prolegomena to a Scientific Philosophy of Religion and a Scientific Theology*, 1972. A Swedish translation did not appear until 1982 (*Mening och metod*). Nygren is an excellent *point de départ* since his philosophy has bearing on many philosophic trends in Sweden and in Finland today — some elaborating his line of thought, others in opposition.

Outside Scandinavia, Nygren seems to be best-known as a systematic theologian, especially because of his work Eros and Agape, but in my opinion his most original contributions lie in the field of philosophy of religion. This side of Nygren's work has been discussed very little in an international context. However, some instructive papers about his philosophy are included in the volume *The Philosophy and Theology of Anders Nygren*, edited by Charles W. Kegley, 1970. The Swedish debate has been very critical of Anders Nygren during the past several decades. The average theological student in Sweden seems to know little about him except that he 'was wrong'. This is due to a multifaceted opposition in Sweden against Nygren. I will return later to this opposition, but can mention at this point that it is a theological criticism which has been influential in the churches. The theologian Gustaf Wingren, while neglecting philosophical questions, strongly opposed Nygren's interpretation of Christianity from a Lutheran religious perspective. The early Swedish debate about Nygren has been analyzed by Jarl Hemberg in his book *Religion och metafysik*, 1966. A symposium held in Lund in 1991 to celebrate the one hundredth anniversary of Nygren's birth can be seen as a starting point for a new, positive interest in Nygren's philosophy in Sweden. An interesting report from this symposium was published by the theological faculty in Lund: *Anders Nygren som teolog och filosof*, 1991. Anders Nygren's son, Gotthard Nygren, held a professorship at the Swedish university at Åbo, Finland, and I believe that interest in Nygren has been greater in Finland than in Sweden. Tage Kurtén, who is discussed below, included Nygren in his dissertation *Vetenskaplig teologi och dess samhällsrelevans*, 1982; (the summary in English is titled 'Scientific Theology and its Relation to Society').

It is not possible to discuss Nygren's philosophy at length in a survey of this type. I intend however to point out six traits in his philosophy and use these as starting points for a presentation of recent Swedish and Finnish tendencies in our field.

1. The background to Nygren's philosophy is the neo-Kantian tradition in Germany. In his early work Nygren was especially interested in

developing the Kantian concept of a priori; and indeed his whole philosophy right up to his last book is dominated by a Kantian approach. As a Kantian scholar, he strongly opposes a psychological interpretation of Kant's epistemology and his way of interpreting Kant influenced his understanding of Schleiermacher.

Now, a superficial view of the situation in Sweden and Finland may give the impression that Nygren was the last philosopher who had an in-depth knowledge of Kant and who tried to make Kantian philosophy fruitful in his own philosophy of religion. It is true that during recent decades, most philosophers have been oriented toward the English-speaking world and that the main influences in philosophy have come from England and the United States. But we must bear in mind that there is an on-going study of the Kantian tradition in Sweden and in Finland. Two instances of this should be especially mentioned.

The first is a study by Hans Olof Kvist, currently professor at the faculty of theology in Åbo: *Zum Verhältniss von Wissen und Glauben in der kritischen Philosophie Immanuel Kants*, 1978. Kvist does not deal explicitly with Kant's philosophy of religion, but he analyzes a more fundamental aspect of Kant's philosophy which is of utmost importance for an understanding of religion — the borderline between theoretical and practical reason. Religion belongs, says Kant, to the realm of practical reason. Kant sees it as a great mistake to try to refer religion to theoretical reason as is done by those who try to prove the existence of God. Therefore, Kant claims, it is by clarifying the realm and limits of theoretical reason that we can find adequate room for religion in human knowledge. Kvist closely adheres to this Kantian line of thought, and in doing so sheds light on a perpetual problem of a general nature: how to explain the differences between science and religion. The Kantian limitation of theoretical reason in order to give religion a legitimate place outside its realm is in a way parallel to what Wittgenstein does in the *Tractatus*. For my own part, I think that the early Wittgenstein has been neglected too much in recent philosophy of religion despite the constant tedious referrals to the final statements of the Tractatus.

My next example of Kant studies is a recent dissertation of Mats G. Hansson at the university in Uppsala: *Human Dignity and Animal Well-Being. A Kantian Contribution to Biomedical Ethics*, 1991, even though it too deals only indirectly with Kant's main work on religion. This work is primarily a study in Kantian ethics, but the author deals with Kant's imperatives and formulates a view of mankind which is of basic interest also from a perspective of philosophy of religion. The author gives an interesting alternative to those anthropological and ethical systems which reduce the ethical differences between treatment of humans and treatment of animals, for instance, the philosophy of Peter Singer. I think the significance of the study, as it relates to the purpose of this paper, lies in its showing the shortcomings of a simple positivistic view of human knowledge and human drives. Now however we run a risk of drifting away from Nygren and his kind of Kantianism, so let's look at another trait in Nygren's philosophy.

2. An important point for Nygren is his attempt to show that there is what he calls 'a religious category'. Kant meant to show, as we know, that our knowledge is based partly on certain structures of reason which he called categories. One of these is cause-and-effect, and the argument used by Kant to establish such a category is called a transcendental deduction. Influenced by the discussion among neo-Kantians, Nygren believed that such categories exist as a basis not only for scientific knowledge, but also for knowledge in the fields of ethics, aesthetics and religion. Nygren wanted to make a transcendental deduction in the religious realm. To this end, he tried to find a formal supposition, or necessary condition, for the possibility of religion in general. This necessary condition for the possibility of religion is the category of eternity, according to Nygren. Sometimes he also seems to mean that this religious category is a presupposition not simply for religious knowledge, but for knowledge in general. This is, of course, a grandiose thought, but Nygren's argument is only given as a sketch, and I do not feel it unfair to say that he never worked out his transcendental deduction of religion. Nor has any scholar in Sweden or Finland attempted later on to fulfill Nygren's project in this direction. There exists nonetheless a link between this part of Nygren's philosophy and the present philosophical situation. This link is the interest in the formal aspects of knowledge. There is a group of philosophers who agree with Nygren in his Kantian criticism of the pure empirical tradition and who want to analyze the structure of human reason in our formation of religious knowledge. Their starting point is not the same Kantian tradition as Nygren uses; rather it is a philosopher who has an affinity to Kant, i.e. Edmund Husserl.

The recent professor of philosophy of religion in Lund, Dick Haglund, is a well-known Husserl scholar, (*Perception, Time, and the Unity of Mind. Problems in Edmund Husserl's Philosophy*, 1977). Significant in the present context is that he has shown how phenomenology in Husserl's sense can help us understand religious knowledge and religious experiences. He gives several examples in his book *Tro — upplevelse — språk*, 1990. It is not possible to give even a short summary of his detailed reasoning here. Let me just point to one line of thought: the only objects we can come into direct contact with according to Husserl are the phenomenological objects in our intentional acts such as experiencing, thinking, imaging. We can analyze how the objects of such acts are constituted, but we can never go outside the bounds of the phenomenological world. This is in accordance with the Kantian idea of the impossibility to have knowledge of das Ding an sich. A consequence of this view, which Haglund seems to accept, is that a religious person, who constitutes a religious world-view, can never compare this world-view with a world outside the one constituted by his knowledge-acts. There is no unformed experiential material to refer to. This means that a comparison between a religious and a nonreligous view must take part inside the phenomenological worlds which we constitute. According to this philosophy, the reasonableness of religion depends on to what extent a religious view can give a consistent interpretation of our experiences. From a quite different starting point, I have argued for a similar position in my book *Vägar till teologi*, 1981.

Among the philosphers in Sweden who have been inspired by Haglund's interest in Husserl, I want to mention Åke Sander from the university in Gothenburg. He has published a two-volume study which is a phenomeno-logical analysis of 'what it is to be a typically religious person in a typically religious world': (*En tro — en livsvärld. En fenomenologisk undersökning av religiös erfarenhet, religiöst medvetande och deras roller i livsvärldskonstitutionen*, 1988). Sander has links not only to Husserl, but also to such scholars as Mircea Eliade, William James and Rudolf Otto. Eliade has moreover been a starting point for a study from Uppsala written by Antonio Barbosa da Silva, *The Phenomenology of Religion as a Philosophical Problem*, 1982.

As pointed out above, Nygren's epistemological ambition has been taken up and developed in a new direction by phenomenological philosphers. But in Sweden there is another and related way of dealing with the epistemology of religion. It is represented by Eberhard Herrmann, professor at the Uppsala university. His first book investigates a continental tradition which, like phenomenology, can be both critically and positively related to the English analytical tradition (*Die religionsphilosophische Standpunkt Bernard Bolzanos unter Berücksichtigung seiner Semantik, Wissenschaftstheorie und Moralphilosophie*, 1977). Bolzano clearly consigns religion to what Kant called the realm of practical reason. Thus far, Eberhard Herrmann seems to agree with Bolzano, and in his further philosophy he attempts to develop an epistemological standpoint which will help us clarify the specific character of religious knowedge-claims. Eberhard Herrmann seems to agree with Bolzano thus far, and in his further philosophy he tries to develop an epistemological standpoint which can help us clarify the specific character of religious knowedge-claims. Thereby he connects to the German philosopher W. Stegmüller and to Popper (*Erkenntnisansprüche. Eine orientierende erkenntnistheoretische Untersuchung über Fragen zum Verhältnis zwischen Religion und Wissenschaft*, 1984.) According to Herrman's line of thought, religion provides us with a basic structure which can help us generate scientific hypotheses and which can be creative in the field of values. In a recent essay in *Nederlands Theologische Tijdschrift*, 1991 no. 3, he writes: 'It is rational to adhere to an ideology or religion only if it can function both in creating and sustaining values. And it can do this when it contains a utopian concept of human life on the basis of which we know both what disappointment, failure, guilt and so means, and what course to follow in deciding which attitude to adopt toward reality'.

3. To return to a main line in Nygren's philosophy, that part of our knowledge which is based on a category of eternity establishes what Nygren calls a 'context of meaning' (*meningssammanhang*). Religion, then, is a context of meaning. There are at least four such general contexts of meaning, says Nygren: the theoretical (with the basic categorical question 'What is true?'), the ethical, the aesthetical and the religious. To understand the language of religion, we must see every religious sentence in its context of meaning and in its relation to the religious category. But if we disengage a religious sentence from its own context of meaning and look at it as if it belonged to the theoretical context of meaning, thus answering the categorical question 'What is true?', then, according to Nygren, the sentence is distorted. What we in fact do, he says, is to transform religion into metaphysics and doing so is a serious mistake. Nygren is a staunch enemy of what he calls metaphysical philosophy. There is an essential difference between the theoretical and other contexts of meaning he claims further. Scientific theory can provide direct answers to the basic categorical question, but in ethics and religion it is quite a different matter. Inside these contexts of meaning, certain clusters are held together by a leading idea which in the language of Nygren is a 'basic motif' (*grundmotiv*). This is where his theological reasoning starts. He wants to prove that *agape* is the basic motif of true Christianity. The significant thing here is that Nygren, in his last book, explicitly refers these thoughts to the

philosophy of Wittgenstein's Investigations. Contexts of meaning and their subcontexts are language-games. He more or less makes the claim to have been a 'Swedish Wittgenstein' in the 1920s. Be that as it may, my intention is to make clear that in both Sweden and Finland there has long been a discussion of language-games and of the relevance of a Wittgensteinian analysis of religion.

In 1977, Lars Haikola published his book *Religion as Language-Game. A Critical Study with Special Regard to D.Z. Phillips*. The word 'critical' is pivotal. Haikola makes a detailed analysis of Phillips' way of applying Wittgenstein's theory of language games to religion and points out many difficulties in Phillips' position starting with the observation that it is far from clear which of the religious linguistic units really are language-games. A more modest criticism of Phillips is to be found in Carl Reinhold Bråkenhielm's book *How Philosophy Shapes Theories of Religion. An Analysis of Contemporary Philosophies of Religion with Special Regard to the Thought of John Wilson, John Hick and D.Z. Phillips*, 1975. I cannot here discuss the Swedish debate on language-games, but it is symptomatic that John Hick was elected honorary doctor in Uppsala. Personally I am not against the use of Wittgensteinian tools, but have argued against a tendency to make religious discourse into an intellectual protectorate. This position is reflected in the title of one of my books: *Religion and Integration*, 1987.

On the opposite side of the Baltic Sea, we find a quite different situation. A strong interest in Wittgensteinian philosophy has been in development in Åbo during the past decade. In the field of philosophy of religion, this is especially apparent in the publications of Tage Kurtén. One of his books, *Grunder för en kontextuell teologi. Ett wittgensteinskt sätt att närma sig teologin i diskussion med Anders Jeffner* (1987; summary in English: Foundations for a Contextual Theology. A Wittgensteinian approach to theology in discussion with Anders Jeffner), takes a stance against my line of reasoning. Allow me to briefly comment on this by saying that the discussion between Swedish and Finnish scholars concerning language-games and related matters is held in a very friendly atmosphere and we find the slightly different points of view to be mutually enriching. One of the doctoral students from the university in Uppsala recently spent a year in Åbo to deepen his knowledge of Wittgensteinian philosophy. There are a number of articles concerning Wittgenstein and theology in existence in the Finnish language, but as previously mentioned I am unable to comment them.

4. Can religion be true, according to Nygren's line of reasoning? The

answer is clearly that it cannot. Truth belongs to the theoretical context of meaning. Nor, continuing this line of thought, can ethical sentences be true. But, says Nygren, religions and ethical systems can be legitimate or valid as they are rooted in a category of reason. However, as previously mentioned, the transcendental deduction of the categories in Nygren's philosophy starts from a supposition that religion is a given human activity which we are obliged to accept. This is quite obvious in his final book *Mening och method*. Nygren's philosophy contains other tendencies as well, for instance the idea that the category of eternity is necessary for all kinds of human knowledge. But it is hardly unfair to say that Nygren's philosophy has as its starting point the claim that religion is not an illusion and his argument is intended to show that religion is not true. Viewed thus, Nygren's philosophy might seem trivial and in conflict with common sense. These two opposing charac- teristics of Nygrenian thought were taken up by the Swedish philosopher Ingemar Hedenius who formulated a devastating critique of Nygren in two of his books, *Tro och vetande* (1949) and *AAtt välja livsåskådning* (1951). Hedenius' works had an enormous impact in Sweden. An entire generation of intellectuals came to be influenced by Hedenius. *Tro och vetande* was recently reprinted, and is still regarded as a bible of atheism.

Ingemar Hedenius was, in certain respects, a Swedish counterpart to Bertrand Russell. He was strongly influenced by the English empirical tradition and was a very witty writer. The structure of his argument against Christianity is in brief as follows. His starting point is what he called the principle of intellectual morality, expressed thus: Do not believe in anything for which you cannot give good reason. Then he tried to demonstrate that there are no good reasons for accepting Christianity. The conclusion is, of course, that it is against intellectual morality to believe in Christianity. (I have dealt with this kind of argument in more detail in my contribution to the handbook *The World's Religions*, edited by Stewart Sutherland et al, 1988.) A major debate about the reasonableness of Christianity followed the publication of *Tro och vetande*. At that time, Sweden had many distinguished theologians. In addition to Nygren, there were scholarly bishops such as Gustaf Aulén, John Cullberg and Torsten Bohlin. All of them took part in the debate, but none were very successful. For most Swedes, Hedenius appeared to be the winner.

I myself was one of Hedenius' students, and I admire him as a philo- sopher and as an individual. He had a profound knowledge of many philoso- phical traditions and always argued with clarity. Religion was to him of utmost importance. He struggled very hard to come to clarity in religious questions. To simply suppose that religion is valid was to him an intellectual crime. However I believe that his position in philosophy of religion is totally wrong, and I have tried to show this in many of my works. In my first study, I went back to the roots of the British empirical tradition (*Butler and Hume on Religion*, 1966) and later connected to lines of thought expressed in the debate after the classic *New Essays in Philosophical Theology* (*Filosofisk religionsdebatt*, 1967; *The Study of Religious Language*, 1972). I believe that the question of good reasons is basically a normative question at the roots of epistemology. To answer it deserves an ultimate decision which never can be totally well-guarded. According to this view, it can be intellectually fair to be religious, but you cannot avoid an element of intellectual risk in taking up a religious view of life. I can mention that I have to some extent been influenced by the existentialist tradition despite the fact that existentialists have played a minor role in Swedish philosophy of religion.

Among the reasons for being religious, reference to religious experience is greatly significant. This was ignored by Hedenius, but there is a lively discussion about religious experiences in Sweden. Here special mention must be made of a study by Carl Reinhold Bråkienhielm, now professor at Uppsala, *Problems of Religious Experience*, 1985. Experiential aspects of the mystical tradition has been dealt with by Hans Hof (Myt och symbol, 1967) and Catharina Stenquist (*Simone Weil om livets tragik — och dess skönhet*, 1984).

5. One of the functions of philosophy of religion for Nygren was to be a prolegomena to a scientific theology. When a philosophical analysis had shown the importance of basic motifs, the task of theology was to do motif research. In a way this is a purely descriptive task. Theology cannot say anything about God directly, not even that God exists. Nygren therefore thought that such theologians as Bultmann and Tillich had misunderstood the task of a theologian. Nygren's descriptive theology still has some adherents in Sweden, but I think that most theologians, myself included, hold some other view of the relationship between philosophy and theology. This school believes that philosophy can give theologians tools to clarify the meaning and reasons for different doctrinal standpoints. With help of philosophical argument, theology can also construct and compare models for Christian thinking and thereby help develop a Christian doctrine. This can be termed a kind of philosophical theology. A brief list of examples of this genre might include: Anders Jeffner, *Kriterien Christlicher Glaubenslehre*, 1976, and *Theology and Integration*, 1987; Ulf Görman, *A Good God?* 1977; Carl

Reinhold Bråkenhielm, *Förlåtelse*, 1987; Mats Hansson (not the Kant-scholar mentioned above) *Understanding an Act of God*, 1991. A somewhat different tendency can be found in Sten Philipson, *A Metaphysics for Theology* (1982) which has links to Whitehead and the American process-tradition. Other theologians have tried to find a foundation for theology in continental philosophical traditions. An example is Henry Cöster's discussion of Ernst Bloch in his *Människa, hopp, befrielse. En systematisk studie i Ernst Blochs spekulativa marxism med speciell hänsyn till hans kristendomstolkning*, 1975.

Beside these works, many studies have been published in which the various authors analyse basic theological concepts without explicitly applying their results to theology. I must restrict myself to two good examples, one from Sweden and one from Finland. The first is Urban Forell's *Wunderbegriffe und logische Analyse*, 1967. Forell is now professor in Copenhagen but his book was published in Lund. The second is Heikki Kirjavainen, 'The Simultaneity of Faith and Knowledge: Tendencies in Epistemic Logic from Antiquity to High Scholasticism' in Heikki Kirjavainen (ed.) *Faith, Will and Grammar*, 1986. Both Forell and Kirjavainen show how tools drawn not only from philosophical conceptual analysis but also from formal logic can bring important clarification in a theological context.

In concluding the discussion on this fifth trait, it might be mentioned that a new kind of theological description is now emerging in Sweden and Finland which however has nothing to do with Nygren's motif research. It is an empirical study of world views and value systems among ordinary citizens in a secularized society. This is done in cooperation with sociologists of religion, but is not pure sociology. In analyzing the findings, philosphers of religion can make many interesting observations concerning the function of religious language and the construction of world views. In Finland, Tage Kurtén is involved in such studies and in Sweden, Carl Reinhold Bråkenhielm and myself. I have given a glimpse of some results in my contribution to *Christian Faith and Philosophical Theology*, edited by G. van den Brink, L.J. van den Brom and M. Sarot, 1992.

6. Now we have come to a discussion of the sixth and final trait. Many books and authors could have been mentioned above but I must emphasize that this survey is in no way complete. However one last kind of study remains to be addressed if we are to obtain a reasonably correct description of the situation in Sweden and Finland. This too can be related to Nygren. As mentioned above, Nygren is best known in international circles for his historical studies in the Christian tradition. After Nygren, interest in the

history of Christian doctrine has been strong in both Sweden and Finland, and the findings often run contrary to Nygren's *Eros and Agape*. The historically oriented studies attempt to understand and interpret the major thinkers of tradition in a way which will make them fruitful for the contemporary debate, including the philosophical debate. Of special importance here is the study of medieval philosophy which is going on in Helsinki under the guidance of professor Simo Knuuttila. Of his many publications I restrict myself to mentioning his forthcoming book *Modalities in Medieval Philosophy*, (Routledge, London, 1992). It might also be noted that Simo Knuuttila is the chairman of the Commission for Finnish translation of teh works of Aristoteles. This translation will give Finland a unique position among the Nordic countries. A Swedish example of an important historical study is Ragnar Holte's lucid book about St. Augustine's relation to the classical schools of philosophy (1958). Holte deals mainly with the ethical aspects, but Hampus Lyttkens goes right to the heart of philosophy of religion in his *The Analogy between God and the World. An Investigation of its Background and Interpretation of its Use by Thomas of Aquino*, 1952. Hampus Lyttkens has meant a great deal to the development of different aspects of the philosophy of religion in Sweden and also other countries. I am pleased to end my survey with this reminder of one of the great books by the founder of our European conference.

Philosophy of Religion in Denmark

Svend Andersen

The following is my first attempt to establish a survey of my own intellectual background. It reflects of course my point of view, seen from others' it would have appeared differently.[1]

General background

In order to understand what philosophy of religion means in a Danish context, some important facts must be kept in mind. First, Denmark has been a protestant country since 1536, when it joined the Lutheran reformation. Since then, Lutheranism has been the all-dominating religion, the Evangelical-Lutheran Church still written into the constitution as 'the Danish Folk Church'.

Since the Reformation, the *theological faculty* at the University of Copenhagen was the place where ministers for the Lutheran Church were educated.[2] In 1942, a second faculty was established at the University of Aarhus. Thus theological teaching and research is primarily carried out at the two major state universities.

A consequence of the Lutheran domination has of course been a strong German influence. Thus, over the years, in Denmark you find all the well-known theological positions: Lutheran Orthodoxy, Pietism, Rationalism, Enlightenment Theology, Hegelianism etc.

---

1. In the original version I had included some remarks on philosophy of religion in Norway. As some collegues from that country rightly pointed out, the picture I gave was not satisfactory. As it has not been possible for me to improve that part of the paper I have preferred to remove it. I have, however, retained some remarks and a list of some Norwegian publications.
2. Until the end of the Napoleonic Wars Denmark and Norway formed a double monarchy. In 1814 they were separated, and only then a Norwegian university was founded. Thus, until 1814, Danish and Norwegian university theology are one and the same thing. A Norwegian peculiarity is the founding of a socalled 'Congregation Faculty' (Det teologiske Menighetsfakultet) at the beginning of this century. The background was a controversy over the confessional commitment of theology professors.

Originally then, the Danish university was primarily an institution for educating Lutheran ministers. This influenced the status of *philosophy* in the sense that in the first centuries after the Reformation it was not independent from theology. Also, Danish philosophy was originally strongly German-oriented.

Things changed in the 19th century: philosophy emancipated itself from theology, and English and French influence was enhanced. But still, at the beginning of our century, it was not unusual for Danish philosophy professors to have had a theological training. This has a significant bearing on Danish philosophy of religion: within the field of philosophy, all treatises of philosophy of religion were written by authors with a theological background.

What is Philosophy of Religion?

When does 'philosophy of religion' appear? This is an ambiguous question. As to the *problems* normally treated under this label, philosophy of religion has always been with us. As to philosophy of religion as an academic *discipline*, the case is of course different. But it is hard to trace it back exactly to its origin — at least, I have not been able to do so in a Danish context. As to theology, the historians tell us that in the 1740s, a new discipline within systematic theology appeared when one of the professors (J.F. Reuss) lectured on the relationship between contemporary philosophy and theology.[3] During the same period, the character of theological controversy changed from polemics (against e.g. Calvinism) to *apologetics*. It seems reasonable to connect the origins of the type of reasoning called philosophy of religion to the changes in intellectual culture which created criticism of Christian religion and the following efforts to defend Christianity rationally. Although these changes began in the 18th century, in Denmark they manifested themselves strongly only by the middle of the 19th century. At that time, criticism of Christianity was connected with the breakdown of idealistic philosophy and the growing importance of empirical sciences.[4]

3. Cf. Knud Banning, Det teologiske Fakultet 1732-1830, in *Københavns Universitet 1479-1979*, Copenhagen 1980, vol. V, p. 237.
4. The very designation 'philosophy of religion' for a specific field of tehological teaching and research seems to have appeared about the turn of the century. What in Germany is united under the heading 'systematic theology' was then split up

It is during this period that we find the most important Danish contributor to the philosophy of religion at work: Søren Kierkegaard.

Kierkegaard and after Kierkegaard

For various reasons, it would be futile to give a presentation of Kierkegaard's own philosophico-theological thinking. Nor do I find it appropriate in this paper to give a survey over Danish contributions to Kierkegaard research. Rather, I want to take Kierkegaard as a starting point for my presentation of some features of Danish work in philosophy of religion. It would not be totally wrong to claim that all succeeding authors in some way are influenced by his thinking.

To start with then, I want to indicate how Kierkegaard created some fundamental problems which the following philosophers of religion had to face. A crucial claim in Kierkegaard is that the religious attitude (i) is practical of character, i.e. it is an attitude of choice and action; (ii) is an attitude of the individual person; (iii) cannot be adequately grasped or described by theoretical concepts. As is well known, in the 'Postscript' Kierkegaard distinguishes between two kinds of religious attitude: *Religiosity A* and *Religiosity B*, the latter being the specific Christian attitude involving a relation to the paradox, the appearance of God in time.

Now, although Kierkegaard incessantly fights against Hegel, it is — as far as I can see — essential to his thoughts that he expresses them with the help of terms and concepts of German Idealism. The question which underlies the following positions of Danish philosophy of religion is: what happens to Kierkegaardian thinking when those concepts lose their meaning?

One of Kierkegaard's few real pupils was the philosophy professor *Rasmus Nielsen* (1809-83). Inspired by Kierkegaard, he (in the book *Gospel faith and Modern Consciousness*, 1849) started an important argument on *faith and knowledge*. What he did was, so to speak, to transpose the thoughts of

into two fields: *dogmatics* and *ethics with philosophy of religion*. The 'with' indicates that, in the beginning, philosophy of religion had the status of a minor subject within the curriculum. Today the combination of ethics and philosophy of religion still exists, but the latter is now a full subject. Both in Copenhagen and in Århus an introductory course in philosophy of religion is obligatory in the first part of the theological curriculum.

Kierkegaard into the academic controversies about Christianity.[5] In 1869, Nielsen published the first Danish exposition of philosophy of religion (Nielsen 1869). In it, he develops his version of the Kierkegaardian position: faith and (scientific) knowledge are based on totally different principles, so there can be no conflict between them. Nevertheless, philosophy of religion is a kind of science, viz. what Nielsen calls 'reversed science': in the case of philosophy of religion, scientific thinking abolishes knowledge to let faith manifest itself. The foundation of this enterprise is the miraculous God-relation of the believer. All statements about God and his attributes acquire their meaning in relation to the believing/faithful self.

Although Nielsen taught philosophy, his philosophy of religion must be regarded as a kind of theology. Thus the main parts of his book deal with 'The Belief in the Father', 'The Belief in the Son' and 'The Belief in the Spirit'.

Psychologism

The most important contribution to philosophy of religion by a professional Danish philosopher is 'Religionsfilosofi' by *Harald Høffding* (1843-1931). Although he too was trained as a theologian, his approach is genuinely philosophical.

In a way Høffding, like Nielsen, takes the faith – knowledge contradiction as the starting-point for his exposition. More precisely, he starts with the fact that at his time, human cultural and intellectual life had undergone a strong differentiation, leading to the situation that explanation and evaluation had been separated. This process is, according to Høffding, primarily caused by the new scientific world-view. Now, every 'power' of intellectual and cultural life has to serve the development of this life. And the question is, whether or not religion can retain this kind of cultural signficance — and if not, whether equivalent powers are thinkable, i.e. powers which can serve the function previously occupied by religion.

This 'problem of religion' is closely connected with Høffding's *definition of religion*; it is contained in the following passage:

.. in its inner essence, religion does not have to do with understanding reality, but with the evaluation of it, and the religious ideas express the relation between reality

---

5. Important participants in the arguments were the left-Hegelian philosopher Hans Brøchner and the literary critic Georg Brandes.

as we know it, and that which to us gives life its highest value. The core of religion is ... a belief in the endurance of value in reality.[6]

Philosophy of religion, in Høffding's version, is not thinking based upon religion but rather thinking with religion as its subject matter. It is an investigation of the problem of religion defined by the cultural situation; more specifically, it deals with the conditions of every kind of belief. Such conditions, according to Høffding, are either epistemological, psychological or ethical. The vocabulary of conditions sounds Kantian, but in Høffding there is no theory of *a priori* conditions, rather the emphasis lies on psychology, which is why I label his position 'psychologistic'.

It is no surprise then, that there is a good deal of psychology of religion in Høffdings 'Religionsfilosofi'. And as his definition of religion is intended as a general one, he draws in a lot of material from the history of religion.

Høffding defines the central concept *'value'* in the following way:

Value is the property of something so that it causes real satisfaction or can be a means for (satisfaction). (Høffding 1924, p. 10).[7]

This concept of value is manifestly psychological in character. It is not surprising, then, that Høffding regards feeling so to speek as the 'receptor' of value. Further, he distinguishes between three types of value: the values (i) of self-assertion, (ii) of devotion, and of (iii) religion. The latter are in a way second order values insofar as they are values based on the acquisition and retention of values (i) and (ii).

A central element in Høffding's definition of religion is *belief*. By belief, he understands a 'conviction about a continuity, an endurance beyond the horizon shown by experience'.[8] This is not a cognitive or theoretical kind of belief but rather what could be called personal belief, the model being the belief in the faithfulness of another person. In the case of religious belief, the target is 'objective continuity in reality' (ibid.).

The *scientific* world-view too is directed towards continuity, viz. the continuity of causal connections. It is different from, but compatible with religious belief, the compatibility resting on the possibility

6. Harald Høfding, *Religionsfilosofi*, 3rd ed., Copenhagen 1924, p. 6f.
7. Høffding, *op.cit.*, p. 10.
8. Høffding, *op.cit.*, p. 70.

.. that the great causal connection which science more and more reveals is a framework or foundation for the development of a valuable content, going on through the laws and forms which scientific research has detected.[9]

Thus Høffding does not agree with Nielsen in his claim about the totally heterogeneous character of science and religion respectively.[10]

Høffding's concept of *God* has two aspects: epistemologically and metaphysically speaking, God is the principle of continuity and comprehensibility of reality; to religion, however, God is the principle of endurance of value, the 'principle of faithfulness'.

The psychological character of Høffding's thinking has the consequence that he lays much emphasis on phenomena like religious feeling and religious experience. Religious *feeling* in his view is — in accordance with his basic definitions — the feeling connected with the fate of values in reality. *Experience* (erfaring) in Høffding is primarily awareness of mental states, but it also includes a causal and an expressive aspect. Thus Høffding seems to presuppose that what an experience is *of*, is its cause. With the help of a representation or idea (forestilling) an experience can be interpreted, which strangely enough equals it being explained. The reason for this terminology is clear: an interpretation determines what the experience is *of* and according to Høffding this can only be done by giving the *cause* of it. And giving the cause of something is the same as explaining it.

Now in the case of religious experience, the emphasis is not on causal interpretation/explanation, but rather on expression. Høffding regards *symbol* as the most adequate means of expression for religious experience, more adequate than dogma, myth and legend. Symbolism is non-cognitive; it is founded on *analogy*: ideas from other domains of human psychology — self-affirmation and devotion — are transposed to the religious sphere. This is what happens e.g. when the value-sustaining power is called 'Father'. In the end, to Høffding, there is a strong affinity between religion and poetry at the level of expression.

What a symbol expresses is in the last resort 'the *urge to live*'. Here we find in Høffding an important echo of Kierkegaard: the claim that life is more fundamental than theory. In religion, the urge to live is superior to the urge

9. Høffding, *op.cit.*, p. 166.
10. Høffding has interesting considerations on the parallels between science and religion, i.a. in relation to verifiablility. But I cannot go into details here.

to know. The term Høffding uses to designate the subject of individual life is 'personality'. The individual personality is the center of experience and value; he lives his life as an individual work of art. 'Personality' is also the basic ethical concept insofar as Høffding uses it to express Kant's principle: a personality must always be treated also as an end in itself. Høffding regards religion as connected with ethics, but not simply as a condition for ethics. Religion is more fundamental; in a way it is pre-ethical. Thus Christianity does not give us an ethic, rather it is a 'source of life'.

Høffding's definition of religion as belief in the endurance of values mirrors his view that religion is fundamentally 'optimistic' of character. An attitude towards life according to which life is devoid of value could not be called religious. On the contrary, 'pessimism' presupposes the existence of value. Accordingly, an absolute pessimism has never been articulated. The contrast to religion is not pessimism, but what Høffding calls neutralism, i.e. the attitude of pure observance, the conviction that the course of the world has an 'infinite indifference towards what human beings call value'.[11] I regard this as one of the crucial sentences in Høffdings 'Religionsfilosofi' and I will come back to the thought it contains.

Until now, I have presented Høffding's philosophy of religion as if its outlook were totally anthropologically restricted. However, a recurring question in it is: What is the relationship between the human desire for value and reality as a whole?

In the first place, Høffding emphasizes that it is not possible to separate totally human personal beings from reality as a whole: the human person with his/her experience and knowledge is part of reality. This fact might be an explanation of the open-endedness of experience. On the other hand, reality in itself might be unfinished. In any case, Høffding emphasizes the *limitations* of human experience, part of the cause of which the abundance and richness of reality.

Høffding sums up the thought about the relationship between the value-oriented human personality on the one hand and reality as a whole on the other in the following way:

Reality appears to man as a battle field on which the fate of the values is decided.

11. Høffding, *op.cit.*, p. 152

It is a big drama that is performed, in relation to which man is both participant and observer.[12]

Høffding uses the drama metaphor to emphasize another feature of reality, viz. its uniqueness a character resembling that of an individual. There is a similarity between the individual human being and reality as a whole: neither of them can be reduced to instances of general laws. Also in this respect human knowledge is limited. Religious symbolism mirrors this connection between individuality and uniqueness: 'the individual phenomenon stands as typical — as a nutshell in which the worlds content is hidden'.[13]

To Høffding, the problem about the relationship between value-dependent human beings and reality as a whole, in a way is concentrated in the concept of *evolution*. The question at the core of religion is whether the general evolution of reality furthers the values of human beings.

In my opinion, Høffding here articulates a problem which is still central to philosophy of religion. Yet instead of developing this further, I want to conclude the section on Høffding with a fine expression of his optimistic, life-oriented attitude:

In all areas life anticipates experience. Life begins with a reserve of power. We live in expectation before living in remembrance .. We are born with faith and start with trustful anticipation .. This is the great art of life.[14]

This is not the Kierkegaardian mood. Rather it is an anticipation of the outlook of another great figure of Danish philosophy of religion.

Neokantianism

The exposition of the philosophy of religion by the theologian F.C. *Krarup* (1852-1931) stands in the Danish tradition insofar as he takes the faith-knowledge problem as his starting-point. Unlike Høffding, however, his

---

12. Høffding, *op.cit.*, p. 62. As is well known, the observer-participant topic plays an important role in *Niels Bohr's* philosophical reflexions on quantum theory. It is a widespread conjecture that he was in fact influenced by Høffding. The topic is connected with the concept of complementarity which can be applied within philosophy of religion. On some aspects of this, see Andersen 1985.
13. Høffding, *op.cit.*, p. 140.
14. Høffding, *op.cit.*, p. 168f.

point of view is explicitly Christian. In his *Religionsfilosofi*,[15] he attempts to solve the problem as it presents itself to a Christian on modern conditions.

As to the philosophical framework, Krarup is very much on Høffding's line. Thus, in order to identify a domain for religion, different from the area of science, he points at the concept of *value*. And he too regards value as the counterpart to the human person: the individual human being is a 'self-purpose'.

Like art and ethics then, *religion* involves value-judgements. In general, religion is a relationship between human beings and the 'powers who support life and control what happens'.[16] Religious attitude is characterized by the certainty that '..the human soul will not disappear in the great, wild world, but that there is .. a meaning and plan to reality ...'[17]

In value-terminology, the religious motif is the idea that the value defined by the self-purpose of the human person is an expression of the inner purpose of the world as a whole.

Krarup's formal definition of religion is the following: Religion is 'the perfect awe of the life-conditions by which we are determined'.[18] The reason for talking of 'awe' — and not e.g. respect or acceptance — is that religion understands the fundamental powers of reality in terms of the human self-purposive person.

But isn't the religious value judgement subjective? Krarup denies this and tries to make his case by using Kantian arguments. His strategy is not to regard religion as a precondition for ethics: religion is a human attitude of its own.[19] He uses what he regards as the Kantian method in taking religion as a datum in human consciousness and searching for the necessary and general component in it. In other words: without using the term, Krarup is looking for the *a priori* element in the religious consciousness. He claims that this consciousness, like the ethical, presents itself with a kind of necessity and general validity. Accordingly, in his view, religious assertions can be regarded as true and referring to a kind of objective reality. Thus, to Krarup, the Kantian, transcendental argument is a way to escape the kind of

15. Krarup, F.C., *Religionsfilosofi. En bog om det religiøse Livs Væsen og Ret*, Copenhagen 1905.
16. Krarup, *op.cit.*, p. 129f.
17. Krarup, *op.cit.*, p. 131.
18. Krarup, *op.cit.*, p. 129f.
19. In this connection, Krarup criticizes the Ritschl-school for making religion dependent upon ethics.

psychological relativism which is a threat to Høffding's position. On the other hand, his way of using the Kantian method differs significantly from Nygren's.[20]

Logical Positivism

Within Danish philosophy, Neokantianism had an adherent in *Jørgen Jørgensen* (1894-1969). His most important contribution, however, is to have introduced modern logic and logical positivism into our intellectual life. With Jørgensen, analytical philosophy in a broad sense began to determine the agenda of philosophical work in Denmark.

In Jørgensen we find the same kind of criticism of religion as in his contemporary A.J. Ayer. But it might be indicative of more mildness in the intellectual climate that we find the criticism in a correspondance with an archdeacon.[21]

Against archdeacon Brodersen's Krarup-like talk about religious experience, Jørgensen counters:

.. religious assumptions can with no right claim to be true, they can only be regarded as subjective convictions in certain people ...[22]

Religious experiences, then, have to be studied by the methods of experimental science, in the same way as a botanist studies the 'richness of flora'.[23]

The most serious challenge of Jørgensen's positivism in my opinion is that it tries to destroy the very conceptual framework which underlies the thinking of Høffding and Krarup. The concept of *personality* simply vanishes into scientific psychology:

20. Another way of relating to German 'Liberal Theology' is found in the little work by *Glarbo* (Glarbo 1916). It deals with the relationship between religion and history from the standpoint of philosophy of religion — with lengthy discussions of Troeltsch.
21. P. Brodersen, & J. Jørgensen, *Er Gud en Virkelighed? Brevveksling om Religion og Videnskab mellem Paul Brodersen og Jørgen Jørgensen.* Copenhagen 1935.
22. *Op.cit.*, p. 34.
23. *Op.cit.*, p. 27.

.. what we understand in this complicated field [of life and personality] seems to me to be the result of scientific well-controlled observations and analyses, and of nothing else ..[24]

Thus, instead of Kierkegaard's idealistic 'theory' of the existing individual, we now have empirical psychology.

However, Jørgensen's version of the positivistic approach did not give rise to a tradition of philosophy of religion. In this respect he cannot be seen as a Danish counterpart to Ingemar Hedenius.

Barthianism

The problem about how to proceed when the philosophical conceptuality Kierkegaard presupposed is no longer convincing, can be solved in a very drastic way by simply claiming that theology does not need any philosophical framework at all. This was, as far as I can see, the position of 'Dialectical Theology' in the version of the young Karl Barth. In Kierkegaardian terms, the claim is that you can analyse Christian faith without reference to 'Religiosity A': faith is based upon the Word of God which totally contradicts 'natural' human efforts to think about or experience God.

Within Danish philosophy of religion, the challenge of Barthianism was first taken up by the theology professor *Eduard Geismar* (1871-1939). In Geismar's exposition[25] philosophy of religion is a specifically theological discipline. He describes it as a statement of principles for dogmatics and ethics. Its task is to clarify the essence of Christianity by comparing it with other 'intellectual powers' like philosophical doctrine of God, and other religions. Geismar does not, as did Høffding and Krarup, presuppose a general defintion of religion. As a theological discipline, philosophy of religion has to take its concept of religion from Christianity. Christianity is actually the religion with which 'we' are acquainted; and as philosophy of religion has to describe religion on its own conditions, taking its object-relatedness seriously,[26] it must start with Christianity.

---

24. *Op.cit.*, p. 41. The *opus magnum* of Jørgensen has the significant title: *Psykologi på biologisk grundlag* [Psychology on Biological Foundation] published 1941-1946.
25. E. Geismar, *Religionsfilosofi. En Undersøgelse af hvad religion og Kristendom er.* 2nd ed., Copenhagen 1930.
26. In this connection Geismar talks about the '*phenomenological*' standpoint of philosophy of religion. He is indeed the first Danish author who makes

To be more specific: the model of religious belief, according to Geismar, is Christ's relation to God. Geismar agrees with the 'Barthians' that belief thus understood involves judgment of the believing person. He cannot, however, follow them in totally rejecting the idea that Christian faith is connected with 'ethical idealism'. Geismar tries to establish a kind of synthesis, claiming that Christianity stands to ethical idealism both in the relation of judgment and of continuation. His argument for not abandoning the connection between christianity and human idealism is that the Gospel needs a 'point of contact' with human nature. Also, the very concept of judgment would be meaningless, if id did not presuppose some kind of ideal.

Thus, Geismar retains Kierkegaard's two types of religiosity. He recognizes a kind of religiosity immanent in human culture which is distinct from, but not separated from, 'specific Christian religiosity'.

Athough Geismar's arguments against Barthianism are important, I do not find his 'synthesis' satisfactory. Its main weakness is that it contains no contribution to the crucial question about the philosophical framework within which to explicate human religiousness.

A different way of dealing with Barthianism is found in N.H.Søe (1895-1978), the successor of Geismar. His exposition of the philosophy of religion[27] is a piece of Christian theology in the sense that it takes as its starting point God's revelation in Christ. Unlike Geismar, Søe totally rejects the way of thinking we found in Høffding and Krarup. The most important question in his Religionsfilosofi is whether man is able to understand revelation, which is the only 'bridge' between God and the human sphere. Accordingly, there is not much reflexion on the philosophical foundation of the elucidation of religious faith.[28]

Existentialism

Besides Barthianism, Dialectical Theology has an existential line, represented in Germany by Rudolf Bultmann. It can be called more genuinely Kierke-

comprehensive references to Husserl, Scheler and Heidegger. But it would not be adequate to characterize his own philosophical position as phenomenological.
27. Søe, N.H., Religionsfilosofi, Copenhagen 1955.
28. On the line of Søe is th dissertation by P.H. Jørgensen, Die Bedeutung des Subjekt-Objektverhältnisses für die Theologie. Der theo-ontologische Konflikt mit der Existenzphilosophie, Hamburg-Bergstedt 1967. As a Norwegian example one can mention Reidar Hauge.

gaardian insofar as it recognises the necessity of analysing human existence in philosophical terms. As is well known, in Bultmann's case the philosophical work was, so to speak, handed over to Martin Heidegger.[29] In his theological work, Bultmann presupposes rather than exercises philosophy.

If there is such a thing as an Aarhus School of philosophy of religion, it is distinguished in the following point from Bultmann. Like Bultmann, philosophers of religion in Aarhus very much acted against a Heideggerian background; but unlike him, they involved themselves in philosophical work.

The first representative of this approach I want to mention is *Johannes Sløk* (b. 1916). He has produced a large amount of books and perhaps changed his mind several times, so I will concentrate on his textbook.[30]

In it, Sløk realizes that the very concept of philosophy is ambiguous: on the one hand, there is the standpoint, represented by e.g. Jørgensen, that philosophy can only investigate the conceptual foundation of empirical science (and formal systems) — on the other hand, there is the existential point of view, that philosophy is part of man's attitude to 'his existence as a whole'. As an heir to Kierkegaard, Sløk of course holds the latter view. But in an interesting way, he shares some of the claims of positivism. As he faces the crucial problem: How to found the conceptual framework of human existence, Sløk turns to scientific anthropology.

Put briefly, his argument runs as follows: What distinguishes human beings from animal is that we are not instinct-directed into a fixed pattern of behaviour. The openness of the human brain makes the child flexible, so that its behaviour can be shaped by the norms of the culture into which it is born. Hence, human beings live in an environment created by convention; but that means that the environment is created by human beings themselves. These facts about the human species are the conditions of the 'self-contradiction of human existence': we experience the framework of our life as something given — but on the other hand we know that we are free to change them.

Human beings, then, are conscious about the fact that the norms they follow have only relative validity. But they have a desire to have normative validity secured by some kind of transcendent power. This desire, given with the structure of human existence, is one of the decisive roots of *religious*

---

29. A critical presentation of the relation between Bultmann and Heidegger is given in a *Norwegian* study: Valen-Sendstadt 1969, *Eksistensialfolosofien som fundamental-ontologi for åbenbaringsteologien*, Oslo 1969.
30. J. Sløk, *religionsfilosofiske problemer* I, Århus 1956.

phenomena. One of the tasks, then, of philosophy of religion is to show how religious phenomena are rooted in human existence. In doing so philosophy of religion is not necessarily part of Christian theology.

In order to understand Christianity we have, according to Sløk, to take into account a very specific category, viz. the category of *preaching* [forkyndelse; Verkündigung]. In every important respect preaching differs from the *views* [anskuelser] we find in (other) religions: it is personal, it has an obliging character, and it is outside the control of the hearer. Thus, preaching provokes the hearer to choose either to obey or to reject. In obeying, the hearer recognizes a kind of validity differing from the relative validity of cultural norms.

In a way, then, one could characterize Sløk's philosophical position as 'Existential analysis on biological foundation'.

Løgstrup

If there is such a thing as an 'Aarhus School', the most outstanding representative of it was the first professor of philosophy of religion at the faculty, *Knud E. Løgstrup* (1905-81).

Philosophically, Løgstrup was brought up in the athmosphere of Neo-kantianism, i.e. a way of thinking in which epistemology was so to speak *prima philosophia*.[31] In theology, his teacher was Geismar, and it was Geismar who directed his interest towards phenomenology. Husserl's phenomenology can, I think, be seen as the most important effort to escape psychologism beside Frege's philosophy of language. But what Husserl did not escape, according to Løgstrup, was the view of human beings as primarily conscious beings, separated from the world. A way of thinking which avoided this weakness he found in the *existential* variety of phenomenology. In other words, he found it in Heidegger, but even more impressively articulated in a contemporary of Heidegger, *Hans Lipps* (1889-1941), he too a pupil of Husserl.

As is well known, an important element in this approach is the thought that to be a human being is to be situated in a world and be placed within relations to other human beings. Situation and relation are constitutive of human existence. Philosophical analysis, according to this existential

---

31. Løgstrup's most important philosophical teacher was *Frithiof Brandt*, who is still well known for his book on the natural philosophy of Hobbes.

phenomenological approach, to a large extent means description of the typical ways in which a human being is involved in such relationships. Particularly in Lipps, the descriptions often consist in linguistic analysis. And thus,
this kind of philosophy has very much in common with the kind of analytical
philosophy which followed the late Wittgenstein.

I think one could say that for Løgstrup, existential phenomenology was
a means to retain a fundamental Kierkegaardian idea: the primacy of the
living human being over theory. This kind of phenomenology gave him the
tool to elucidate what living as a human being means.

In his philosophy of religion, Løgstrup in a way returns to Kierkegaard's
distinction between religiosity A and B. One must, he claims, distinguish
between a universal and a specific component of Christianity. The universal
component is the doctrine of *creation*, and as it is universal, it must be open
to philosphical analysis and reasoning. The specific component, on the other
hand, is the claim that God has acted in an uforeseeable way in the life and
fate of Jesus.

Thus, to Løgstrup philosophy of religion is part of theology. It is to a
large extent philosophical explication of the doctrine of creation, facing the
challenges from the various types of irreligious thinking in modern Western
culture. The philosophical argument has not so much the character of
demonstrating the existence of a Creator as to point at features of human life
which make the thought of creation plausible. The intellectual form of belief
in creation is not demonstration, but rather interpretation. The features in
question are, i.a. trust, love, mercy, sensual and esthetic experience —
features or phenomena which bear human life and make it good life.

In emphasizing such features, Løgstrup is on the same line as Høffding.
One of the challenges he faces is nihilism; and his claim is that nihilism in
order to make sense must presuppose the goodness of life.

The way of thinking I have just sketched gives rise to two important
questions: (i) Is not existential phenomenology a kind af Kantianism, in the
sense that in it human existence plays the role of the transcendental subject
as creative/constitutive of the structure of the surrounding world? (ii) Is the
doctrine of creation adequately explicated so long as you only point at
features of *human* life which can be interpreted as indications of createdness?
The two questions are closely connected in that they both pose the problem
about the place of *nature* and *the universe* in the philosophy of religion.

In the case of Løgstrup, the questions led him into a direction of thinking,
which he himself labelled 'metaphysics'. The basic idea behind this enterprise

is that human existence is not only situated in a surrounding world, but founded in nature and, in the last resort, in the universe. In order to show this, Løgstrup in fact involves himself in 'considerations' about classical metaphysical topics such as time, space, universals etc. His aim is to give reasons for the claim that not only human existence, but the universe — rather: the universe-as-source-of-human-existence — can be interpreted as created. One important argument which shows how Løgstrup moves away from existential phenomenology concerns *time*. In his analysis of time he takes as his point of departure the 'subjective' views of Husserl and Heidegger. But, Løgstrup asks, is it really the end of the story about time that its future-past-present structure is constituted by human conscious-ness/human existence? His answer is no: time as experienced by humans has a 'cosmological' foundation; experienced time is a manifestation of the fact that human life has the character of a 'revolt' against an irreversible process of annihilation. If this is true, not only human being, but being/existence in general means being annihilated. But then every existing thing raises the question: Where does it get the power to be? And this question leads to the idea of *God* as 'the power to be in everything that is'.

In arguing this way, Løgstrup again takes up a problem we found in Høffding, viz. the problem about the relationship between man seeking value or meaning, and reality as a whole. Løgstrup too regards this as the funda-mental question of religion:

If we move from the statement that the universe concerns us to the question whether we concern the universe, we have moved from metaphysics to religion.[32]

In order to have an adequate analytical tool to explicate this metaphysical understanding of creation, Løgstrup had to change his conception of pheno-menology. In his metaphysics, he presents what he calls 'cosmo-phenomenology', and one of the tasks he has left for his followers is to develop this method further.

Løgstrup was well aware of the similarities between his original version of phenomenology and Oxford philosophy. Especially in his ethical works he dealt with authors such as Ryle, Nowell-Smith, and Hare. As to philosophy

32. Løgstrup 1978, p. 211.

of religion, he read Ian Ramsey who was a personal friend of his.[33] But in his writings he did not take into account the debates within analytical philosophy of religion.

Recent Work

It is true in general of Danish philosophy of religion that but little notice is taken of the analytical tradition. There are, however, some exceptions.

As early as 1969, *Jens Glebe-Møller* published a comprehensive study of 'Wittgenstein and Religion'.[34] More recently, *Benny Grey Schuster* has published a number of articles in which he points at parallels between Wittgenstein and Kierkegaard.[35]

I myself have tried to compare the foundations of philosophy of language within the phenomenological and the analytical traditions respectively, and to draw some consequences for the understanding of religious language.[36] My book is a contribution to the understanding of Løgstrup's position, and it is only one of a whole series of works on his philosophy of religion. Thus, *Jakob Wolf* tries to find a line of influence from the phenomenology of Goethe's theory of colors to Hans Lipps and further to Løgstrup.[37]

In *Norway*, too, important work has been done on Løgstrup. *Svein Aage Christoffersen* has written several articles. And in his doctoral thesis, *Karstein M. Hansen* presents many early unpublished manuscripts by Løgstrup which indicate his philosophical road from epistemological philosophy to existential phenomenology, and his reaction to Dialectical Theology (Hansen 1990).[38]

I regard it as an original contribution to philosophy in general that

33. Løgstrup participated in the European conference in Oxford 1978, where he read the paper printed as Løgstrup 1979.
34. J. Glebe-Møller, *Wittgenstein og religionen*, Copenhagen 1969.
35. B.G. Schuster, Hvis kristendommen er sandheden, er al filosofi derom falsk, in *Sprog, Moral & Livsform. Ludwig Wittgensteins filosofi*, ed. by Steen Brock and Klaus K. Hansen, Aarhus 1986.
36. S. Andersen, *Sprog og skabelse. Fænomenologisk sprogopfattelse i lyset af analytisk filosofi, med henblik på det religiøse sprog.* Copenhagen 1989.
37. Wolf, J.: *Den farvede verden.* Copenhagen 1990.
38. K.M. Hansen, Skapelse ok kritikk, Skapelsestankens kritiske funksjon i K.E. Løgstrups forfatterskab med særlig henblikk på den unge Løgstrup (unpublished). Also in Finland a dissertation on Løgstrup has been published: Svante Ewalds, *Metafysik och religionsfilosofi. Det universella i K.E. Løgstrups teologisk-filosofiska tänkande 1971-1981.* Åbo 1993.

Løgstrup tried to develop phenomenology further. The dominating trend in German influenced philosophy, however, has been away from phenomenology to something else. For instance to hermeneutical philosophy. This branch has generated important Danish contributions to philosophy of religion among which I want to mention *Andersen 1979, Hahn 1979* and *Wind 1987*. One of the very few writers who try to make the French hermenutical tradition fruitful in philosophy of religion is *Peter Kemp*.[39] From *Norway*, we must mention *Christoffersen 1984* in connection with German hermeneutical philosophy.

Wind characterizes the claim of hermeneutical philosophy in the following way:

.. the truth is that we who live now, are ourselves history; socially, mentally and linguistically, we are conditioned by what has been and has happened.[40]

If this is the truth, it seems futile to ask whether or not sentences within religious language can be true. From this point of view it looks more reasonable to investigate into the ways in which religious language is conditioned e.g. by traditions, and to accept a non-assertoric character for it. Hence the growing interest in narration, rhetoric and literature. In Denmark important work in this field has been done by *Svend Bjerg*, *Peter Kemp* and *Jan Lindhardt*.

The work on literature has resulted in the creation of a *Theology and Literature Forum* [Forum for Teologi og Litteratur] in Århus. In a way, another Århus forum in a way keeps alive the tradition from the faith-knowledge argument: The *Theology and Science Forum* [Forum Teologi Naturvidenskab]. One of the most important results of the work in this forum is Mortensen 1989.

Concluding remarks

To conclude, I want to emphasize some characteristic features in the work within *Danish* philosophy of religion after Kierkegaard.

(1) By far the largest part has been done within *Lutheran theology*.

(2) Of the very few *philosophical* constristions, only Jørgensen claims to

39. Peter Kemp, *Théorie de l'engagement* I-II, Paris 1973.
40. H.C. Wind, *religion og kommunikation. Teologisk hermeneutik*, Aarhus 1987, p. 5.

treat religion from a neutral, objctive standpoint (the 'botanist' point of view), but actually he is critically biased.

(3) These two points are part of the explanation why in Denmark – unlike Sweden – there is *no* tradition at all of *'objective'* or *'scientific'* philosophy of religion.

(4) This has also to do with the philosophical orientation; the main influence has come from *German (continental)* philosophy: Neokantianism, phenomenology, existential analysis, hermeneutics.

(5) Many Danish philosophers of religion have not just taken philosophical positions for granted and applied them to religious problems. Rather, they have contributed to developing philosophical positions. One important aspect of this is the search for parallels and connections between the continental and the analytical traditions.

(6) Important continuous 'threads' in Danish philosophy of religion are the emphasis on the individual human being and her experience, and the effort to clarify the distinction between faith and knowledge.

Bibliography

Denmark

Andersen, S. (1985): *Niels Bohr og sproget*. In V.Mortensen (ed.): Kontrast og harmoni. Niels Bohr som fysiker og tænker. Århus.

Andersen, S. (1989): *Sprog og skabelse. Fænomenologisk sprogopfattelse i lyset af analytisk filosofi, med henblik på det religiøse sprog*. Copenhagen.

Andersen, V. (1979): *Historicitet og natur. En undersøgelse af de ideologikritiske indvendinger mod den hermeneutiske filosofi*. Århus (not published).

Banning, K. (1980): Det teologiske Fakultet 1732-1830, in *Københavns Universitet 1479-1979* vol. V. Copenhagen.

Bjerg, S. (1981): *Den kristne grundfortælling*. Århus.

Brodersen, P. & Jørgensen, J. (1935): *Er Gud en Virkelighed? Brevveksling om Religion og Videnskab mellem Paul Brodersen og Jørgen Jørgensen*. Copenhagen.

Geismar, E. (1930): *Religionsfilosofi. En Undersøgelse af hvad Religion og Kristendom er*. 2nd ed. Copenhagen.

Glarbo, Chr. (1916): *Religionshistorie og Teologi. En principiel Undersøgelse*. Copenhagen.

Glebe-Møller, J. (1969): *Wittgenstein og religionen*. Copenhagen.

Hahn, B. (1979). *Hermeneutik og Religionsfilosofi*. Copenhagen.

Holm, S. (1955): *Religionsfilosofi*. Copenhagen.

Høffding, H. (1924): Religionsfilosofi. Tredie Udgave. Copenhagen.

Jørgensen, P.H. (1967): *Die Bedeutung des Subjekt-Objektverhältnisses für die Theologie. Der theo-onto-logische Konflikt mit der Existenzphilosophie*. Hamburg-Bergstedt.

Krarup, F.C. (1905): Religionsfilosofi. En Bog om det religiøse Livs Væsen og Ret. Copenhagen.

Kemp, P. (1973): *Théorie de l'engagement I, II*. Paris.

Lindhardt, J. (1983): *Martin Luther. Renæssance og reformation*. Copenhagen.

Løgstrup, K.E. (1979): The Metaphysical and Ethical Triad, in *Religious Studies* 15, p. 227-37

Løgstrup, K.E. (1971): *The Ethical Demand*. Philadelphia.

Løgstrup, K.E. (1978): *Skabelse og tilintetgørelse. Religionsfilosofiske betragtninger. Metafysik IV*. Copenhagen.

Løgstrup, K.E. (1990): *Schöpfung und Vernichtung. Religionsphilosophische Betrachtungen. Metaphysik IV*. Tübingen.

Mortensen, V. (1989): *Teologi og naturvidenskab. Hinsides restriktion og ekspansion*. Copenhagen.

Nielsen, R. (1849): *Evangelietroen og den moderne Bevidsthed. Forelæsninger over Jesu Liv*.

Nielsen, R. (1869): *Religionsphilosophie*. Copenhagen.

Nielsen, R. (1881): *Om det oprindelge Forhold mellem Religion og Videnskab*.

Schuster, B.G. (1986): Hvis kristendommen er sandheden, er al filosofi derom falsk, in *Sprog, Moral & Livsform. Ludwig Wittgensteins filosofi*. En artikelsamling ved Steen Brock og Klaus K. Hansen. Århus.

Sløk, J. (1956): *Religionsfilosofiske problemer I*. Århus.

Stybe, S.E. (1980): 'Filosofi', in *Københavns Universitet 1479-1979*, vol. X. Copenhagen.

Søe, N.H. (1955): *Religionsfilosofi*. Copenhagen.

Wind, H.C. (1987): *Religion og kommunikation. Teologisk hermeneutik*. Århus.

Wolf, J. (1990): *Den farvede verden. Om Goethes farvelære, Hans Lipps' fænomenologi og K.E. Løgstrups religionsfilosofi*. Copenhagen.

Norway

Aukrust, T. (1956): *Kristendom og verdensbilde*. Oslo.

Aukrust, T. (1958): *Mennesket i kulturen*. Oslo.

Christoffersen, S.Aa. (1984): *Identifikation og verifikation*. Oslo.

Dokka, T.S. (1989): Å gjenkjenne den ukjente. Om menneskets mulighet for å kjenne Gud. (Unpublished).

Hansen, K.M. (1989): Skapelse og kritikk. Skapelsestankens kritiske funksjon i K.E. Løgstrups forfatterskap med særlig henblikk på den unge Løgstrup. (Unpublished).

Hauge, R. (1952): *Gudsåpenbaring og troslydighet. Om forholdet mellem det subjektive og det objektive i den kristne tro.* Oslo.

Hygen, J.B. (1973): *Guds allmakt og det ondes problem.* Oslo.

Hygen, J.B. (1977): *Trekk av religionsfilosofien.* Oslo.

Lønning, I. (1984): 'Gott', in *Theologische Realenzyklopädie.*

Lønning, P. (1985): *Der begreiflich Unergreifbare. 'Sein Gottes' und modern-theologische Denstrukturen.* Oslo.

Nome, J. (1970): *Kritisk forskerholdning i etikk og religionsfilosofi.* Oslo.

Valen-Sendstadt, A. (1969): *Eksistensialfilosofien som fundamentalontologi for åpenbaringsteologien.* Oslo.

Valen-Sendstadt, A. (1973): *Filosofi for kristentroen.* Oslo.

Wigen, T. (1975): *Erfaringsimmanens og gudtro. Religionsapologetikken hos en del nykantiansk influerte teologer, med særlig hensyn til Anders Nygren.* Oslo.

About the Authors

Henrik John Adriaanse was born in 1940 and studied theology at Leyden University. After some years of ministry in two parishes of the Remonstrant Brotherhood, he took his doctoral degree in 1974 and became a lecturer in the theological faculty at Leyden. Since 1978, he holds the Leyden chair in philosophy of religion and ethics. His publications focus on the relationship between theological discourse and present-day standards of truth.

Svend Andersen was born in 1948 and studied theology and philosophy in Aarhus, Heidelberg and Oxford. He received doctoral degrees from the university of Heidelberg (1980) and Aarhus (1989). He has been a lecturer in the faculty of theology at Aarhus; since 1989, he holds the chair in philosophy of religion and since 1993, he is director of the Centre for Bioethics at the University of Aarhus. Recent publications include *Sprog og Skabelse* (1989) and *Som dig selv. En indføring i etik* (1993).

I.U. Dalferth was born in 1948 and studied theology, philosophy and linguistics in Tübingen, Edinburgh, Vienna and Cambridge, before receiving his doctoral degree in systematic theology in 1982. From 1987 to 1990, he served as a minister in the Evangelical Church of Württemberg; since 1990, he is professor of dogmatics and philosophy of religion at the University of Frankfurt. Recent publications include *Kombinatorische Theologie* (1991), *Gott. Philosopisch-theologische Denkversuche* (1992) and *Jenseits von Mythos und Logos* (1993).

Anders Jeffner was born in 1934, received his doctoral degree in 1966 for the dissertation *Butler and Hume on Religion*, and has been a professor at Uppsala University since 1976. His latest publication is *Six Cartesian Meditations* (1993); has has also published many articles and reports in the fields of philosophy, ethics and philosophical theology.

Klaus-M. Kodalle was born in 1943. He was professor of philosophy of religion and ethics at Hamburg University, since 1992 professor of practical philosophy at the Friedrich-Schiller-Universität Jena. Recent publications include *Die Eroberung des Nutzlosen. Kritik des Wunschdenkens und der Zweckrationalität im Anschluß an Kierkegaard* (1988) and *Dietrich Bonhoeffer. Zur Kritik seiner Theologie* (1991).

Günter Meckenstock was born in 1948 and studied at Göttingen and Munich, receiving the dr.theol.habil. degree in 1986 from the university of Kiel, where he is now professor of systematic theology and director of the Schleiermacher Research Institute. Recent publications include *Deterministische Ethik und kritische Theologie* (1988) and *Schleiermachers Bibliothek* (1993).

David A. Pailin was born in 1936 and studied history and then theology at Cambridge, Dallas and Manchester, where he received his Ph.D. From 1961 to 1966 he was a Methodist minister; since 1966 he has taught philosophy of religion in the University of Manchester, where he is now Head of the department of philosophy and professor of the Philosophy of Religion. His publications include *Probing the Foundations: a study in Theistic Reconstruction* (in press).

D.Z. Phillips was born in 1934, graduating from the University of Wales in 1956. He is professor of philosophy in the University of Wales, Swansea and Danforth Professor of the Philosophy of Religion at the Claremont Graduate School, California. Recent pbooks include *From Fantasy to Faith* (1991), *Interventions in Ethics* (1992), *Wittgenstein and Religion* (1993).

Christoph Schwöbel taught at the university of Marburg from 1981 to 1986; from 1986 to 1993 he was lecturer in systematic theology at King's College, University of London. He is now professor of Systematic Theology and director of the Institute for Systematic Theology and Social Ethics at the university of Kiel. Recent publications include *God: Action and Revelation* (1992) and *Persons – Divine and Human* (edited with Colin Gunton, 1991).

Jan van der Veken was born 1932. He holds degrees in philosophy, classical philology, and history, and has been a visiting professor in San Francisco, Claremont, Lublin, Budapest and the Netherlands. He is now professor of philosophy and director of the Center for Metaphysics and Philosophy of God at the Catholic University of Leuven, Belgium. His publications deal with process thought, phenomenology and religious language.

John Stephen Keith Ward was born 1938 and studied at the University of Wales and at Oxford, where he graduated in 1964. He has taught philosophy at Glasgow, St. Andrews, London and Cambridge; since 1991, he is Regius professor of divinity at the University of Oxford. Recent publications include *Images of Eternity* (1993) and *Religion and Revelation* (1994).

Index

240